McGraw-Hill Education

500 Review Questions for the MCAT: Critical Analysis and Reasoning Skills

Also in McGraw-Hill's 500 Questions Series

McGraw-Hill Education

500 Review Questions for the MCAT: Critical Analysis and Reasoning Skills

Kevin Langford, PhD

New York Chicago San Francisco Athens London Madrid
Mexico City Milan New Delhi Singapore Sydney Toronto

1 2 3 4 5 6 7 8 9 10   DOC/DOC   1 2 1 0 9 8 7 6 5

ISBN   978-0-07-184659-2
MHID   0-07-184659-X

e-ISBN   978-0-07-184660-8
e-MHID   0-07-184660-3

MCAT is a registered trademark of the Association of American Medical Colleges, which was not involved in the production of, and does not endorse, this product.

McGraw-Hill Education products are available at special quantity discounts to use as premiums and sales promotions or for use in corporate training programs. To contact a representative, please visit the Contact Us pages at www.mhprofessional.com.

CONTENTS

INTRODUCTION

You've taken a big step toward MCAT success by purchasing *500 Review Questions for the MCAT: Critical Analysis and Reasoning Skills*. We are here to help you take the next step and score high on the MCAT so you can get into the medical school of your choice.

This book gives you 500 multiple-choice questions that cover all the most essential course material. Each question is clearly explained in the answer key.

Two parts, Humanities and Social Sciences, reflect the two main subject areas presented by the Critical Analysis and Reasoning Skills section of the MCAT. These parts cover a range of disciplines, from architecture to theater and anthropology to sociology. Eighty reading passages across these disciplines will show what you might expect to find on the actual exam. The 500 questions that follow these passages represent the three principal critical analysis and reading skills evaluated by the MCAT: Foundations of Comprehension, Reasoning within the Text, and Reasoning beyond the Text.

This book and the others in the series were written by expert teachers who know the MCAT inside and out and can indentify crucial information as well as the kinds of questions that are most likely to appear on the exam.

You might be the kind of student who needs to study extra a few weeks before the exam for a final review. Or you might be the kind of student who puts off preparing until the last minute before the exam. No matter what your preparation style, you will benefit from reviewing these 500 questions, which parallel the content and degree of difficulty of the questions on the actual MCAT. These questions and the explanations in the answer key are the ideal last-minute study tool for those final weeks before the test.

If you practice with all the questions and answers in this book, we are certain you will build the skills and confidence needed to excel on the MCAT. Good luck!

—*The Editors of McGraw-Hill Education*

ABOUT THE AUTHOR

Dr. Kevin Langford is an Associate Professor of Biology and the Director of the Pre Health Professions Program at Stephen F. Austin State University. He has served as Chairman of the Texas Association of Advisors of the Health Professions. In addition to his teaching, Dr. Langford also has an active research program investigating the cellular and molecular events that occur during early cardiac development.

Humanities

CHAPTER 1

Architecture

USPS Historic Properties

The USPS's inventory of historic properties spans two centuries. The architectural styles of the post offices, the fine art they house, and the function the buildings provide in the community tell the history of the agency and of rural and urban development in 19th and 20th century America. This history is important to understanding not just the architectural significance of these facilities, but also their value and their significance to the communities they have served for decades.

History

Post offices constitute the most common form of federal government buildings in the nation. Located in large cities, small towns, and rural areas, post offices are an important presence of the federal government in communities. They play an essential role in facilitating communication and promoting economic development, reducing the isolation of rural locales, and disseminating products, information, and ideas across geographical areas. Historically, in times of economic stress, the construction of post offices has stimulated local economic recovery and provided work.

Many post offices are significant civic monuments that beautify the cities and towns in which they are located. Architecturally, post offices have served as symbols of the federal government's authority, conveyed regional historical themes, and exemplified high art forms. Some post offices were designed in an "official" national style and serve as notable examples of classicism in their respective communities. During other phases in the federal government's public building program, post offices were designed to reflect regional styles and influences. For much of the 19th century and throughout the Depression, artwork, such as ornamental sculptures and murals, was integrated into the architectural design of post offices.

While many post offices functioned as community meeting places, they were and are also an integral part of the governmental presence in the community, providing not only a functional role but a symbolic presence. In some communities, post offices, along with a courthouse, city hall, or other public buildings, collectively form a civic core that generates pedestrian traffic, contributes to the vitality of the downtown area, and provides a sense of community identity and civic pride. For many of America's smaller towns the post office remains the only federal presence in the community.

Historically, governments have maintained control over postal systems, since the effective organization and control of society depend upon the ability to communicate. The United States government also assumed control over mail service, but incorporated democratic principles by constitutionally placing the power to establish post offices and post roads in the hands of Congress. The establishment of the postal service throughout the country provided an example of democracy at work: citizens petitioned Congress, which established post roads and instructed the Postmaster General to provide postal service along the routes.

The buildings constructed for use as post offices have reflected various government and architectural philosophies. From the establishment of the Office of the Supervising Architect of the Treasury in the 1850s until the 1890s, the style of federal buildings tended to follow the favorite style of the incumbent Supervising Architect. During the tenure of James Knox Taylor (1897-1912) as Supervising Architect of the Treasury, the federal government promoted the concept that government buildings should be monumental and beautiful, and should represent the ideals of democracy and high standards of architectural sophistication in their communities. Taylor preferred styles derived from classical or early American traditions. Believing that federal buildings should be built to last, he also emphasized the use of high quality construction materials. Private architects worked on many of the larger projects, but the Office of the Supervising Architect produced smaller buildings, including many of the post offices that are found in small towns across the nation. The buildings were individually designed; Taylor firmly resisted suggestions that designs be standardized.

1. According to the passage, which of the following would NOT be a benefit of the post office to the community as a whole?

   (A) Promoting economic development
   (B) Generating pedestrian traffic
   (C) Being the sole government office in communities
   (D) Disseminating ideas across geographical areas

2. The author's use of the term "classicism" (paragraph three) to describe the design of post offices most likely refers to the buildings':

   (A) High quality of design
   (B) Less frequent use by people from lower economic classes
   (C) Taste and station of post office designers incorporated the style of ancient Greece and Rome into the architecture
   (D) Only upper class individuals designing and building post offices

3. Which of the following statements most supports the information given in the passage?

   (A) Post offices reflect the state of the community in their design.
   (B) Post offices enable government control of communication.
   (C) Post offices lead to community growth.
   (D) Post offices provide more than mail to communities.

4. Which of the following roles of the post office would the author agree remains important even in the electronic messaging age?

   (A) Sending and receiving documents
   (B) Providing a sense of community
   (C) Government presence in community
   (D) Economic development

5. With the decline in the use and usefulness of the post office in modern times, which of the following would the author most likely agree provides many of the same benefits to the modern digital community as did the old walk-in post offices?

   (A) Modern post office
   (B) Department of motor vehicles
   (C) Court house
   (D) Voter registration office

6. Of the following list of adjectives, which best describes the tone of the author in this passage?

   (A) Informative
   (B) Excited
   (C) Nostalgic
   (D) Progressive

Building Big

An urbanite hurrying to work may take for granted the skyscrapers overshadowing her, and a harried commuter may travel across a bridge several times daily without thinking it unusual. But when we stop to contemplate how the cityscape became what it is, the mystery of mammoth structures such as skyscrapers and bridges prompts many questions.

"For all of us, young or old, real learning begins with a sense of curiosity—about the natural world, the world of our ancestors, and the world we build for ourselves," says Larry Klein. "If someone begins to wonder, for example, how a bridge is built, a river tamed, or a tunnel created, that person is now more receptive to understanding and appreciating the achievements of the past and the principles of physical science and technology."

Larry Klein is the executive producer of the upcoming television documentary, *Building Big,* which takes on these questions. . . .

What's all the commotion over large structures? "There's the image issue—big has always signified strength, stability, and longevity—a talisman for public confidence," says Klein. "Building tall can be spiritually uplifting, like the great cathedrals of Europe; a matter of civic and national pride, like the Washington Monument; or the outward expression of a profound inner drive—called vision by some and ego by others—to simply build as big and as tall as humanly possible."

The series takes a look at five architectural wonders of the modern world and how they came to be, including the Golden Gate Bridge, the Toronto Skydome, the Petronas Towers in Kuala Lumpur, Malaysia, the Aswan Dam, and the English Channel Tunnel.

While the five segments show many examples of architectural innovation, each focuses on a structure selected for its relative importance in the world and the difficulty of its architectural achievement. "When they appeared on the world's landscape, each of our structures influenced society and galvanized global attention," says Klein. "The stories of their respective creations are truly dramatic. And each became . . . a signpost of achievement that other builders immediately strove to match or even surpass. . . ."

The series tells dramatic stories such as the construction of the Brooklyn Bridge, highlighting the ambition of the architects and the fearlessness of workers who labored in perilous conditions.

For John Roebling and his son, Washington, the engineers who designed it, the Brooklyn Bridge became a symbol of their shared vision and misfortune.

Not long into the project, John Roebling was seriously injured on the site and developed lockjaw. After his death, his son took up the reins.

The Roeblings' many innovations, such as the first steel suspension cables, made it possible to build a bridge 50 percent longer than any other existing bridge.

Another invention, the pneumatic caisson, provided an airtight, underwater construction site 78 feet below the East River. In dim light and a precarious air supply, workers dug the bridge's foundation. Many died from the bends, also known as caisson disease or decompression sickness, caused by emerging too quickly from the compressed atmosphere.

Washington Roebling developed the bends and was forced to monitor construction through binoculars from his room nearby. But in 1883 the Roeblings' dream was realized and the bridge was completed. Spanning 1,595 feet and able to bear 18,700 tons, the Brooklyn Bridge broke all records.

Project Director Paula Apsell says, "I think what most interests me is getting an understanding of how our ability to build these massive structures is really built on layers of effort. I'm always interested in people seeing science and technology as a process that evolves over many generations." Apsell adds that the monumental feats of engineering we see today owe a great deal to the great mistakes and tragedies that have occurred in the development of such structures over the years.

"We marvel today at the Gothic cathedrals. Yet many medieval churches collapsed during or soon after construction and were never completed," agrees Klein. "Massive building projects always carry such risks."

7. Based on information provided in the passage, which of the following is NOT suggested to be represented by large structures?
    (A) Affluence
    (B) Stability
    (C) Longevity
    (D) Power

8. Which of the following best reflects the main theme of the passage?
    (A) The challenge of building big
    (B) An introduction for the TV series "Building Big"
    (C) "Building Big" and the achievement of the Brooklyn Bridge
    (D) Human achievement always pushing forward from the success and failures of the past

9. The passage includes a listing of the five wonders of the modern world. In the list below, which is NOT one of those listed?
    (A) Brooklyn Bridge
    (B) English Channel Tunnel
    (C) Aswan Dam
    (D) Toronto Skydome

10. From information gleaned in the passage, in the list below, which achievement would the author most agree should be added to wonders of the modern world?
    (A) Curiosity rover on Mars
    (B) Massive offshore drilling platforms
    (C) International Space Station
    (D) Deep ocean submersibles

11. As recounted in the section on the Brooklyn Bridge construction, in addition to the architectural and physical triumphs included, which human character trait would most likely account for the ultimate success of the project?
    (A) Persistence and determination
    (B) Quest for economic gain
    (C) Human ingenuity and creativity
    (D) Meeting the needs of others

12. In considering large structures representing the most creative and ingenious designs of mankind, of the following list, which would the author most agree would represent the biggest failure of human building projects?

    (A) Hindenburg
    (B) Titanic
    (C) Bent Pyramid
    (D) Leaning Tower of Pisa

The Supreme Court Building

"The Republic endures and this is the symbol of its faith." These words, spoken by Chief Justice Charles Evans Hughes in laying the cornerstone for the Supreme Court Building on October 13, 1932, express the importance of the Supreme Court in the American system.

Yet surprisingly, despite its role as a coequal branch of government, the Supreme Court was not provided with a building of its own until 1935, the 146th year of its existence. Initially, the Court met in the Merchants Exchange Building in New York City. When the National Capital moved to Philadelphia in 1790, the Court moved with it, establishing Chambers first in the State House (Independence Hall) and later in the City Hall.

When the Federal Government moved, in 1800, to the permanent Capital, Washington, the District of Columbia, the Court again moved with it. Since no provision had been made for a Supreme Court Building, Congress lent the Court space in the new Capitol Building. The Court was to change its meeting place a half dozen times within the Capitol. Additionally, the Court convened for a short period in a private house after the British set fire to the Capitol during the War of 1812. Following this episode, the Court returned to the Capitol and met from 1819 to 1860 in a chamber now restored as the "Old Supreme Court Chamber." Then from 1860 until 1935, the Court sat in what is now known as the "Old Senate Chamber."

Finally in 1929, Chief Justice William Howard Taft, who had been President of the United States from 1909 to 1913, persuaded Congress to end this arrangement and authorize the construction of a permanent home for the Court. Architect Cass Gilbert was charged by Chief Justice Taft to design "a building of dignity and importance suitable for its use as the permanent home of the Supreme Court of the United States."

Neither Taft nor Gilbert survived to see the Supreme Court Building completed. Construction proceeded under the direction of Chief Justice Hughes and architects Cass Gilbert, Jr., and John R. Rockart. The construction, begun in 1932, was completed in 1935, when the Court was finally able to occupy its own building.

The classical Corinthian architectural style was selected because it best harmonized with nearby congressional buildings. The building was designed on a scale in keeping with the importance and dignity of the Court and the Judiciary as a coequal, independent branch of the United States Government, and as a symbol of "the national ideal of justice in the highest sphere of activity."

The general dimensions of the foundation are 385 feet from east to west, (front to back) and 304 feet from north to south. At its greatest height, the building rises four stories above the terrace or ground floor. Marble was chosen as the principal material to be used and $3 million worth was gathered from foreign and domestic quarries. Vermont marble was used for the exterior, while the four inner courtyards are of crystalline flaked, white Georgia marble. Above the basement level, the walls and floors of all corridors and entrance halls are either wholly or partially of creamy Alabama marble. The wood in offices throughout the building, such as doors, trim, paneled walls, and some floors, is American quartered white oak.

The Court Building cost less than the $9,740,000 Congress authorized for its construction. Not only was the final and complete cost of the building within the appropriation, but all furnishings were also procured, even though planners had initially expected that the project would require additional appropriations. Upon completion of the project, $94,000 was returned to the Treasury.

13. The quote from Chief Justice Charles E. Hughes when he stated that the Supreme Court Building, ". . . is the symbol of its faith" appears to blend government and religion together. Which of the following would most represent what the speaker (and author in using this quote) meant by this statement?

    (A) The judicial system was founded upon the precepts of the Bible.
    (B) The American people believed the republic would last.
    (C) It commemorated the earliest settlers to America who came in search of religious freedom.
    (D) Americans had faith in the government and its elected officials.

14. As the federal government grows, more funds are appropriated to diverse projects and programs. In recent years, many of these building programs have been documented and publicized (and/or criticized) in the media. Of the following things that happened during the construction of the supreme court building, which would be the least likely to occur if the building were constructed today?

    (A) Marble would not be used because it would be too expensive.
    (B) Today the building would be constructed much larger.
    (C) The project would come in under budget.
    (D) The structure would be made to distinguish itself from the congressional building rather than be made in a similar manner.

15. William Howard Taft, who served as Chief Justice of the Supreme Court during its construction, had a major influence on its design and architecture. However, Taft also has another notable distinction to his credit. Which of the following applies to Chief Justice Taft?

    (A) Former congressman
    (B) Former president
    (C) Former vice president
    (D) Former governor

16. The current Supreme Court Building began housing the Supreme Court in the 146th year of its existence. Of the following, which would the author most agree was responsible for the delay in obtaining a separate but equal residence for the third branch of the federal government?

    (A) The court was seen as the least of the three branches of government.
    (B) Funding was unavailable.
    (C) Sufficient space had always been allocated elsewhere.
    (D) There were only nine justices of the Supreme Court and they did not require as much space as the 100 senators and over 400 congressional leaders.

17. In a similar way, of the following, which would the author most agree served as the impetus for building a Supreme Court Building after all those years in other places?

    (A) There was increased demand for space in the capital from more and more congressmen.
    (B) Taft was extremely influential and moved the project forward to successful completion.
    (C) The government was well enough established to be able to afford a new building.
    (D) Land was donated to the government for the purpose of a Supreme Court Building.

18. For the look and structure of the Supreme Court Building, which was decided to be the final style of the building?

    (A) Grecian
    (B) Colonial
    (C) Renaissance
    (D) Corinthian

CHAPTER 2

Art

The Serious and the Smirk: The Smile in Portraiture

Today when someone points a camera at us, we smile. This is the cultural and social reflex of our time, and such are our expectations of a picture portrait. But in the long history of portraiture the open smile has been largely, as it were, frowned upon.

In Charles Dickens' *Nicholas Nickleby* (1838-1839) the portrait painter Miss La Creevy ponders the problem:

. . . People are so dissatisfied and unreasonable, that, nine times out of ten, there's no pleasure in painting them. Sometimes they say, "Oh, how very serious you have made me look, Miss La Creevy!" and at others, "La, Miss La Creevy, how very smirking!". . . In fact, there are only two styles of portrait painting; the serious and the smirk; and we always use the serious for professional people (except actors sometimes), and the smirk for private ladies and gentlemen who don't care so much about looking clever.

A walk around any art gallery will reveal that the image of the open smile has, for a very long time, been deeply unfashionable. Miss La Creevy's equivocal 'smirks' do however make more frequent appearances: a smirk may offer artists an opportunity for ambiguity that the open smile cannot. Such a subtle and complex facial expression may convey almost anything—piqued interest, condescension, flirtation, wistfulness, boredom, discomfort, contentment, or mild embarrassment. This equivocation allows the artist to offer us a lasting emotional engagement with the image. An open smile, however, is unequivocal, a signal moment of unselfconsciousness. Such is the field upon which the mouth in portraiture has been debated: an ongoing conflict between the serious and the smirk.

The most famous and enduring portrait in the world functions around this very conflict. Millions of words have been devoted to the *Mona Lisa* and her smirk—more generously known as her 'enigmatic smile'—and so today it's difficult to write about her without sensing that you're at the back of a very long and noisy queue that stretches all the way back to 16th century Florence. But to write about the smile in portraiture without mentioning her is perverse, for the effect of the *Mona Lisa* has always been in its inherent ability to demand further examination. Leonardo impels us to do this using a combination of skillful sfumato (the effect of blurriness, or smokiness) and his profound understanding of human desire. It is a kind of magic: when you first glimpse her, she appears to be issuing a wanton invitation, so alive is the smile. But when you look again, and the sfumato clears in focus, she seems to have changed her mind about you. This is interactive stuff, and paradoxical: the effect of the painting only occurs in dialogue, yet she is only really there when you're not really looking. The *Mona Lisa* is thus, in many ways, designed to frustrate—and frustrate she did.

19. When conveying emotion in a portrait, a smirk would allow which of the following for the artist?

    (A) Ambiguity
    (B) Consistency
    (C) Uniformity
    (D) Acceptability

20. The serious facial expression is said to be widely preferred in the 1800s for professionals. In our contemporary society, as stated in the beginning of the passage, when a camera is pointed in your direction you reflexively smile. In which of the following scenarios would the portrait rule of the 1800s still apply today?

    (A) Presidential portrait
    (B) Portfolio photos of a model
    (C) Advertising promotional pictures
    (D) Family portraits

21. Of the following list of emotions, which was NOT included in the passage as a possible emotion conveyed by the smirk?

    (A) Boredom
    (B) Flirtation
    (C) Condescension
    (D) Calculating

22. In what manner does the author refer to the *Mona Lisa* being an example of the skillful "sfumato" used by Leonardo?

    (A) The colors and brush strokes made her face blurry or foggy and prevented an exact interpretation of her smile.
    (B) His ability to convey emotion was unknown and thus unclear.
    (C) The expression of her smile could be seen either as a smile or a smirk, serious or playful, depending on the moment or person who observed her.
    (D) Only people trained in the arts can truly appreciate the real expression and meaning of the *Mona Lisa*.

23. At the end of the passage, the author states that the *Mona Lisa* is intended to frustrate the viewer and she does. Which of the following would the author agree was the intent of this statement?

(A) He doesn't know how Leonardo did it.
(B) No one knows who she actually was.
(C) Her expression seems to change every time he looks at her.
(D) He can't figure out what she is thinking and feeling.

24. In paragraph four, the author defines *Mona Lisa's* smirk as an "enigmatic smile." Based on the passage, which of the following best describes the author's meaning in choosing this term?

(A) Famous
(B) Definite
(C) Mysterious
(D) Classical

25. The "selfie" may, in the minds of some, be equivalent to the portraits described in the passage. Considering the instant modern photo snapped each and every day by individuals, with which of the following would the author most agree about modern photography and the smirk?

(A) Facial expression is less important today due to the sheer numbers of photos that can be taken.
(B) Modern portraits are still captured moments in time and would be influenced in much the same way as those in Da Vinci's time.
(C) The smile/smirk is only important in modern times for professional portraits of high ranking officials such as the president.
(D) Smiles are even more important with the multitude of photos on social media that share and show emotion.

The Highwaymen, A School of African-American Artists Who Exhibited Their Work Where Tourists Would See It

It was an era when most African Americans in Fort Pierce were relegated to working in kitchens or fields, when Jim Crow prevented them from using the same water fountains as whites, and few, if any, black artists could be found in history books. Despite the obstacles, a loose group of creative and entrepreneurial African Americans dared to break the bounds of poverty and segregation by capturing the rugged natural beauty that they saw around them. With quick strokes of their brushes and swift sweeps of bold colors with palette knives, they captured vibrant coastal sunsets framed by palms, Royal Poinciana trees in flaming red bloom, and interior wetlands touched by egrets, ibis, and roseate spoonbills.

Since most galleries in the 1950s and 1960s refused to sell African-American art, these artists sold their creations for about twenty-five dollars apiece out of the trunks of their cars along Florida's Atlantic coast. They went door-to-door at white-owned businesses and residences; they set up along U.S. 1 and peddled to passing tourists.

Decades later, after many had stopped painting, a prominent art collector declared their style distinctly Floridian and coined them the "Florida Highwaymen" because of where they commonly sold their art. *The New York Times* wrote about them. Prices soared. People started discovering old Florida landscape paintings in attics, yard sales, and thrift stores. Fakes appeared on eBay.

Today paintings by noted Florida Highwaymen sell for anywhere from $500 to $45,000 in galleries, antique stores, and art shows.

To University of Central Florida humanities scholar Kristin Congdon, they are significant because of their determination and success in using art to escape poverty and combat racial boundaries. "The times were changing with civil rights. They had an inkling that freedom was in the air," she said. "They didn't sit at the counters in protest, but they were doing the same kind of thing while saying I can bring you a gift."

In 2004, a core group of twenty-six Highwaymen were inducted into the Florida Artists Hall of Fame. The City of Fort Pierce, with the help of a Florida Humanities Council grant, is establishing a website and a Highwaymen Heritage Trail that traces significant sites of the artists' development, lives, and, in a few cases, their deaths. Directed by Libby Woodruff, the trail officially opens in December with commemorative signs marking each site.

26. In paragraph one, the author mentions "Jim Crow." How is this name used in regard to this passage?

   (A) It was used as an example because of what happened to the man named Jim Crow.
   (B) He was the author of legislation to restrict the mixing of blacks and whites.
   (C) It was the law that segregated blacks and whites completely.
   (D) It was a means with which to integrate blacks and whites in the South.

27. Why were the African American artists called the Florida Highwaymen?

   (A) Most lived in Florida.
   (B) Florida had a busy interstate highway on which the artists sold their paintings from the trunks of their cars.
   (C) Florida had less strict laws regarding the interaction of blacks and whites.
   (D) Few African American artists practiced in other areas of the country.

28. What is the main theme of this passage?

(A) People will find a way to express themselves in spite of planned restrictions.

(B) Law can restrict action, but a passion for the arts cannot be silenced.

(C) Florida is the most permissive state for the arts.

(D) The Florida Highwaymen represents a foundation of historic black artists in America.

29. In contemporary society, which of the following artistic genres may most closely compare to that of the Florida Highwaymen?

(A) Hip Hop / Rap music

(B) Graffiti artists in the cities

(C) African American poets writing about their history

(D) Dancers who demonstrate traditional African dance styles in America

30. Of the following explanations, which would be most likely to account for the increase in the value of the paintings of the Florida Highwaymen as stated in the passage?

(A) Exposure of their paintings by *The New York Times*

(B) No other African American artists came after them

(C) Supply and demand

(D) Older paintings are always worth more than new paintings

31. The Florida Highwaymen, like many African Americans of the time, experienced great hardship; however, they endured and overcame those social obstacles and were inducted into the Florida Artists Hall of Fame. From the list below, which would be the most likely argument supported by this author for the induction of these gentlemen into the hall of fame?

(A) Exceptional quality of the art

(B) The capture of raw emotion and hardship on the canvases

(C) The skill of the artists with the lack of extensive materials

(D) All of the above

The Importance of Taking Children to Museums

There's no shortage of research indicating the benefits of museum visits for children. They can provide memorable, immersive learning experiences, provoke imagination, introduce unknown worlds and subject matter, and offer unique environments for quality time with family. Curious to hear more from people in the field, we asked educators from Blue Star Museums around the country to tell us why they think it's important to take children to museums. Here's what they had to say:

> "Museums offer a dynamic opportunity to expose children to experiences and explore new things in a rich and educational environment. Through interactive exhibits and hands-on play, children have the ability to take ownership of their own learning and develop and explore their own curiosities. This unique exposure provides the foundation for creativity, critical thinking, and connection to the world around them."
>
> —*Sara Choi, Education Program Manager, Zimmer Children's Museum*

> "Art gives us an experience like nothing else can, a chance to connect, understand, and explore perceptions, feelings, and innovative thoughts. Museums provide a space for reflection, experimentation, inspiration, creativity, enjoyment and allow for authentic learning experiences and play. Bringing children to the museum reveals children and adults as being equally active in learning, putting them on equal standing as they create a shared understanding. It's a democratic process."
>
> —*Jamee Yung, Education Coordinator, Weisman Art Museum*

> "Families come to the Vermont History Museum to get a glimpse of different times and places, helping the children gain a broad understanding of the past. When parents and grandparents bring children to the museum, they spend family time together, sharing conversations about favorite objects, family stories, and historic events. Lifelong learning begins at a young age and museums are a great place to spark an interest in history, art, and science."
>
> —*Victoria Hughes, Education Coordinator, Vermont Historical Society*

> "Many of our guests are novice adult visitors who are nervous about bringing children to museums. They express concern that the children will ask questions they can't answer. We always encourage them to look at it as a shared intergenerational learning experience in which they grow together. Simply asking a child what piece he or she likes best in a particular gallery and then exploring it together, talking about what the child likes, what the adult likes, what they each think is going on in the work, if it is narrative or how the work makes them feel, if it is more abstract. This can evoke discussions of memories (for instance, a landscape that reminds an adult of a lake visited in childhood) or of dreams (a child saying that he or she would like to be as strong and big as a figure depicted in a sculpture) and can lead to a very natural free-flowing dialogue that often gets missed in the day-to-day busy-ness of life. This is particularly valuable I think for our Blue Star families—those cherishing last moments before deployment, those reconnecting after a long

time apart, and those newly blended as family scenarios change. Use the art as a way to talk, open up, explore, and learn from each other, and from there you will grow and your comfort in the museum will grow too."

—*Adera Causey, Curator of Education, Hunter Museum of American Art*

"As the mother to an almost four-year-old boy and a museum professional, I believe that early exposure to museums fosters curiosity in children. Our first visit to a museum was when my son was only six weeks old, and over the past few years we have visited science centers, natural history museums, traditional history museums, art museums, botanical gardens, and of course children's museums. His curiosity about the world around him, and the people and things that make up our world is in large part due to these visits exploring museums and their exhibits. I have always believed that early exposure to museums creates lifelong museum visitors and now I have the proof."

—*Kate Whitman, Vice President of Public Programs, Atlanta History Center*

32. According to the author, there are many benefits from taking children to the museum. From the list below, which of the following was NOT mentioned in the passage as a benefit to museum visits?
   (A) Foster creativity
   (B) Enhance critical thinking skills
   (C) Form a closer world view
   (D) Break from the "busy-ness" of life

33. What if no museum is possible? What do students in rural schools do that can be comparable?
   (A) Visits to local businesses
   (B) Field trip to a zoo
   (C) Interactive exhibits that come to the school
   (D) Guest speakers visiting the school

34. Visits to the museum aren't just for the children but are an important part of the adult learning experience as well as an opportunity for interaction between children and adults. In a museum setting, how does the author describe a similarity between the experiences of the adults and children?
   (A) Children and adults are equally active in the learning process at the museum.
   (B) Both adults and children are actively communicating.
   (C) Each group has a similar level of interest in the exhibits.
   (D) Both are in the same role as observers.

35. What does the author mean by "intergenerational learning experience"?
    (A) Adults and children contributing different elements to the learning experience
    (B) Adults teaching and children learning
    (C) People of all ages learning at the same time
    (D) Children learning about older people from history

36. Of the following, which would be a Blue Star family?
    (A) Children of a soldier going off to war
    (B) A newly married couple with their children and step children
    (C) Family and foster children
    (D) Rural students and their families

37. Which of the following would the author agree should MOST occur in the early formative years of a child's life?
    (A) Visiting a museum
    (B) Early exposure to science, history, and art
    (C) Spending time with adults
    (D) Gaining new experiences

To Make Beautiful the Capitol

Over a span of 25 years, Constantino Brumidi (1805–1880) decorated the walls and ceilings of the United States Capitol in a manner befitting a great public building. In the Senate wing, he designed and painted murals, some in the traditional fresco medium, for important spaces such as the President's Room, the Senate Reception Room, and the renowned Brumidi Corridors—the august hallways that today bear the artist's name. Brumidi's monumental fresco in the Capitol Rotunda, The *Apotheosis of Washington*, covers an impressive 4,664 square feet and yet took just 11 months to complete. His prodigious efforts at the Capitol were truly a labor of love. When Brumidi died in February of 1880, *The Washington Post* reflected: "He was the genius of the Capitol. So many of its stateliest rooms bear the touch of his tireless brush that he shall always be associated with it."

Brumidi accepted his first assignment for the Capitol in December of 1854, when he was a mature 49 years of age. Having emigrated from Italy just two years earlier, the Italian-born artist arrived in Washington, D.C., as construction progressed on the Capitol extension, which comprised the Senate and House wings.

Shortly thereafter, in March of 1855, a new cast-iron dome for the building was authorized. Brumidi possessed the skills, temperament, and motivation to take on the demanding challenge of designing and painting historical frescoes and decorative murals for the building's new interiors. He became a naturalized U.S. citizen in 1857, and in later years, was something of a fixture at the Capitol. Members of the press and visitors to the building often observed "Signor Brumidi" at work and engaged the amiable artist in conversation about the subjects of his paintings.

During the two and a half decades that Brumidi ornamented the Capitol with his "tireless brush," he worked through six presidents' terms and 13 Congresses, and the young nation grew from 31 to 38 states. Changes in administration, controversies about his decorative style, the turmoil of the Civil War, and his own advancing age did not deter him from his life's work. Brumidi's son Laurence reflected on his father's efforts: "All labor was given freely out of pride in the Capitol Building of the United States and love for the land of his adoption."

After Brumidi's death, his murals were altered by artists hired to repair and restore the paintings in the era before modern conservation. These alterations managed only to diminish Brumidi's originals, in many cases quite severely, and his reputation suffered accordingly.

In recent decades, Brumidi's artistic contribution to the Capitol has become a subject of serious study for scholars and a primary occupation for fine art conservators. Starting in the 1980s, Congress supported an extensive and long-term conservation program to restore Brumidi's work in the Capitol. As a result of a decade of researching Brumidi's life and of managing the mural conservation program, Architect of the Capitol Curator Barbara A. Wolanin published *Constantino Brumidi: Artist of the Capitol* in 1998. This book discusses Brumidi's background and painting techniques, as well as the political context in which the artist worked at the Capitol; the book also highlights the conservation and restoration efforts that had been accomplished by the mid-1990s.

Since then, the mural conservation program has made sweeping changes to the appearance of the Senate wing of the Capitol and has allowed a fresh examination of Brumidi's artwork. These changes are most evident in the Brumidi Corridors, where the reemergence of the historical detail in Brumidi's original murals has opened doors for new research, discoveries, and interpretations. What we know about the artist has been enhanced by the addition of several of Brumidi's preliminary sketches to the Senate collection and by the transcription of a key journal detailing the building of the Capitol extension, as well as by recently digitized resources that point to the inspiration for Brumidi's work.

38. The painting that covers the Capitol Rotunda ceiling is called the *Apotheosis of Washington*. Of the following, which would be the best definition of the word apotheosis as used in this instance?

(A) Elevation to the highest level
(B) Remembrance of his life
(C) In memorial
(D) Marking the beginning

39. The *Apotheosis of Washington* one was of Brumidi's greatest accomplishments. While it is a beautiful work in its own right, which of the following would the author most agree would be the most impressive thing about Brumidi's *Apotheosis of Washington*?

    (A) It was on the ceiling of the Rotunda.
    (B) It was huge; 4,664 square feet.
    (C) It was completed in only 11 months.
    (D) Rumidi was 60 years old when the painting was complete.

40. Throughout the text, the author states Brumidi's work was a "labor of love" and quotes his son Laurence who said, "All labor was given freely out of pride in the Capitol Building of the United States and love for the land of his adoption." Of the following, which would the author most agree was the driving force behind Brumidi's sense of loyalty and pride, having only come to the United States two years prior to beginning work on the Capitol?

    (A) The money he would earn for working on the Capitol
    (B) America's provision of a sanctuary, freedom, and opportunity not available in his country
    (C) The prestige he would engender having his work displayed in the Capitol
    (D) His becoming part of the American culture and history

41. In paragraph three, the author states that Brumidi was assigned the task of painting the Capitol Rotunda because he had the . . . "temperament" to take on the challenge. Based on the passage, why would the temperament of an artist be important for such a task?

    (A) He needed patience because of the project's length.
    (B) He would have to deal with the long hours and difficult conditions.
    (C) He would be directing many other artists to finish the project.
    (D) As politicians came and went, he needed to be able to work with them all.

42. As a dedication to the artists whose brush strokes are present throughout the Capitol building, which area is specifically named after him?

    (A) President's room
    (B) Senate Reception room
    (C) The corridors
    (D) Rotunda

43. The conservation of historical works of art takes much skill and meticulous effort to preserve the art in its original form. Often the damage is so extensive that the work may not be recoverable. In the passage, the early conservation of Brumidi's work in the Capitol was said to be poor and resulted in the severe damage to his art and his reputation. Which of the following would best explain how the conversation efforts made it worse?

   (A) The conservators didn't have the technology to conserve as we do today.
   (B) They only restored the damaged areas.
   (C) Paints currently available were used rather than those used by Brumidi.
   (D) The damaged areas were covered more than they were repaired.

44. Through which tumultuous period did Brumidi work on the paintings in the Capitol?

   (A) Revolutionary War
   (B) Civil War
   (C) World War I
   (D) Great Depression

Cosmic Creativity: An Artist's View of Space

When Dan Goods was studying graphic design, he figured he'd probably end up at an ad agency or some sort of commercial corporation. But these days, his artistic concerns are bigger than choosing the appropriate typeface, layout, and color. Much bigger. Like Jupiter-sized big. For the past ten years, Goods has worked as a visual strategist at the National Aeronautics and Space Administration's (NASA) Jet Propulsion Laboratory (JPL) in Pasadena, California. His job is to translate the technical, data-driven language of JPL's missions into engaging, public-friendly works of art. When negotiating his position, the original idea was that Goods would create visualizations communicating JPL's work. But Goods pushed back: he didn't want people simply to see the universe; he wanted them to feel it.

"What is great about being here is that I get to work with content that is, in its essence, mind-blowing. But you still have to express it in a way that's mind-blowing as well," said Goods, who was named "one of the most interesting people in Los Angeles" by *LA Weekly* in 2012. "I want to be able to give people a moment of awe about the universe that we live in."

Take his piece "Beneath the Surface," inspired by the Juno spacecraft's mission to Jupiter. Launched in 2011, Juno will penetrate Jupiter's thick cloud cover for the first time, allowing scientists to study the planet's evolution and properties, including the depth of its powerful lightning storms. Intrigued by the idea of these massive storms, Goods used vaporized tap water, ultrasonic misters, infrared lights, and audio of thunder to simulate what it might be like when Juno descends upon the gas giant.

He filled a darkened room with a vast, amorphous cloud, backlit by an eerie reddish glow. In a nod to the instruments needed to see below Jupiter's clouds, the installation's "lightning" was created using infrared lights, which are invisible to the naked eye but can be seen with a cell phone camera. As thunder crashed all around, people were able to use their phones to embark on their own exploratory mission of the lightning storm.

"That experience of going into this room, seeing this crazy cloud, touching it, using their cell phone—it's all an experience I like to hope people take with them for a long time," Goods said. Although Goods said he has always been fascinated by space, he didn't consider pursuing science professionally until he arrived at the Art Center College of Design, also in Pasadena. When nearby California Institute of Technology opened its summer research program to Art Center students for the first time, Goods became one of the first three artists accepted. He found himself working alongside conceptual artist David Kremers to help create the "Mouse Atlas," a digital tool that visually mapped the development of mice. While a far cry from astrophysics, it left a profound impression on Goods. "The experience of hanging out with scientists was fascinating for me," he said. "I loved the big ideas that science works with, and I felt like I was doing something meaningful."

The experience was so positive that after graduation, Goods focused his job search within the world of science. After a number of false starts, he was invited on a tour of JPL with the president of Art Center and the director of the NASA facility. "I had about two seconds to sell myself," Goods remembered. Eventually, he was able to show JPL's top brass the "Mouse Atlas" and a traveling pipe organ he had invented by rigging soda bottles to a car. The projects were innovative enough to convince JPL staff that he had more to offer than the animations they had in mind.

"Most of the time, if someone says, 'Do you want to do animations?' You say, 'Yes,' when you need a job. You don't usually say, 'Hey look at this bottle project,' to a person from NASA, expecting them to be enticed by it. But I took the risk, and it paid off," said Goods. He was told he'd get six months and then they'd re-evaluate. That was ten years ago.

45. Although Dan Goods was a trained artist and had experience with scientific projects, which of the following was the most important factor that landed him the job at JPL?

  (A) The "Mouse Atlas"
  (B) The soda bottle pipe organ
  (C) His science knowledge
  (D) His creative and innovative style

46. What is the name of the JPL project, created by Goods, that illustrates the atmosphere of Jupiter?

(A) Juno
(B) "Beneath the Surface"
(C) Lightening in Space
(D) The Red Storm

47. For the past 10 years, Dan Goods worked as a "visual strategist" at NASA's Jet Propulsion Lab (JPL). Which of the following would the author agree is the best description of his position?

(A) An artist illustrating astronomical data
(B) An engineer designing exhibits for the public
(C) A creator of meaningful, visual, and experiential illustrations of JPL projects
(D) A computer animator illustrating spacecraft missions

48. Working with soda bottles and cell phones seems a far distance away from the technology required to communicate with a spacecraft at the edge of our solar system. In what way does Dan Goods most contribute to science and our understanding of the world around us?

(A) He simplifies and demonstrates the end results of the highly complex missions in understandable ways.
(B) He condenses the data into packets more easily understood by most people.
(C) His animations illustrate in a short period the milestones and long range goals of the missions.
(D) His work only demonstrates those concepts which are easily understood and illustrated.

49. For his interactive exhibit on cloud lightning on Jupiter, Goods had visitors use their cell phones to capture images of the clouds and lightning. In what way was this experience unique for his exhibit as compared to simply capturing a photo of lightning in nature?

(A) He used backlit red lights.
(B) Infrared light was used.
(C) The lightning was UV light, only detectable by cell phone cameras.
(D) Strobe lights were used to mimic the lightning in the room.

50. As the author interacts with Goods, she enables the reader to truly see the heart and the mind of this creative individual. However, he isn't simply an artist or a computer animator. In fact he states in the passage his one goal and the aspect which sets his work apart from all others. Which of the following would the author agree is that greatest distinction for Goods?

(A) His illustrations are cutting edge and breathtaking.
(B) He wants to blow your mind with the science.
(C) He attempts to awe the viewer with graphical information.
(D) He wants visitors to experience science, not just see it.

51. The worlds of biology and astrophysics seem to be a universe apart from one another. Yet, Goods has spanned those two diverse fields of science and accomplished similar goals for each. When the "Mouse Atlas" and the "Beneath the Surface" projects are compared, which of the following do you think they have most in common with each other?

(A) Each takes highly complex scenarios and produces simple interactive exhibits.
(B) Both are explanations of science.
(C) Computer animations are used in both.
(D) Each uses state of the art technology to illustrate the projects and missions.

CHAPTER 3

Dance

Full Exposure: Ballet East Brings Modern Dance to East Austin

"Ballet East shatters the myth that one has to live west of Interstate 35 to be a highly trained dancer," said dance critic Sondra Lomax. This is a testament to the work of Rodolfo Mendez, who in 1978 founded the Ballet East Dance Company. Mendez's determination exposed the low-income neighborhood of East Austin to modern dance, providing opportunities for local dancers and choreographers to develop their skills.

Ballet East presents a minimum of eight performances a year, including new works and restagings set on the company by local and nationally recognized choreographers. The company also provides youth internships in stagecraft, presents community-wide folk and traditional arts festivals, and runs Dare to Dance, an after school dance program for students ages 7 to 15 who are at risk of dropping out of school. Dare to Dance was recognized in 2002 and 2003 as a Coming Up Taller semifinalist.

In order to broaden its reach among East Austin youth, Ballet East partnered with East Memorial High School (formerly Johnston High School) for the 2007-2008 school year. In partnership with the school, the company presented two dance demonstrations and seven in-school performances for the entire student body. With 80 percent of the students coming from families with limited economic means, this opportunity to view live, professional dance was rare. "You wonder if the kids will be interested," said Mendez. "But they sat through all the performances. . . . Seeing dance live keeps their attention better than viewing a tape."

The company also took 240 eleventh- and twelfth-grade students to dance productions by Ballet East and fellow local companies Ballet Austin and Tapestry Dance Company, an opportunity Mendez said would not have been possible without NEA grant support. For many of the students, this was their first experience in a professional theater, seeing how the lighting, sound, and set all contribute to the final production. As part of the field trips, Ballet East arranged for the students to meet the dancers and choreographers.

Through the school's Arts Academy, company dancers and choreographers held in-school classes in dance fundamentals and Horton modern technique.

Ballet East also opened up master classes to the entire school, which were taught by Regina Larkin, artistic director of New York City's Joyce Trisler Danscompany, and Francisco Gella, a freelance choreographer who has worked with Philadanco.

"Exposure" was the key word for Ballet East's year at East Memorial High School. From in-school demonstrations to master classes to field trips to professional productions, Ballet East was invested in providing the students with as much access to the world of dance as possible, creating a new generation of dance audiences, and—for the students who have gone on to take Ballet East classes full-time—perhaps a future as a dancer.

52. When considering dance in the area described in the passage, which of the following is the most surprising about people in this area learning about in modern dance?

   (A) Ballet isn't popular in Texas.
   (B) Rural communities rarely have modern cultural exposure.
   (C) It is a low-income area.
   (D) Austin is known for music more than dance.

53. Of the following list, which was the key vehicle through which Ballet East was successful in reaching its goal?

   (A) Exposing students to the art of dancing
   (B) Training students in various aspects of artistic dance
   (C) Generating interest in dance as a profession
   (D) Providing opportunities for students to stay out of trouble

54. When attending a live performance, the extra cost to the program is offset by the benefits the live performance will bring to the students versus a recorded performance to be viewed later. Which of the following best describes the added benefit to the students of the live performance?

   (A) Students paid more attention.
   (B) The ability to see behind the scenes is not possible with film.
   (C) Students were able to speak with performers.
   (D) Visual effects are better in a live performance.

55. Which of the following best represents the main theme of the passage?

   (A) Exposure to the arts always produces an interest in the arts.
   (B) Low income communities benefit when provided exposure to the arts.
   (C) Ballet East provides opportunities to experience the arts which may turn into a lifetime of enjoyment and interest.
   (D) Exposure at an early age is important in stimulating interest in the arts.

56. Considering all of the positive aspects of Ballet East for the students and the communities, which of the following was a principle goal of the project?

(A) To prepare dancers for a career in the arts
(B) To provide opportunities for individuals to learn valuable skills in the arts
(C) To develop an appreciation and interest in the arts
(D) To bring the arts to the area to increase the attractiveness of the community

57. Of the following, which would most weaken the argument for the success of Ballet East?

(A) None of the students ever attended a ballet performance after graduation.
(B) No graduates of Ballet East chose a career in professional dance.
(C) Crime rates among Ballet East participants were as high as those of the population in general.
(D) Grades of Ballet East participants did not improve.

The Healing Power of Dance

Dance/Movement Therapy is the psychotherapeutic use of dance and movement processes to bring about healing and recovery for individuals of all ages and cultural groups. It is practiced by trained, masters level professionals: mental health clinicians who specialize in this creative arts therapy. Since 1966, the ADTA [American Dance Therapy Association] has advanced this mind/body integrated form of psychotherapy, with member services, educational standards, professional credentialing, continuing education, and public action to advocate for the needs of those we serve in hospitals, after-school programs, mental health centers, schools, rehabilitation facilities, wellness programs, and other settings.

One of the benefits of dancing is an increased sense of vitality—an awakening and renewal of one's life energy. Studies have shown that dance interventions by trained professionals can decrease depression, improve mood, and strengthen positive feelings about one's self. Dance/movement therapy (or DMT) harnesses the many elements of dance that have therapeutic potential. DMT does not emphasize dance technique and it is not about the artistic product (a performance). Rather, it is very much about improvisation, the mobilization and exchange of energy, and the creative, expressive process. DMT clients learn to move in ways that are authentic to how they are feeling and experiencing life, in the context of a supportive therapeutic relationship.

We dance/movement therapists focus on rhythms and phrases, and on the quality of the movement: space, weight, and time. We rely on Laban Movement Analysis for assessing movement in relation to health and human development. We work with transforming fragmentation into connectedness, and giving the silenced a voice through the medium of dance. Dance forms and structures are modified for release of tension and for helping people become comfortable moving. While the dance/movement experience is the main focus of a DMT session, dance/movement therapists will also use verbalization and discussion in sessions, and sometimes DMT sessions can be noisy with music, rhythm instruments, foot stomping, hand-clapping, or laughter and all kinds of vocalizing.

Dance is movement, and movement is essentially a process of ongoing change. Moving with one's whole body, with and against gravity, one learns to both yield and resist, to feel one's strength and to feel one's vulnerability, to try on new qualities of action and behavior. This is what it means to be fully human. DMT can improve body image. Paul Schilder, a developmental neuroscientist, once said that dance is a loosening up of the body schema. He was describing how when we dance, the movement activates a dynamic and constant feedback loop back and forth between our brains and our bodies, so that our experience of our felt and living selves is one of change.

It has been reported that children who have been traumatized can live on the alert, anxious and fearful. Dance-based methods for getting grounded, for sensing the body's energy and position, and for developing breath support can help with learning to pay attention to one's own needs, and for feeling more in control, and for regulating fearful or angry reactions.

As dancers know, dancing and moving rhythmically with other people creates a powerful sense of "with-ness." This is a basic principle of DMT, as noted by dance therapy pioneer Marian Chace, and group cohesion is formed very quickly through what she called "shared rhythmic action." Unlike most dance classes, group dance/movement therapy sessions will often start and end in a circle formation. In a circle, everyone can see everyone else; we connect visually with the people across the circle and kinesthetically with the people on either side. Everyone is of equal status: the circle encourages participation by everyone, and invites each person to contribute movement ideas.

58. In the passage, the author states that dance gives "the silenced a voice." From the list below, find the statement that the author would MOST AGREE represents his meaning for that statement?

(A) Dance enables those who are mute to express themselves.
(B) Those who have difficulty putting their emotions into words can express them through dance.
(C) People who have been abused often do not share through words but will through dance.
(D) People are inherently more expressive through dance and music than through words.

59. For healthcare, many individuals seek the aid of a physical therapist. From the passage, dance therapy would most contrast with traditional physical therapy in which aspect?

    (A) Physical therapy works with range of motion while dance is artistic technique.
    (B) Dance therapy is more cardiovascular than physical therapy.
    (C) Physical therapy is a certified approach to healing, dance therapy is not.
    (D) Dance deals with the emotional aspect of the patient while physical therapy deals with the mechanical.

60. While there are many approaches to help a patient obtain a better quality of life, dance therapy is suggested to help individuals in many ways, with the EXCEPTION of which of the following?

    (A) Decreasing depression
    (B) Improving body image
    (C) Regaining strength
    (D) Better at controlling emotions

61. Of the benefits of dance therapy, the author mentions that dance assists with an individual's "with-ness." In the list below, find the example that the author would most agree represents his meaning of this term?

    (A) Being part of a team
    (B) Joining a social media group
    (C) Contributing to a group blog
    (D) Staying up to date on the social norms (i.e., fashion, music, etc.)

62. Based on the passage, which of the following would most WEAKEN the argument for the therapeutic value of dance?

    (A) The "wallflower" who fears dancing in public until they give it a try
    (B) A professional dancer who has devoted years to dance
    (C) Someone dancing to be seen and attract others
    (D) Married couples learning to ballroom dance together

63. Considering the passage, which of the following statements would the author most agree reflects the meaning of "movement is essentially a process of ongoing change"?

    (A) Change is inevitable.
    (B) Change is part of growing.
    (C) Dance is constantly moving.
    (D) To dance you must move.

Grassroots Modern

The dance revolution was fought on many fronts, but the key battle took place at Vermont's Bennington College. It was here in the 1930s, amid the cow farms in the bucolic Green Mountains, that the giants of modern dance—Graham, Humphrey, Holm, Weidman—fine-tuned their techniques and trained their dancer armies to spread the revolution across the country.

"There could not have been a more felicitous falling out of circumstances—the time, the place, the people—for the creation of a new center for the burgeoning American dance," wrote dancer and educator Martha Hill. It was Hill's determination and finesse that took the study of dance from places like the Kellogg School of Physical Education (of which Hill was a graduate) to the fine arts departments of America's top universities. And it was her vision that transformed summer vacation into an intense crucible of dance, the kind now replicated at hundreds of colleges every summer, but quite radical at the time.

Hill had been lured to Bennington in 1932 by Robert Devore Leigh, Bennington's first president, who had seen the maverick educator at a dance workshop in New York City. Hill was dancing with Martha Graham's company and teaching at New York University. She kept her New York teaching gig and commuted back and forth on the "Up-Flier" to her faculty job at Bennington when the college opened that year, in the midst of the Depression.

Leigh shared Hill's idea that dance should be "in the commonwealth of the arts," not relegated to PE departments. He secured permission from Bennington's trustees to seek an appropriate summer enterprise for dance, putting Hill in charge of making it a success. And the whirlwind began.

The launching of the Bennington Summer School of Dance in 1934 resembled more an act of faith than a predestined success. Hill's motto became, "Go do whatever comes next, and do it fast."

Leigh told Hill, "If you get sixty students, you'll be able to pay your bills." When the forty-third registration came, she relaxed. When the sixty-fifth came, she celebrated, and with the arrival of the hundred and third, she closed enrollment. They had run out of beds. Hill recalled, "We knew we had an original, and world-shaking, and timely idea."

For a faculty, Leigh instructed Hill to "get the best there is" and she did, creating her own temple for dance with a bevy of handpicked talents serving as both artists and teachers.

Martha Graham, of course, was the first choice—an appointment no one questioned. Graham had been Hill's mentor and was emerging as a leader in modern dance with a cultish following. Hanya Holm had danced with Mary Wigman's company in Germany before setting up a New York City branch of the influential Wigman School. Doris Humphrey's considerable choreographic talent had been evident throughout her years with the Denishawn dance company. After breaking away and establishing a company in 1928 with her partner, Charles Weidman, she was producing some of the most respected dance work on the recital scene. All of these artists happily agreed to join the Bennington staff—the prospect of a steady salary for these perpetually broke dancers was too much to resist.

Hill wisely invited a spokesman for the new movement, *New York Times* dance critic John Martin, to develop a dance history and critical writing course for the curriculum. Louis Horst would be the school's authoritative figure for anything pertaining to music for dance. The "pessimistically hopeful" Horst had just begun to publish *Dance Observer* as an advocacy sheet for modern dance that year. The presence of working critics on campus immediately raised the bar for the choreographers and their dancers.

Enrolled in that first season was a small but valiant platoon ready to serve in the name of a rapidly growing American art form. They were all women. Less than one-third were undergraduate students coming from other colleges; the rest were teachers. Hill predicted that this impressive array of "professional" women would take their experiences back to their own universities and schools. And Bennington's first program—a six-week session with the study of dance techniques, dance composition, music for dance, teaching methods, and production, as well as a survey of dance history and critical theory—became the model for programs around the nation.

64. The author describes the very beginnings of the modern dance movement and mentions the "felicitous falling out of circumstances" in paragraph one. Of the following, which would be the best synonym to use for felicitous in this sentence?

   (A) Planned
   (B) Angry
   (C) Covert
   (D) Fortunate

65. Many individuals are mentioned in the passage as playing essential roles in the modern dance revolution. Of the following, which were not considered as among the "Giants" of modern dance?

   (A) Graham
   (B) Hill
   (C) Weidman
   (D) Humphrey

66. From what we learned about Martha Hill, which of the following was the most likely reason for her to have kept her NY University teaching appointment while commuting to Bennington college?

   (A) Job security at NYU
   (B) More prestigious position at NYU
   (C) More money during the depression
   (D) Bennington was a brand new college

67. When Hill began the dance program at Bennington College, it was offered as the Summer School of Dance. Which of the follow would the author agree would be the most likely explanation for the promotion of this new program in the summer, rather than during the regular school term?

    (A) In 1932, college was all year long.
    (B) It would not interfere with regular course offerings during the regular school term.
    (C) Courses were cheaper in the summer and might attract more students.
    (D) Students from other colleges could attend during the summer when their school was not in session.

68. Louis Horst is described as "pessimistically hopeful." Which of the statements below would best reconcile this apparent oxymoron?

    (A) He did not think the program would last.
    (B) He helped the program but was not interested in dance.
    (C) He expected the worst but hoped for the best.
    (D) He was always negative even in the best of times.

69. During the six-week summer session on dance many aspects important to understanding and teaching dance were taught to the students. Of the following, which was NOT part of the summer curriculum?

    (A) Staging
    (B) Production
    (C) Critical theory
    (D) Dance techniques

70. Of the 103 students enrolled in the summer dance program at Bennington College, all were female. Of the following, which would the author most agree would account for this lack of male participants?

    (A) Men were busy earning wages to support their families during the Depression.
    (B) Professional dance was seen as a predominantly female oriented activity.
    (C) Other artistic endeavors more interested men.
    (D) Dance was only offered to females.

CHAPTER 4

Ethics

"I want to Be an English Teacher!"

"I want to be an English teacher!"
"A journalist!"
"I will be a doctor!"

A dozen Yemeni girls sit on the floor of a *diwan* in Al Sawd village, giggling and smiling bashfully as they describe what they hope to be doing in 10 years. They are between 8 and 15 years old and fortunate to attend one of the few local schools for girls.

In this remote corner of northwest Yemen, most of their female peers have already ended their schooling. While this group can still afford to dream, the grim reality is that most girls their age will soon be married, without a chance to complete their education or have a career.

Yemen is one of 20 "hot spot" countries for child marriage, a conservative Muslim nation where a seventh of all girls are married by age 14 and nearly half by age 17. In rural districts, girls as young as 9 are often betrothed. Most "hot spot" countries are clustered in central Africa, with other pockets in Southeast Asia and Central America.

Various factors have institutionalized child marriage. For some, it is a tribal custom. For others, exchanging daughters without dowries in "trade marriages" makes economic sense.

Regardless of its causes, child marriage represents a human rights infringement and a public health problem. It deprives young girls of a childhood, enhances their risk of domestic abuse, and entraps them in a cycle of poverty.

The health consequences are also dire. According to the World Health Organization, the maternal mortality rate is five times higher for adolescent girls under age 15 than those over 20, and the health outcomes for their infants are similarly poor.

USAID has confronted this issue with its Safe Age of Marriage (SAM) program, designed to change social norms around early marriage, girls' education, and children's rights. In partnership with the Yemeni Women's Union, the pilot program was implemented in two districts in the Amran governorate starting in 2009.

Leaders of the Community

A land of treacherous roads and dust-colored houses built into the mountain steppes, the Al Sawd and Al Soodah districts in Amran represent some of the most isolated regions in Yemen. Most of the population is illiterate and 71 percent of mothers are married before age 18. In these rural communities, USAID support trained 40 community leaders on the social and health benefits of delaying marriage. It also taught them how to share this knowledge with others.

"The community educators themselves decided the best way to talk about early marriage," explains Leah Freij, a senior gender adviser with the USAID-funded Extending Service Delivery Project. "They went to schools. They distributed newsletters. They talked to women in their homes."

They also garnered support from the Ministries of Education and Public Health and Population, which spoke at monthly fairs on the safe age of marriage. As the program gained traction, even the governor of Amran got involved—he personally awarded 12 "model families" in a ceremony for not only delaying their daughters' marriages, but also for educating them through 12th grade.

Piloting Results

The initial results of this pilot are promising. In one year, community educators reached 29,000 people, leading to an 18 percent jump in awareness in the benefits of delaying marriage. The program was instrumental in preventing 53 girl-child marriages.

It shifted the peak age of girls' marriage from 14 to 18 years old in the project area. Several villagers asked community educators to help them annul their daughters' marriages, and in one instance a community educator ended an engagement by paying back the family's dowry himself. In addition, the Ministry of Endowment and Guidance in Amran directed all religious leaders in the governorate to speak about the consequences of child marriage in their Friday sermons. Not long afterwards, the entire Al Soodah community took an oath to forbid child marriage for girls under 18.

"This is a big accomplishment," says Freij. "This is changing social norms."

71. Based upon the passage, which of the following would the author most agree represents the main point of this passage?

   (A) Child marriage is a practice that should be abolished throughout the world.
   (B) Yemen is the worst place in the world for child marriage.
   (C) Child marriage should only be allowed in Muslim communities.
   (D) Delays in child marriage can have lasting positive effects on individual lives and communities.

72. Based on the passage, what is the most likely rationale for child marriages perpetuating a cycle of poverty?

    (A) With no dowry, child brides are likely to be treated as less worthy.
    (B) In the remote community most people live below the poverty level.
    (C) Wealth is discouraged in the social setting of Yemen.
    (D) Men agreeing to a marriage with no dowry are likely to be impoverished and remain that way.

73. Which of the following approaches to changing a well-established and socially acceptable practice would the author of this passage agree to be most successful?

    (A) Governmental prohibition of the social practice
    (B) Shared information with the community through mass media sources
    (C) Honest and personal education about the negative factors of the practice
    (D) Punishing those who continue the old practice and rewarding those who choose the new standards

74. Given the positive short-term results of this educational program, which of the following would the author most agree will be a likely long-term, positive result of this change in the Yemen culture?

    (A) Greater role of women in the functioning and shaping of the society
    (B) Increase growth of the community due to lower infant mortality rate
    (C) Better healthcare provisions for women in Yemen
    (D) More communities being reached through programs like the one described here

75. Of the following, which is NOT a negative consequence of child marriages in Yemen as stated in the passage?

    (A) Increased prenatal mortality
    (B) Lost childhood of the girl
    (C) Increase in domestic abuse
    (D) Perpetuation of poverty

76. According to the initial results of the program, after one year, the mean age of girl marriages shifted from 14 to 18. Of the following statements about these results, with which do you believe the author would most agree.

    (A) Success will only result when child marriages are eliminated.
    (B) The mean age must shift above 18.
    (C) The program will only be successful when it reaches the entire country.
    (D) Governments should also supply health and educational support to child brides.

All Countries Must Speak Out Against Anti-Semitism

It's been dubbed the "longest hatred" by some, the "oldest hatred" by others. And this past summer, the world witnessed the latest chapter in the age-old story of anti-Semitism.

We saw it unfold in Paris, where protestors lobbed a Molotov cocktail at a synagogue and looted Jewish-owned shops amid shouts of "Death to the Jews." We saw it in Sydney, where a group of teenagers boarded a bus of Jewish primary school-children and unleashed a stream of invectives capped off with a "Heil Hitler" shout. We saw it in Casablanca, where the rabbi of the Jewish community was beaten while walking to synagogue.

The swastika graffiti recently found on buildings in places ranging from South Florida to Copenhagen are not isolated anecdotes; they are worrisome statistical trends. In the United Kingdom, the Community Security Trust recorded 130 anti-Semitic incidents in July—the highest monthly total in more than five years. In the San Giovanni neighborhood in Italy, Jewish community members counted more than 70 disturbing messages and posters.

These and other incidents are of deep concern to the United States government. That is why we convened a roundtable discussion yesterday, September 2, with a group of American and European Jewish community leaders at the U.S. Department of State. Secretary John Kerry, who participated in the conversation, emphasized that monitoring and combatting anti-Semitism is a global State Department priority, and reaffirmed our commitment to speaking out against this scourge whenever and wherever it exists. For Secretary Kerry, whose own grandparents came to the United States escaping anti-Semitism in what is today the Czech Republic—and whose own ancestors who stayed behind lost their lives in the Holocaust—this cause is very personal.

In recent weeks and throughout the year, we have reached out to leaders of beleaguered Jewish communities around the world to assess conditions on the ground. Our Embassies in the field use diplomatic channels to advocate with foreign governments. We also speak out unabashedly as National Security Advisor Susan E. Rice recently did when she remarked, "[We] see anti-Semitism flaring up around the world, including in Europe. The pretext is the passions coming out of the current conflict, but we all know it has its roots in something ancient and ugly—and we should not shy away from calling it by its name."

We have been heartened that representatives of other governments at the national and local level feel the same way. Earlier this summer, the foreign ministers of France, Germany, and Italy issued a strong joint statement condemning "outrageous anti-Semitic statements, demonstrations, and attacks." Dutch Prime Minister Rutte signed a joint statement with Jewish groups rejecting anti-Semitism. The mayor of Rome said swastikas and other anti-Jewish graffiti were "shameful and offensive to all Romans"; the mayor of The Hague met with Jewish groups to hear their concerns; and the mayor of Rotterdam is organizing an inter-faith discussion to address the issue.

These are positive and courageous steps, and we will continue to encourage governmental leaders, civil society activists, and every day citizens alike to condemn anti-Semitic rhetoric, threats, or violence.

The troubling truth is that anti-Semitism is not a historical fact, but a factual reality—one that continues to play out too often in too many places around the world. No one country is immune, and so all countries must continue to speak out. Let us all work toward closing the book on this ancient hatred.

About the Author: Ira N. Forman serves as Special Envoy to Monitor and Combat Anti-Semitism.

77. The author makes the statement that anti-Semitism is considered either the longest or oldest hatred in society. Is he trying to draw emphasis to this statement by using synonyms or is there a distinction he is trying to draw between these two phrases? Which of the following best reflects his likely intent?

   (A) Of contemporary bigotry, anti-Semitism was the first and has consistently over time been exercised by individuals.
   (B) Anti-Semitism has been occurring longer than any other form of prejudice.
   (C) Longest and oldest refer to the extent of the prejudice against Jews.
   (D) The violence against the Jewish people has occurred for generations.

78. Which of the following list of countries did NOT have government officials participating in joint statements speaking against anti-Semitism as discussed in the passage?

   (A) Netherlands
   (B) Germany
   (C) India
   (D) Italy

79. The author included a statement by Susan Rice that says, ". . . it (anti-Semitism) has its roots in something ancient and ugly," while she notes that the contemporary problems are the pretext for this situation. However, which of the following would represent her feelings about the true core of the anti-Semitism problem?

   (A) Nazi anti-Semitism and the Holocaust of WWII
   (B) Human nature and an inherent resentment for anyone different than ourselves
   (C) The long lasting struggle and violence that has occurred over religion and between ethnicities throughout human history
   (D) The religious crusades and the violence and death that occurred in the name of religion

80. When discussing violent and extreme anti-Semitism in modern times, the author included examples from all the countries in the list below except for which one?

    (A) Germany
    (B) France
    (C) Australia
    (D) Morocco

81. Which of the following U.S. government officials lost Jewish grandparents during WWII due to anti-Semitic violence of the Nazis?

    (A) Susan Rice
    (B) John Kerry
    (C) Hilary Clinton
    (D) John Boehner

82. The U.S. State Department is very concerned with the increase in anti-Semitic activity in the country. With more and more violence occurring related to race relations in the country, of the following, which statement would the author most likely agree is the leading cause of the increased racial tension in the U.S.?

    (A) Evil is color blind and comes in all shapes and forms.
    (B) Increased demand for freedoms is pushing fringe groups into a corner and they are fighting to survive.
    (C) Much like radical Islamic groups, the anti-Semitic groups have chosen a target for their frustration and fears.
    (D) Jewish people are easy peaceful targets and present a low risk of retaliation.

The Importance of Press Freedom

On May 3, 2011, we marked the 18th observance of World Press Freedom Day. And this year, there is much to celebrate. Thanks to new forums for public opinion, such as the Internet and social media, voices have been heard in countries across North Africa, and repressive regimes are crumbling. It is as if Thomas Jefferson's words from 1823 are echoing throughout the world, "The formidable censure of the public functionaries, by arraigning them at the tribunal of public opinion, produces reform peaceably, which must otherwise have been done by revolution."

A fundamental axiom of democracy is that citizens must have information and knowledge. People must be informed if they are to play an active role in the life of their country. Free and responsible media are critical sources of information for citizens who want to choose the best leaders for their country and make sound decisions about the issues in their nation and in their communities.

The information the media provide is just as critical for intelligent economic and personal decisions as for good political choices. There is a strong relationship between open media and free and effective economies. In fact, recent studies conducted by the World Bank have shown that free media are essential for successful economic progress in developing countries.

The Human Rights Report on Kenya, released on April 7, says the following, "The constitution provides for freedom of speech and of the press, but [in 2010] the government sometimes restricted these rights. Unlike the previous year, there were no reports that security forces killed members of the media. However, during the year security forces harassed members of the media, and journalists practiced self-censorship." What Kenya needs to support the reform agenda is a free and professional press corps that can work unhindered by harassment to bring necessary information to the Kenyan people.

The failure of the Kenyan media to report accurately and responsibly both before and after the election often had less to do with malicious intent than with lack of experience and training on how to report on conflict. Vernacular radio stations in particular, often identified as being most at fault, are often staffed by highly motivated but untrained volunteers. "Reporting for Peace" and "Land and Conflict Sensitive Journalism" are USAID projects to train journalists to create a more professional Kenyan media.

The Nairobi Media Resource Center, a place where journalists can come to access equipment, mentorship, information, and apply for travel grants, was established through USAID-support. Following its success, another center was opened in Eldoret in the Rift Valley. This area experienced horrific ethnic violence during the post-election period. The area remains one of the most vulnerable to violence and ethnic tension in Kenya. The U.S. Embassy is focusing on training local journalists in conflict-sensitive reporting. The Eldoret Media Resource Center better equips local journalists to produce stronger and more balanced stories.

It has long been the policy of the U.S. government to support the development of open and responsible media abroad and to assist in building the infrastructure needed for a free press to operate—legislative infrastructure, financial independence, transparency in government, and journalists trained in objective and fair reporting. Achieving a free and responsible media is a constant, challenging, vital and ongoing activity. We must keep in sight the ultimate objective—a citizenry able to make informed decisions that shape their lives.

I want to close with another quote from Thomas Jefferson: "The only security of all is in a free press."

83. The author makes the statement that "a fundamental axiom of democracy is that citizens must have information and knowledge. . . . if they are to play an active role in the life of their country." For the U.S., which of the following statements would most go against this statement?

    (A) Fewer than 10% of Americans get any news via any medium.
    (B) Less than 1/3 of Americans vote in any given election.
    (C) Only two major political parties have been in existence for more than 100 years.
    (D) Less than 30% of Americans will earn a degree from an institute of higher education.

84. Free and responsible media are stressed by the author as being critical for Americans to make the best decisions about the direction of our government. Which of the following adjectives would be most important to media outlets today?

    (A) Responsible
    (B) Accurate
    (C) Popular
    (D) Fair

85. Based on the passage and the importance of media to the general public, which of the following is NOT a listed provision of effective media for the people?

    (A) Career opportunities
    (B) Economic decisions
    (C) Personal decisions
    (D) Political choices

86. Vernacular radio stations in Kenya are most blamed by the author as perpetuating the relaying of inaccurate or false information to the Kenyan people. This is suggested to be due to their lack of training. Which of the following statements would the author most agree caused this problem in these stations?

    (A) Unfamiliarity with the equipment
    (B) Understanding how to deal with harassment
    (C) Lack of knowledge on laws that protect journalists and free speech
    (D) Poor understanding of governmental agencies

87. While the U.S. Constitution provides for free press in our country, which of the following most likely is still used by our government as a means by which to control media outlets and thus control the news provided to the American people?
    (A) Using the IRS to punish news agencies who do not align themselves with the administration
    (B) Restricting press conferences and news briefings only to those agencies friendly to the administration
    (C) Initiating FBI investigations into the leadership of newspapers who are against the administration
    (D) Allowing illegal surveillance on reporters who are antigovernment

88. The Nairobi Media Resource Center provides services to journalists in Kenya. Of the following, which is NOT a service or resource provided by this center?
    (A) Equipment
    (B) Visa assistance
    (C) Travel grants
    (D) Mentorship

89. In paragraph six of the passage, the author states that the federal government seeks to train Kenyan journalists in "conflict-sensitive reporting." Of the following, which statement most reflects the intent of the author's statement?
    (A) Fair, balanced, and nonaccusatory tone to the reporting
    (B) An avoidance of reporting about any conflict
    (C) Only reporting on conflicts that do not directly impact the readership
    (D) Not providing names and photographs of the dead out of sensitivity to the families

Franklin D. Roosevelt: First Inaugural Address, March 4, 1933

Plenty is at our doorstep, but a generous use of it languishes in the very sight of the supply. Primarily this is because the rulers of the exchange of mankind's goods have failed, through their own stubbornness and their own incompetence, have admitted their failure, and abdicated. Practices of the unscrupulous money changers stand indicted in the court of public opinion, rejected by the hearts and minds of men.

The money changers have fled from their high seats in the temple of our civilization. We may now restore that temple to the ancient truths. The measure of the restoration lies in the extent to which we apply social values more noble than mere monetary profit.

Happiness lies not in the mere possession of money; it lies in the joy of achievement, in the thrill of creative effort. The joy and moral stimulation of work no longer must be forgotten in the mad chase of evanescent profits. These dark days will be worth all they cost us if they teach us that our true destiny is not to be ministered unto but to minister to ourselves and to our fellow men. Recognition of the falsity of material wealth as the standard of success goes hand in hand with the abandonment of the false belief that public office and high political position are to be valued only by the standards of pride of place and personal profit; and there must be an end to a conduct in banking and in business which too often has given to a sacred trust the likeness of callous and selfish wrongdoing. Small wonder that confidence languishes, for it thrives only on honesty, on honor, on the sacredness of obligations, on faithful protection, on unselfish performance; without them it cannot live.

Restoration calls, however, not for changes in ethics alone. This Nation asks for action, and action now.

Our greatest primary task is to put people to work. This is no unsolvable problem if we face it wisely and courageously. It can be accomplished in part by direct recruiting by the Government itself, treating the task as we would treat the emergency of a war, but at the same time, through this employment, accomplishing greatly needed projects to stimulate and reorganize the use of our natural resources.

Hand in hand with this we must frankly recognize the overbalance of population in our industrial centers and, by engaging on a national scale in a redistribution, endeavor to provide a better use of the land for those best fitted for the land. The task can be helped by definite efforts to raise the values of agricultural products and with this the power to purchase the output of our cities. It can be helped by preventing realistically the tragedy of the growing loss through foreclosure of our small homes and our farms. It can be helped by insistence that the Federal, State, and local governments act forthwith on the demand that their cost be drastically reduced. It can be helped by the unifying of relief activities which today are often scattered, uneconomical, and unequal. It can be helped by national planning for and supervision of all forms of transportation and of communications and other utilities which have a definitely public character. There are many ways in which it can be helped, but it can never be helped merely by talking about it. We must act and act quickly.

Finally, in our progress toward a resumption of work we require two safeguards against a return of the evils of the old order; there must be a strict supervision of all banking and credits and investments; there must be an end to speculation with other people's money, and there must be provision for an adequate but sound currency.

90. In the opening sentence, President Roosevelt states that "plenty is at our doorstep." This was at the lowest point of the Great Depression. Of the following, which best paraphrases what President Roosevelt meant?

    (A) The end of the depression was close.
    (B) It was up to Americans to act to return to prosperity.
    (C) The financial relief from the Depression was within reach.
    (D) He was planning a "bailout" of the American people.

91. In order to divert the minds of Americans from their bleak financial situation, President Roosevelt states that happiness lies in many things and not only in money. Which of the following was NOT a means to happiness as stated by the President?

    (A) Quest for employment
    (B) Joy of achievement
    (C) Creative effort
    (D) Moral stimulation of work

92. Roosevelt mentions that through this trial Americans have the opportunity to learn an important lesson, that we are "not to be ministered unto but to minister to ourselves and to our fellow men." To what lesson is Roosevelt referring in this statement?

    (A) The government shouldn't provide for the people.
    (B) It's better for people to help themselves and others.
    (C) Welfare should only be for the most destitute.
    (D) The dole will only make people reliant on the government.

93. While there are several specific points made by Roosevelt in his address, there is a very powerful underlying theme. Of the following, which most reflects his main message for the American people?

    (A) We the people will work our way out of the Depression.
    (B) The government will lead you through this difficult time.
    (C) Help in the form of government aid is available if needed.
    (D) Have confidence in the leaders to overcome the Depression.

94. Much discussion occurs today about the redistribution of wealth. Roosevelt also discusses redistribution within the nation. Which of the following does he suggest required redistribution?

    (A) Wealth equally to all people
    (B) Employment spread throughout the nation
    (C) Equal opportunity for loans
    (D) Population shift from urban to rural areas

95. Within recent years, we have watched the U.S. economy and the World economy balance on the brink of another disastrous financial collapse. Of the following, which event would the author most agree came close to causing another depression much like the stock market crash of 1929?

    (A) Housing market inflated prices
    (B) Banking failures remedied by government bailouts
    (C) Foreign currency (Euro) collapse
    (D) Falling oil prices in recent months

96. In addition to his proposal to put Americans back in the workplace, Roosevelt also proposed several measures that had to be enacted to prevent such a depression from ever happening again. Of the following, which was NOT included in his address?

(A) Increase unemployment benefits
(B) End to speculation
(C) Strict supervision of banks
(D) Ensure sound currency

CHAPTER 5

Literature

Literature's Invisible Art: A Look at Literary Translation

Translation is an invisible art: the better it is, the less you notice it. At the art form's pinnacle, a text reads so naturally that one might not even realize it is a translation at all. Few people, for example, stop to think that well-known phrases such as "all for one and one for all," "ye who enter, abandon all hope," and "all happy families are alike; each unhappy family is unhappy in its own way" were originally written in a language other than English (they appear in *The Three Musketeers*, "Inferno", and *Anna Karenina*, respectively). These lines, and the works they are from, have become as much a part of American culture as the culture of their mother tongue.

Yet even with translation's clear importance to cultural life, American translations are exceedingly few. According to the University of Rochester's Three Percent website, only three percent or so of all books published in the U.S. each year are works of translation. When calculating only literary fiction and poetry, this figure dwindles to 0.7 percent, or 517 titles in 2013. Even this paltry amount requires hours of painstaking, time-intensive, and frequently thankless work, overlaid by the anxiety of choosing the correct word, the right tone, and the proper syntax.

Nancy Naomi Carlson is no stranger to these labors of language. She has translated works of poetry by René Char and Suzanne Dracius from French into English, and also serves as the translation editor for the Blue Lyra Review. Her latest project, supported by a 2014 NEA Translation Fellowship, is the translation of Abdourahman Waberi's first collection of poetry. Like his novels, which include *Passage of Tears* and *In the United States of Africa*, the poems in *The Nomads, My Brothers, Go Out to Drink from the Big Dipper* draw on Waberi's experience as a youth in Djibouti, and later, as something of a self-imposed exile based in France. The collection, published in French in 2000 and reissued in 2013, will be published in English by Seagull Books next spring.

Like Carlson's past projects, the translation process for *The Nomads* follows an arduous path. For all her translations, she works with two French-English dictionaries, an English-English dictionary, two online French-English dictionaries, two online French-French dictionaries, and a thesaurus. Her initial drafts include all possible word choices, which she narrows down according to the original verse's style and meaning. Dracius, for example, writes lengthy poems with flowery language and frequent Greco-Roman references; Carlson chose similarly sumptuous English parallels. On the other hand, "Abdou's work is miniature—just like the Republic of Djibouti," Carlson said. "He says a lot with a few lines and very simple words." In accordance, her Waberi translations are written in succinct, unadorned English.

Many poetry translators stop here; conveying the tone and content of a poem is enough. But for Carlson, who studied music and is a poet herself, sound is almost as significant as content. "Without even trying, [French] is so rich in sound," she said, noting that this quality is amplified by a poet's pen. "How can you ignore that?"

For each poem, Carlson creates what she calls "sound maps," color-coded charts that track alliteration, assonance, and syllabic stresses in the original verse. She replicates these rhythms and sound patterns as best she can, attempting to preserve the poem's musicality. Of course, certain linguistic limitations are unavoidable, which Carlson negotiates with a bit of creative license. "You can't get the exact sound for a line in French," she said. "Many of the sounds—the nasals—don't exist in English, so I couldn't possibly do that. But if I can maybe get another sound pattern going, and maybe it happens to be on this line instead of that line, if it's infused in there, then I've done my job."

Eventually, these words, sounds, and meanings are stitched seamlessly together, ideally creating a text that is at once accurate and beautiful. And yet, "There's always going to be a flaw," said Carlson. No matter how long you might work at it, "It's always going to be imperfect." She invoked a quote by Russian poet Yevgeny Yevtushenko: "Translation is like a woman. If it is beautiful, it is not faithful. If it is faithful, it is most certainly not beautiful."

97. What is meant by the author when they say translation is an "invisible art"?

   (A) When it is read, you can't see it.
   (B) The better the translation, the less you realize it isn't the original work of art.
   (C) The work behind the scenes is never noted.
   (D) Translation is a thankless job because the translator is never seen.

98. If, according to the author, translations will never be fully accurate and will also contain "flaws," which if the following would best explain why translators go to so much difficulty in translating these works?

   (A) The message of the literary work is deemed important.
   (B) Translators love to challenge themselves.
   (C) Poems are art and must be preserved even if the task is difficult.
   (D) Translators attempt to get as close as they can to what the original author was trying to convey.

99. Based on the difficulties of translating poems, as described in the passage, which of the following would aid in making a translation easier?

(A) Translating between languages with similar sounds
(B) Using languages from regionally close groups
(C) Translating from languages with the same origins
(D) Only translating languages based on Latin or Greek

100. Which of the following is NOT a consideration, given in the passage, when a literary work is translated?

(A) Syntax
(B) Grammar
(C) Tone
(D) Word choice

101. The author states that there are few American translators and that only three percent of all books published in the U.S. are translations. With which of the following would the author most agree is an implication for so few translations?

(A) Americans prefer American authors who write in English.
(B) There is a lack of interest in the topics in the U.S.
(C) Translations will never be perfect.
(D) Translating is too difficult.

102. Of the following, which is the only author NOT to have a work translated by Carlson?

(A) Dracius
(B) Waberi
(C) Yevtushenko
(D) Char

Sherman Alexie: Plainspoken Inspiration

"A lot of Native literature is really foo-foo nature crap, and it's written by Indians who don't even live that way." Alexie's own work, however, stays far away from the mythologized, spiritual stereotypes surrounding Native Americans, and focuses instead on the realities he grew up with on the Spokane Indian Reservation in Wellpinit, Washington, which ran thick with poverty, alcoholism, and hopelessness. In Alexie's hands however, these relentless heartbreaks are transformed into lyrical, moving portraits of contemporary Native life, which have garnered the writer a PEN/Faulkner Award for Fiction, a PEN/Malamud Award for Short Fiction, a National Book Award for Young People's Literature, and an NEA Literature Fellowship. We recently spoke with Alexie by phone to hear his thoughts on inspiration, and the role it plays in his creative practice.

What Is Inspiration?

Everything gets written down, everything gets remembered, everything gets catalogued. I don't have that immediate inspiration very often. It is having a moment, a phrase, a line of dialogue and then writing it down and hanging on to it. The inspiration is later when two of those things collide. Then you have to run to a computer, or run to a notebook. That's when it gets exciting, when two things come together that way. . . . I guess you'd say inspiration is something that makes me want to write it down. It's something that makes you want to ask more questions about it.

Where Inspiration Lingers

[Inspiration] is everywhere all of the time. I don't turn it off. I was in New York a few years back and I was walking back to my hotel late night after a literary party, and I saw a 24-hour nail salon. I thought, "Wow, only in New York could you actually have a 24-hour nail salon." As I was walking by, three very lovely drag queens walked into the salon. It was like three in the morning, and they were done up. It was such an amazing moment. I couldn't figure out why they looked so good. Are they on their way to somewhere? Are they on their way back from somewhere? I ended up writing a short story about a 24-hour nail salon in Manhattan. So I can be just as influenced by 3 a.m. drag queens in New York City as I can by a powwow in Oklahoma. I write about basketball and hot dogs and blue-collar jobs. It's plainspoken stuff. I'm not very interested in the ornate. There's a new house built in our neighborhood and it's this modernist masterpiece-looking thing. It does nothing for me. But on the other hand, I wrote a short story because there was once a mattress in my neighborhood that somebody had tossed, and it sat on the curb forever. That abandoned mattress is infinitely more interesting than that house. I was that mattress growing up. I'm a rez Indian. Every rez Indian is an abandoned mattress. When you start at the bottom you're looking at everything above you. When you're a prey animal, you study the horizon. Everything was a potential predator for me.

103. Sherman Alexie decries Native literature as largely "... foo-foo nature crap." This is in stark contrast to the topics and style he chooses for his writings. Which of the following would best capture the contrast that Alexie was attempting to portray in his statement?

    (A) He wrote about real life experiences rather than fictional characters and stories.
    (B) There's a difference between mythologized versus contemporary Native American life.
    (C) Too many Native American writers focus on ecological and conservation issues.
    (D) Alexie did not believe or write about the Spiritual practices of the Native people.

104. When asked about the inspiration for his writing, Alexie said that inspiration to him was each of the following with the exception of which selection?

(A) A moment in time that is special
(B) A phrase and a line of dialogue
(C) Something you have to write down
(D) Something you have more questions about

105. Which of the following would best represent the main theme of this passage?

(A) Native American literature can have a historical or contemporary perspective.
(B) Inspiration is an intangible yet essential player in the writing process.
(C) For success in writing, you must be prepared at any moment and any instance for inspiration to occur.
(D) Sherman Alexie, a writer of Native American descent, finds inspiration everywhere and is always prepared to capture those ideas and put them into his stories.

106. When talking about his life as a Native American, Alexie compares himself, and all "rez Indians", to an abandoned mattress. Which of the following statements best captures the sentiment of his statement?

(A) When you start at the bottom, the only way to go is up.
(B) He was unwanted and made the best of his life on his way to success.
(C) Like articles in the trash, he felt worthless as a person until he started writing.
(D) Coming from such an impoverished area, he is comfortable like an old mattress with the things around him.

107. Of the following list, which was NOT mentioned specifically as an inspiration for one of Alexie's stories?

(A) Old mattress
(B) Nail salon
(C) Hot dogs
(D) A new house

108. Considering Alexie's view on inspiration, which of the following scientific scenarios would most align with his view on true inspiration?

(A) Reading new information in a textbook that makes you ask questions
(B) Combining two or more observations into a testable hypothesis
(C) Obtaining data that results in a new question
(D) Writing a grant based on new experimental techniques

Lewis Carroll and the Hunting of the Snark

This article was originally published in The Public Domain Review under a Creative Commons Attribution-ShareAlike 3.0. If you wish to reuse it, please see: http://public-domainreview.org/legal/.

Although best known as the author of *Alice's Adventures in Wonderland* (1865) and *Through the Looking-Glass* (1871), Lewis Carroll—the pen-name of Charles Lutwidge Dodgson; a mathematical lecturer at Christ Church, Oxford—was also an avid reader and writer of poetry. He greatly enjoyed the poems of Victorian writers such as Alfred, Lord Tennyson, and Christina Rossetti. His own poems were varied—some just humorous nonsense, some filled with hidden meanings, and some serious poems about love and life. Probably his best known is called "Jabberwocky," with its opening line of "'Twas brillig, and the slithy toves . . .", and its many invented words, some that have now entered the English language, such as "chortle" and "galumph". Such nonsense verse is as popular now as it was when first published. His more serious poetry, it must be admitted, is generally inferior to his humorous verse and often over sentimental. Between 1860 and 1863 he contributed a dozen or more poems to College Rhymes, a pamphlet issued each term to members of Oxford and Cambridge universities, and which, for a time, he edited. In 1869, he compiled a book of poems, many of which he had already published elsewhere but now issued in revised form, together with one main new poem, which gives its title to the book, *Phantasmagoria*.

One particular poem stands out from all the others that Carroll wrote. It has inspired parodies, continuations, musical adaptations, and a wide variety of interpretations. It is an epic nonsense poem written at a time when Carroll was struggling with his religious beliefs following the serious illness of his cousin and godson, Charlie Wilcox, who eventually died from tuberculosis. Although the poem concerns death and danger, it is filled with humour and whimsical ideas. Strangely, it was written backwards. After a night nursing his cousin, Carroll went for a long walk over the hills near Guildford, and a solitary line of verse came into his head— "For the Snark was a Boojum, you see!" The rest of the stanza, the last in the poem, came to him a few days later. Over a period of six months, the rest of poem was composed, ending up as 141 stanzas in 8 sections that Carroll called "fits."

The poem concerns a quest by a crew sailing to catch a mysterious creature called a Snark. Each member of the crew has an occupation beginning with the letter "B"—Bellman (the Captain), Baker, Banker, Barrister, Billiard-Marker, Boots, Bonnet-Maker, Broker, and Butcher, accompanied by a Beaver. Their maritime map is an absolute blank. They reach an island, and the hunt for a Snark begins. But the quest is fraught with danger because although Snarks are not in themselves harmful, those that are Boojums are ferocious and will kill. The question that naturally arises is "does the poem have a meaning?" Carroll denied that he meant anything in particular—the poem was all nonsense—but that did not stop people asking him, and it inspired others to give it their own meaning. To some extent, the poem is about the relationships that emerge among the crew, and the interaction between this motley bunch of characters. All behave in odd ways, some have close-shaves, and one completely vanishes—caught by a Boojum.

The poem was entitled "The Hunting of the Snark" with the subtitle, *An Agony in Eight Fits.* Carroll originally intended it as a set of verses to be included in another of his children's stories, but it grew too long and became a book in its own right. He published it on 1 April 1876—the date chosen with care. However, many of his presentation copies to friends are dated 29 March. Although issued in a pictorial buff coloured cloth, he had copies bound in red, blue, green, and white cloth, all with gold decoration, to give away to his friends and family. The book was dedicated to one of his friends, Gertrude Chataway, and a dedicatory acrostic poem that introduces the book embodies her name as the first word of each stanza, Gert, Rude, Chat, Away, and also the first letter of each line . . .

The poem was very popular—it was reprinted many times. In Carroll's lifetime, over 20,000 copies were sold. The poem was incorporated into Carroll's compendium of humorous poetry entitled *Rhyme? and Reason?* (1883). Since then it has been illustrated by a variety of artists and translated into many languages, and the book rarely goes out of print. People are known to memorise and recite the poem. Some people form Snark Clubs. There is a timeless nature about the verses that make it as relevant today as it did in 1876.

109. According to the passage, Lewis Carroll also created literary works using a pen name. Of the following, which was the one used by Carroll?

(A) Alfred
(B) Dodgson
(C) Tennyson
(D) Rossetti

110. While Carroll wrote many literary works, all were not steeped in humor. However, his lighthearted and whimsical works are why he is known today. Which of the following statements would the author most agree accounts for his success in one area and lack of success in others?

(A) Society of the day was looking for something to smile and laugh about.
(B) His more humorous and satirical works were written better than the others.
(C) Carroll's attempts at serious writing were too personal to be interesting to others.
(D) The topics he chose were not interesting to the readership of the time.

111. The "Hunting of the Snark" was an extremely popular work of Carroll's. However, there is one thing that sets this work apart from all of his other literary works. Based on the passage, which of the following would the author most agree is that unique characteristic of this work?

    (A) The work incorporated several invented words.
    (B) It was the longest work of Carroll's career.
    (C) The "snark" was based on his negative religious experiences.
    (D) It was written backwards.

112. Although "Hunting the Snark" clearly appeals to the author, *Alice . . .* is by far Carroll's most famous literary work. Of the following, which would the author most agree would account for its popularity through the years?

    (A) It gained widespread appeal through the medium of television and movies.
    (B) It had whimsical and humorous characters.
    (C) It appeals to both young and old on different levels.
    (D) Individuals can find themselves represented in many of the characters.

113. In *Alice . . .* , the Hatter asks "how is a raven like a writing desk?" After some time, Carroll gave the answer "Both has a B and Neither has an N." How is this much like the example of the "Hunting of the Snark"?

    (A) Both are completely nonsensical.
    (B) The meanings are buried deep within the satire.
    (C) Like a code, only Carroll knows the true meaning.
    (D) Both are about the relationships, not the details.

114. "Hunting the Snark" grew too large to publish in a collection and was released as a separate book. What is significant about its release date?

    (A) It was his cousin's birthday.
    (B) It was the date of his cousin's death.
    (C) It was April Fool's Day.
    (D) It was Easter of 1876.

115. As a dedication of the "snark" to his friend, he wrote an acrostic at the beginning of the book. Of the following, which would NOT have been used in this manner?

    (A) Stay
    (B) Chat
    (C) Gert
    (D) Rude

The White Pages

Elwyn Brooks White was born on July 11, 1899, into a prosperous family in Mount Vernon, New York. He was the youngest of six children, and his father's success as a business executive meant good things for young Elwyn and his siblings.

Elwyn "owned the first small-sized bicycle on the block, and when he was only eleven he was given a sixteen-foot, dark green Old Towne canoe that, as his father might have said, was 'the best that money could buy,'" author Scott Elledge notes in his biography.

White's boyhood home also included a series of memorable dogs, along with pigeons, chickens, a turkey, ducks, and geese. White loved the backyard stable, which had a hutch for his rabbits, too. His affection for animals stayed with White into manhood, leading him to the farm that became his defining landscape, and informing the tales for children still read by millions of youngsters.

"From early childhood, Elwyn found the dark and pungent stable intoxicatingly rich in romantic associations of life and death and adventure," says Michael Sims, the author of a popular study of *Charlotte's Web*. "But it was also a refuge where a thoughtful young boy could spend time by himself." Sometimes painfully reserved, White "felt more at home with animals than with people, and he kept pigeons, dogs, snakes, polliwogs, turtles, rabbits, lizards, singing birds, chameleons, caterpillars, and mice," author Dale Kramer wrote.

As a college student at Cornell, White edited the campus newspaper, but a brief stint at the *Seattle Times* after graduation convinced him that daily journalism wasn't for him. His poetic sensibility didn't square with conventional news reporting, and his exacting, gimlet style was hard to pull off under the pressure of constant deadlines. Like many young dreamers, he eventually migrated to New York City, taking a series of unsatisfying jobs in advertising and freelance journalism. His lyrical worldview didn't seem to have a natural home.

Then, in a providential turn, the *New Yorker* opened its doors in 1925, creating a venue that was tailor-made for White's jeweled prose. Along with contemporaries such as James Thurber and Robert Benchley, he became one of the magazine's formative voices. Harold Ross, the magazine's first editor, quickly realized White's potential.

"White was an individualist and an admirer of nature, especially of Henry Thoreau's writings," Kramer, a historian of the *New Yorker*'s early days, has written. "Whenever he went anywhere he packed his *Walden* as naturally as his toothbrush. But he was aware that solitude was to be found in the city too. His life had fitted him almost perfectly for the wide-eyed yet deep-felt eagerness that Ross needed."

Gotham, teeming with life, ironically seemed a place where White could be inconspicuously alone. Years later, White elaborated on that contradiction in a famous 1948 essay, "Here Is New York":

> *On any person who desires such queer prizes, New York will bestow the gift of loneliness and the gift of privacy. It is this largess that accounts for the presence within the city's walls of a considerable section of the population; for the*

residents of Manhattan are to a large extent strangers who have pulled up stakes somewhere and come to town, seeking sanctuary or fulfillment or some greater or lesser grail. The capacity to make such dubious gifts is a mysterious quality of New York. It can destroy an individual, or it can fulfill him, depending a good deal on luck. No one should come to New York to live unless he is willing to be lucky.

White's essay about New York came to the minds of many Americans after the September 11, 2001, terrorist attack against the World Trade Center. Here's White, writing more than a half a century before that fateful day:

The subtlest change in New York is something people don't speak about much but that is in everyone's mind. The city, for the first time in its long history, is destructible. A single flight of planes no bigger than a wedge of geese can quickly end this island fantasy, burn the towers, crumble the bridges, turn the underground passages into lethal chambers, cremate the millions. The intimation of mortality is part of New York now: in the sound of jets overhead, in the black headlines of the latest edition.

116. Fern Arable is the main character in E.B. White's book *Charlotte's Web*. She spends much time with the animals and is the first to notice the writing in the web. Based on this passage, which of the following would the author most agree was White's inspiration for the character of Fern?

(A) His father
(B) Himself
(C) Harold Ross
(D) Robert Benchley

117. On the White's farm, there were numerous and varied animals that E.B. enjoyed spending time with. Which of the following was a character in *Charlotte's Web* but was NOT mentioned in the passage?

(A) Snake
(B) Rabbit
(C) Geese
(D) Rat

118. White's early formative years on the farm shaped his view of the world and of the animals who became his only friends. If his early life had been in the city, how might *Charlotte's Web* have been different? Which of the following would the author most agree would have been Charlotte's home?

(A) Corner of a stairwell
(B) Alley between buildings
(C) Awning of a storefront
(D) Subway platform

119. In paragraph five the author states that White's exacting "gimlet" style was not conducive to success under constant deadlines. Of the following, which would most represent the meaning intended by the author for this word?

(A) Cautious
(B) Lyrical
(C) Whimsical
(D) Lengthy

120. The author shared many of the experiences that led E.B. White to write many of his works including *Charlotte's Web*. If he were to be of this current generation, which of the following would be true of his life and experiences today?

(A) He would not have been around animals.
(B) His father might not have been as successful.
(C) He would have lived in New York.
(D) He would always have the newest iPhone.

121. In paragraph six, the author describes White's relationship with the New Yorker as a "providential" turn. In what context does the author use this term?

(A) Lucky
(B) Opportune
(C) Fortunate
(D) Profitable

122. Although White's essay about New York appears believably prophetic in light of the 911 tragedy, it was in fact written more than 50 years prior. Thus, which of the following would the author most agree White really meant by this portion of his essay?

(A) The possibility of a tragedy could end the city life.
(B) People can leave the city as quickly as geese fly south for the winter.
(C) The planes, fires, and decay relate to his view of the people in New York.
(D) The city has no substance and can end as quickly as material things can be destroyed in a fire.

Reading in Sunshine: Chicago's Printers Row Lit Fest

Talk to any technophile, and they'll tell you the same thing: books are for dinosaurs; newspapers are dead. Blog posts are the new literary essay, and the only sentences worth reading are those composed of 140 characters or less. If this were true, then a book festival, particularly one owned by a newspaper, is as culturally relevant as the VHS tape.

Yet the Printers Row Lit Fest, produced by the *Chicago Tribune*, has continued to grow, drawing 132,000 people, 200 authors, and 147 booksellers over the course of two days last summer. Next June will mark the festival's 27th year, capping off nearly three decades as one of Chicago's premier literary events. Elizabeth Taylor is the literary editor at the Tribune, and one of the festival's main organizers. While she says that "people are reading really differently" in the digital age, the allure of talking about books with people, not status updates, remains as present as ever. "In this world where everything's really atomized and people communicate online and rarely meet," Taylor said, "there's this place where people can come together in this kind of collective celebration of books, reading, ideas." The success of the festival, she thinks, is proof that "there is this hunger out there."

Of course, when the festival began in 1985, worries about Kindles, iPads, and the loss of independent booksellers were far on the horizon. The event was first created by the Near South Planning Board, a neighborhood organization designed to promote its own corner of downtown Chicago. Printers Row, a historic district located along Dearborn Street just south of the Loop, was a neighborhood of particular focus. At that time, the massive factories and warehouses once responsible for printing books had become dilapidated relics of their turn-of-the-century heyday. The railroad tracks that cut through the neighborhood were abandoned, no longer needed for shipping tomes—or anything else for that matter.

Bette Cerf Hill, president of the Near South Planning Board in the 1980s, was at the forefront of revitalizing Printers Row. "My job was to get people to come to this part of town, which was considered dangerous," she said. "But it was just empty. It wasn't really dangerous. There was nothing going on there. . . ."

"Everybody seems to have some gene, no matter how recessive, that responds to visual art, literature, creating things, doing things with your hands," Cerf Hill said. "They may not respond to all of the various [disciplines], but one or the other of the arts seems to stop people in their tracks, capture their imagination, make them want to hang around or come back."

With this in mind, what was originally called the Printers Row Book Fair was launched. Cerf Hill wanted to "bring books out in the sunshine," which is quite literally what happened given that no vendor tents were used that first year. She hoped that the normally solitary act of reading would, for one weekend, become a catalyst for bringing the community together in its enthusiasm for the written word.

The festival was small that first year; booksellers with new and used wares took up less than a block. But there were authors reading from their work, music was piped in, and a special area was devoted to children's books and writers. "I think the press was surprised that people considered this a fun event," Cerf Hill said. "We were really early in the book fair thing."

Although local authors were—and continue to be—the primary focus, the festival quickly began to attract internationally known names. Susan Sontag came. So did Ralph Ellison. The festival began to creep into adjoining blocks, and attendance rose. Though the festival "barely broke even," a program called Authors in the Schools was started, which brought children's writers into Chicago public schools to give writing workshops. "It was quite fantastic," said Cerf Hill of the program, which is still run by the Near South Planning Board today.

123. In the opening paragraph, the author makes the statement that, to technophiles, "books are for dinosaurs." While this implies people do not read books because of the digital age, which of the following would most disprove the argument about reading in the digital age?

(A) Paper books are still published and sold.
(B) *The New York Times* still has a bestseller listing.
(C) Sales of digital books are at an all-time high.
(D) Textbooks remain in use in colleges and universities.

124. The author paints a picture of the early days of the literary festival and mentions how the press was surprised at the crowds. She quotes Elizabeth Taylor who said that the present world is "atomized". Which of the following best reflects the author's intent in using this term?

(A) Virtual
(B) Electronic
(C) Digital
(D) Dispersed

125. In a statement from the event organizer, Elizabeth Taylor, she says that "people are reading really differently." Which of the following would the author most agree is the meaning of that statement?

(A) People read better when words are on paper.
(B) People are reading digital works.
(C) Eye strain causes people to read less from digital books.
(D) The eyes can move faster when reading digital books.

126. The festival is held on Publishers Row in Chicago and has been an institution of that city since its inception in 1985. Based on the passage, what was the original intent of such a literary festival?

(A) To get people to read more
(B) To get the local community involved in literacy for children
(C) As a means by which to increase book sales for local authors
(D) To increase public awareness and traffic to that part of the city

127. In paragraph five, the author quotes Cerf Hill saying "everybody seems to have some gene . . . that responds to visual art, literature, creating things, doing things with your hands." This was to illustrate that almost every human enjoys some facet of the arts or things considered artistic. Of the following, which would be the best supporting evidence for such a hypothesis?

    (A) People are either artistic or they appreciate something considered artful.
    (B) Children enjoy drawing, music, or making shapes in clay.
    (C) Humans are the only animals to be creative.
    (D) Most people have a favorite kind of music.

128. When considering the beginnings of the festival, organizers hoped that the "solitary act" of reading could bring an entire community together. How can one best align such an apparent contradiction?

    (A) The ideas and feelings stirred by reading the books can be shared with others.
    (B) The festival is a focal point where more books can be obtained.
    (C) Readers and authors can gather and share thoughts and ideas.
    (D) People may read the same books.

CHAPTER 6

Music

Setting Themselves Apart: New World Symphony Mentors a New Generation of Leaders

Twenty-six-year-old Katherine Bormann has been playing violin since age four, but she never dreamed she would one day take lessons with composer John Adams, conductor Emmanuelle Haim, and violinist Christian Tetzlaff. At Miami Beach's New World Symphony (NWS), the country's premier full-time orchestral academy, these once-in-a-lifetime experiences happen all the time. Under Musical Director Michael Tilson Tomas, NWS develops the skills of young musicians to prepare them for positions with the country's top orchestras, including the Chicago Symphony and the Kennedy Center Opera House Orchestra. Dean of Musicians Michael Linville characterizes the NEA's support for the program as crucial. "In terms of the support we've received since the beginning of the institute, it validates what we do educationally and artistically."

The approximately 1,000 post-baccalaureate musicians hoping to get one of 30 coveted three-year NWS fellowships undergo a rigorous application process, including both a video and live audition. Once selected, fellows receive housing, access to world-class facilities, and the occasional travel grant. In addition to daily rehearsals and weekly performances, New World Symphony also facilitates private lessons, master classes, and dress rehearsals via Internet2, an innovative Web-based program. Internet2 allows students an unprecedented opportunity to study and work with internationally known artists, such as cellist Yo-Yo Ma, soprano Renée Fleming, and flautist Paula Robison, via real-time video conferencing. As Borman recalled, "We played the U.S. premiere of a piece by Augusta Read Tomas, "The Soul is Light". The piece was so new, and we had questions about pitches and articulations. For somebody like her, being very busy, we wouldn't have been able to meet with her without Internet2."

NWS coaches students in more than just musicianship. The program also helps the fellows to develop their skills as leaders by having almost all of the musicians sit principal chair throughout the fellowship season, taking responsibility for leading their peers through concerts and rehearsals. The NWS fellowship program also includes a mentor program with local junior high schools. Fellows tutor the junior high schoolers one-on-one, helping the youngsters grow as musicians and individuals, while the musician-instructors benefit from the invaluable teaching experience.

Linville explained that "musicians today need to have a wider range of skills than they did 20 or 30 years ago." This new skill set includes entertaining donors, interacting with the media, and presenting themselves on camera as well as live. Added Linville, "[Musicians] have to be ambassadors for the arts, and ensure that the art form can continue. The skills learned at New World Symphony help to make these young performers extremely marketable, which, combined with superior musicianship, sets them apart at auditions and in the public eye."

129. Of the following list of individuals mentioned in the passage, which is NOT one of the artists mentioned that students were able to work with through Internet2?

    (A) Augusta Read Tomas
    (B) Renée Fleming
    (C) Paula Robinson
    (D) John Adams

130. During their time in the fellowship, participants will learn and develop many skills that will assist them in their careers. Which of the following was NOT mentioned in the passage as a skill fellows will develop during their time in the program?

    (A) Composing
    (B) Musicianship
    (C) Leadership
    (D) Mentoring

131. The author states that musicians today have a wider range of skills that must be learned and mastered than musicians did 20-30 years ago. Of the following skills that were listed, which do you think is the LEAST different now when compared to decades prior?

    (A) Entertaining donors
    (B) Interactions with media
    (C) Performance on camera
    (D) Live performance

132. Which of the following would most likely represent the true value of the fellows learning to become better teachers rather than simply using that time to improve their individual skills and talents as artists?

    (A) Teaching is a means of earning an income while still improving individual skills.
    (B) Music has always been and will always be an apprenticeship where musical talent is passed on from master to student.
    (C) The fellowship was meant to demonstrate teaching skills by exposing the students to masters of the arts.
    (D) One learns a skill or trade better when required to teach rather than simply perform.

133. Of the following artistic venues, which was one of the professional groups in which graduates of the fellows program had obtained positions?

(A) London Symphony
(B) Boston Opera House
(C) New York Philharmonic
(D) Chicago Symphony

134. Most musicians begin playing music at very early ages. While this program will identify and enhance the careers of 30 young adults, which of the following would be the most difficult factor to overcome in identifying these individuals at much earlier ages?

(A) As minor children their travel would be more difficult.
(B) School aged children have educational commitments.
(C) Their skills may not be fully developed.
(D) Parents would be more involved, making logistics difficult and costs increase.

The Reach of African Music

In Africa, musical instruments take on sculptural forms that are serious, sacred, humorous, elaborate, simple, or a mix of the above. Whether beaded, painted, carved, or decorated with skins, instruments send messages about the artistic styles, religious beliefs, and entertainment practices of the people who made them.

"Some instruments are elaborate sculptures that incidentally make music while others have forms that are beautiful and graceful even though they are purely devoted to the sound," says Elizabeth Cameron of the instruments on display in the exhibition, "Music for the Eyes: The Fine Art of African Musical Instruments."

"This exhibit shows these instruments as pieces of art, but there is enough interactivity and enough sound to give a taste that these are not just beautiful pieces," says Cameron, who curated the exhibition before becoming associate curator of African art at the Nelson-Atkins Museum of Art in Kansas City, Missouri. "Almost all are created to be heard."

Among the few instruments in the exhibition not created to be heard is the royal Kuba drum, which is created for the Kuba king. For the Kuba people, who live in the Democratic Republic of Congo, quantity and expense of decoration indicate status. The exterior of royal Kuba drum is covered with a dense layer of cowry shells the make it impossible for musicians to play the instrument without damaging the appearance.

"Essentially the royal drum has been elevated to uselessness," says Cameron. "Its function has been eliminated, but that is okay because the king does not play his own drum anyway. Others play drums for him." Cameron adds that, in the Kuba culture, as in many others, drums sequence up in importance from the village drums that virtually anyone can play, to the drums that only warriors can play, all the way up to the king's drum that no one plays.

African harps can also vary significantly in their visual and aural purposes. Rarer than drums, harps are still found throughout the continent and can range from the portable kora used by itinerant musicians in West Africa, to the lutes found in South Africa, to the human-shaped harps of the Azande and the Mangbetu peoples of the Democratic Republic of Congo.

Illustrating the influence of American and European nineteenth and early twentieth century expeditions into the Mangbetu area, artists created beautiful figured harps because members of those expeditions expressed interest in how the human form appeared in sculpture. Since that time, these shaped harps have become the norm, and, as with the drums, some of the representations of the human form are "wonderful whimsical pieces that you cannot play," says Cameron.

To celebrate the powerful influence that African-based music has had on the rest of the world, the California African American Museum has developed "Rhythms of the Soul: African Instruments in the Diaspora." This exhibition traces the lineage of a distinct African-based heritage in North America and elsewhere from the seventeenth century to the present.

"People brought it here, reconstructed it, built on it, used Western instruments to create new sounds, and created new instruments. I hope people will walk away from here with an understanding that this exhibit is a tribute to one tradition that was left for all of us," says Rick Moss, program manager of history at the California African American Museum. "People need to recognize that music in America did not develop in a vacuum."

"Slaves could not bring possessions," notes Ross. "They could bring their ideas, their religions, their songs." Now, African syncopation, percussion, instrumentation, and vocal patternings are deeply embedded in American music, including gospel, blues, jazz, rock and roll, and rap.

"At heart, what African music brought to the world's music is a complexity of rhythms that make music vibrant and allows us to feel the pulse of life our own heart beats, our own ability to reach deep within and draw from creativity for artistic expression that ultimately helps us survive," says Moss.

135. According to the passage, the Kuba people who produced beautiful musical instruments were from which country?

   (A) Democratic Republic of Congo
   (B) Niger
   (C) Ethiopia
   (D) Africa

136. Based on the passage, with which statement about African musical instruments would the author MOST agree?

(A) They were used primarily in religious practices.

(B) The instruments were exclusively ceremonial; producing sound was of secondary importance.

(C) Musical instruments were ornately decorated.

(D) Most were pieces of art designed to also produce sound.

137. Of all the African musical instruments described in the passage, which were specifically said to be found in South Africa?

(A) Lutes

(B) Kora

(C) Kuba drum

(D) Human-shaped harps

138. After reading the author's description of African instruments, which modern item from the list below would the author compare to those instruments?

(A) Stradivarius Violin

(B) Steinway Grand Piano

(C) Ferrari Sports Car

(D) Waterford Crystal Vase

139. In the history of American music, how was African music most injected into our culture?

(A) African instruments were shared throughout the early U.S.

(B) Slaves brought with them their songs and talent to America.

(C) Europeans traveling to Africa obtained the instruments and then moved to America.

(D) Early settlers in the South developed music similar to that of African cultures.

140. Of the following, which would the author most agree represents the main theme of the passage?

(A) African musical instruments are infused into musical culture of modern music.

(B) African musical instruments are fine art pieces.

(C) American music today has African music within its foundation.

(D) African music remains a distinct genre in modern times.

CHAPTER 7

Philosophy

The Philosopher at Fontana

Those who think of TVA [Tennessee Valley Authority] as a regional power company may not remember that at its founding it was an international sensation, drawing prominent visitors from around the world. Architects, engineers and heads of state visited the TVA region just to see this remarkable coordination of water and power, effort and energy.

Indeed, international visitors still come to study the TVA model. But of all those who have arrived over the years, perhaps the most surprising visitor was neither an architect nor an engineer.

He was a French existentialist.

Jean-Paul Sartre was the shortest man in the party of eight that disembarked from an American B-29 bomber at an airport near Knoxville, Tenn., one winter afternoon 55 years ago. If children stared at him, it was not because he was famous, but because behind his round glasses he was severely walleyed, his nearly blind right eye wandering far away from the other.

In early 1945 few Americans had heard of Sartre, although he had already written most of the books that would make him one of the preeminent philosophers of his century: the novel *Nausea*, the play "No Exit," and the philosophical manifesto "Being and Nothingness."

Sartre came to the TVA region not as an existentialist but as a journalist. A correspondent for French magazines like *Le Figaro* and for Albert Camus's underground journal, *Combat,* he was in Knoxville for one reason: to see the great American experiment that had been famous in France since its founding 12 years earlier, the Tennessee Valley Authority.

Sartre and the seven other reporters with him were guests of the U.S. War Department. The tour had been organized to show America's war effort, to which TVA was making crucial contributions. TVA hydroelectricity powered the manufacture of aluminum to build warplanes. And though at this time neither the French visitors nor the general public knew it, TVA was also providing electricity for the Manhattan Project in Oak Ridge, Tenn.

The morning after the journalists' arrival, guides whisked them to one of TVA's newest hydroelectric dam projects: Fontana, deep in the Great Smoky Mountains.

Sartre's comprehensive description of TVA for the magazine *Combat* isn't readily available in English, but excerpts make it sound like a glowing review. TVA was "a democratic effort," he wrote, "a vast cooperative."

For the mainstream magazine *Le Figaro*, however, Sartre wrote an essay called "American Cities," in which he described the transitory, distinctly un-European quality of New World communities. In his fertile mind, the prefabricated village TVA had built to house the workers at Fontana became the symbolic American city.

"The striking thing," he wrote in *Le Figaro*, "is the lightness, the fragility of these buildings. The village has no weight, it seems barely to rest upon the soil; it has not managed to leave a human imprint on the reddish earth and the dark forest; it is a temporary thing.

"In America, just as any citizen can theoretically become President, so each Fontana can become Detroit or Minneapolis; all that is needed is a bit of luck.... Detroit and Minneapolis, Knoxville and Memphis, were born temporary and have stayed that way."

Then one last metaphysical flourish: "They have never reached an internal temperature of solidification."

Sartre's itinerary, preserved in the National Archives, records that he and his colleagues went on to Norris Dam after visiting Fontana and then flew to Muscle Shoals, Ala., to tour the wartime facility where TVA produced nitrates for use in explosives.

Sartre remained in this country four months before returning to enjoy the next 35 years as an intellectual celebrity in the cafés of Paris. He never forgot his brief tour of the remarkable place called Fontana, and even late in life recalled it as a symbol of the footloose American culture that both fascinated and appalled him.

141. What is the main theme?

    (A) The view of American communities as temporary, nonconnected, and lacking substance as witnessed in the community surrounding the Fontana project
    (B) French existentialism in America as viewed by Jean-Paul Sartre
    (C) The Tennessee Valley Authority as a model for industry and power
    (D) Jean-Paul Sartre and his works surrounding his career as a journalist

142. What does he mean when he talks about American culture being footloose?

    (A) Lacking morals and ethics
    (B) Carefree and immature
    (C) Not connected nor centralized but mobile
    (D) Working without leadership, direction or purpose

143. Visiting which of the following during his trip might have changed Sartre's mind about American culture?

    (A) An established American city such as New York or Boston
    (B) Industrial areas of the country such as Pennsylvania or cities in the Midwest
    (C) Rural areas of the southern U.S.
    (D) Stable nuclear families in the South

144. Which of the following was not listed as a benefit from the TVA project?

    (A) Drinking water for a large portion of the U.S.
    (B) Manufacturing aluminum
    (C) Power for the Manhattan project
    (D) Production of explosive materials

145. Why did Sartre write that four great American cites were "born temporary and have stayed that way"?

    (A) Cities in America lack the spirit and identity that cities in France and Europe possess due to their longevity and heritage.
    (B) Sartre views Americans as fickle and mobile, moving from place to place on a whim and due to a sense of adventure.
    (C) American populations will create cities based on public need and not from a family legacy.
    (D) Success and failure are dictated by the economy that can make or break a city thus the people fail to lay long term and generational ties to the city and the people.

146. Sartre came to see the TVA project in the U.S. Certainly his literary works in Europe had earned him much acclaim, yet in the U.S. he was relatively unknown. In what role was Sartre present in the U.S.?

    (A) Philosopher
    (B) Journalist
    (C) Existentialist
    (D) Author

147. After reading the passage, which of the following would the author most agree represents the underlying theme of the passage?

    (A) American culture viewed through the eyes of a French philosopher
    (B) Thoughts about American ingenuity from a European
    (C) The incredible engineering feat of Fontana hydroelectric facility
    (D) The plight of the workers for the TVA and their poor housing

148. What was the main goal of these companies in bringing foreign correspondents to view these industrial facilities.

(A) To show off America's industrial ingenuity
(B) To display the War effort
(C) To allow the Europeans to use American ideas for their own facilities
(D) To demonstrate a sense of collaboration with other countries

The Islamic Scholar Who Gave Us Modern Philosophy

Abū al-Walīd Muhammad ibn Ahmad ibn Muhammad ibn Rushd—or Averroës, as he was known to Latin readers—was born in 1126 at the far western edge of the Islamic world, in Córdoba, Spain. His father and grandfather were prominent scholars and religious figures, and he, in turn, developed close ties with the Almohad caliphs who reigned over southern Spain and northwestern Africa during the twelfth century. These connections allowed him to serve as an influential religious judge in Seville and Córdoba and, later, as court physician in Marrakesh. Supposedly in response to the caliph's complaint about the obscurity of Aristotle's writings, Averroës devoted much of his scholarly efforts to a series of commentaries on Aristotle, producing both brief epitomes and exhaustive, line-by-line studies. These commentaries would eventually take on a life of their own, but the most striking feature of Averroës's career is how little influence he had on the Islamic world of his time, despite his obvious brilliance. Many of his works no longer survive in Arabic at all, but only in Latin or Hebrew translation. Indeed, even during his life, Averroës became a controversial figure. For in 1195, when the then-reigning caliph felt the need to make concessions to conservative religious figures, he banished Averroës to the small Spanish town of Lucena, and ordered that his philosophical works be burned. Not long after, the caliph moved to Marrakesh, a position from which he evidently was able to restore Averroës to favor. The philosopher rejoined the caliph's court, where he died in 1198.

What made Averroës so controversial, and what does this show us about the way in which philosophy has and has not persisted over the centuries?...we might consider three views in particular that put Averroës outside the mainstream. First, he contends that both philosophy and the text of the Qur'an point toward the conclusion that the world has always existed in some form or another—that although God has shaped the nature of creatures, the physical world itself has eternally existed, just as God himself has. Second, he contends that although our souls survive death, our bodies do not, and will not be resurrected. Averroës seems to believe that our souls will acquire some kind of body in the next life, but he denies that this will be the same body we have now, or even the same kind of body, and he further denies that we should take literally the Qur'an's various enticing pronouncements about the garden of delights that awaits the believer. Third, and most strange to our modern ears, Averroës denies that we each possess our own intellect. Instead, he thinks the intellect is something separate from our souls, some singular, immaterial thing that we are able to access when we think, and that we all share.

Each of these views was disputed, and widely regarded as heretical. Averroës thought that each was at least consistent with religious teachings, if not positively supported by those teachings, and he thought that each could be decisively established on philosophical grounds, drawing on the teachings of Aristotle. Here, then, we can see the importance of philosophy, even in the context of religious questions, since, if not for philosophy, it is likely that the believer would come to the wrong conclusion about each of these problems. In one of his best-known works, the *Decisive Treatise*, Averroës argues at length for the value of philosophy: not just that it should be permitted, but that its study is, in fact, required for those who would truly understand religion. To ban philosophy would be "a wrong to the best sort of people and to the best sort of existing things."

149. According to the passage, Averroës was a great philosopher and an admirer of Aristotle. Yet, his philosophy was unaccepted in his culture and he was largely seen as controversial. Why would Averroës most likely have earned these distinctions?

   (A) He was Muslim while Aristotle was Christian.
   (B) Spaniards and Greeks did not see the world in the same way.
   (C) Aristotle's and Averroës' ideas were seen as contrary to religious practices.
   (D) Most of the people in the area were uneducated and did not understand.

150. During the life of Averroës, which of the following would the author agree had the biggest impact on his belief in philosophy?

   (A) The area where lived provided a more diverse cultural and religious background.
   (B) His political connections allowed for his freedom to explore other ideas and cultures.
   (C) He was raised in a household of learned and spiritual individuals.
   (D) His education was more classical and introduced him to Greek philosophers.

151. Averroës wrote many works and commentaries on Aristotle that were met with resistance or anger by the religious people of his time. Of the following, which was NOT a controversy elicited by Averroës' philosophical ideas?

   (A) The soul is eternal.
   (B) The afterlife is myth.
   (C) The earth is eternal.
   (D) The intellect is communal.

152. Based on the tone of the passage, how do you feel the author views the role of philosophy in culture and religion?

    (A) Negatively—Philosophy is opposed to spirituality.
    (B) Neutrally—They should remain separate but equal.
    (C) Positively—One is supported by the other.
    (D) Indifferently—Neither serve much purpose in the present.

153. In the final paragraph, Averroës states that to ban philosophy would be "a wrong to the best sort of people and to the best sort of existing things"? To what was he referring?

    (A) Faithful people who practice religion
    (B) Educated individuals who are also religious
    (C) Intelligent scholars who support philosophy
    (D) Good people wanting to live the best most moral life possible

154. The author goes into great detail about the role of Averroës' religion and how it influenced his life and philosophy. If he had been Christian, how might his philosophy and acceptance in society been different? Of the following, which would the author most agree would have been the outcome of that shift in religious practice?

    (A) He would have had much more freedom for his philosophy.
    (B) His writings would have gained wide acceptance in the Christian community.
    (C) Only the most extreme Christians would have rejected his teaching.
    (D) Christianity would have been equally as constraining at that time.

CHAPTER 8

Popular Culture

Ethics in the National Pastime Become Subject of Hearings

As baseball took hold not only as an American institution but also as a recognized piece of national identity, Congress began to focus more and more on issues regarding integrity and ethics in the game. Investigations into the impact of expansion in the 1950s and 1960s, as well as the 1994 players strike, brought Congress closer to regulating ethical aspects of the game. During the latter part of the 20th century, Congress tackled more troubling subjects such as the continuing problem of race discrimination in professional sports, drug and tobacco use, violence, and the impact of these issues on fans.

The most famous of these hearings, titled "Restoring Faith in America's Pastime," occurred on March 17, 2005, when several of the game's biggest stars were called before the House Committee on Government Reform to analyze the growing problem of players' use of performance-enhancing drugs. The hearings involved such stars as Mark McGwire, Sammy Sosa, Rafael Palmeiro, and Curt Schilling (appearing to voice his opposition to steroid use). Although none of the players faced accusations of perjury before Congress, popular opinion suggested that few of the stories they told were believable, and the hearings fed a growing sense of outrage among fans.

Though only a few players have ever been convicted of lying to Congress, the steroids investigations have proven to be the closest Congress has come to punishing those in baseball who didn't live up to the high standards required of an iconic sport.

In 2011, Roger Clemens was in court defending himself against charges that he lied to the House Committee on Oversight and Government Reform in February of 2008. The outcome may be one of the first major sanctions of the "steroid era."

Baseball history can be traced through its appearance in the hearings before Congress. Investigating first the vaudevillian and gypsy-like nature of professional baseball, Congress increased its scrutiny as the 20th century ushered in an age of major interstate commerce. As baseball grew into an American institution, Congress investigated how the game influenced the fabric of society, attempting to add a level of government control from the elected voice of the people.

The records of these investigations and hearings, held in the Center for Legislative Archives, demonstrate how baseball is one of the many subjects of American history that can be profitably researched in the records of Congress.

155. Which of the following would the author most likely accept to further support the theme of this passage?

   (A) Pete Rose's ban from the Baseball Hall of Fame for betting on baseball
   (B) Alex Rodriquez's year and a half suspension for use of performance enhancing drugs
   (C) Lance Armstrong's use of performance enhancing drugs during his seven Tour de France victories
   (D) Accusations of PED use by Barry Bonds

156. Since baseball has been played in America for decades, which of the following do you believe the author would most agree is the reason for the move over government regulation and oversight now in the 21st century?

   (A) Impact on interstate commerce increased as professional baseball became more popular.
   (B) Elected officials felt a mandate from the people to "clean up" baseball.
   (C) Both baseball and the federal government have grown sufficiently large and powerful enough to have an impact on each other.
   (D) Big government is always searching for new ways to validate its own existence.

157. Which of the following has resulted in only a few convictions of players by the federal government?

   (A) Gambling
   (B) Use of performance enhancing drugs
   (C) Lying to Congress
   (D) Use of illegal drugs

158. Which player in the modern era was tried in court on charges of perjury before Congress?

   (A) Mark McGwire
   (B) Rafael Palmeiro
   (C) Barry Bonds
   (D) Roger Clemens

159. What reason does the author provide for the federal government investigating ethics and integrity in professional baseball?

(A) Professional baseball is a huge industry with millions of dollars being invested and spent each year.

(B) The players represent American culture to the world.

(C) Criminal activity and illegal gambling was beginning to impact the game.

(D) Baseball is the national pastime.

160. The author describes the role of government oversight in the regulation of America's pastime: baseball. However, the author makes an interesting statement about the history of these hearings and legal actions against baseball. Of the following, which would the author most agree would be interesting to modern historians?

(A) Correcting errors present in the documents

(B) Profitable research

(C) Supplying information for future government action

(D) Preparing a historical timeline for baseball and its legal issues

Conversational Journalism Is Real

The idea of journalism as a conversation has been bandied about since the first newspapers brought their brands into the online space in the late '90s. If traditional journalism has been more akin to a lecture or discourse between elites, what does it mean to bring citizens into the dialogue?

Many traditional journalism distributors have experimented with conversational journalism over the past 20 years, but there has, up to now, been a dearth of data to show editors and publishers whether these plans are resonating with users or, as some fear, damaging credibility.

Doreen Marchionni, a professor at Pacific Lutheran University and 17-year veteran of newspapers, decided to use her doctorate to measure the phenomenon of conversational journalism. What, exactly, is this thing and which real-world applications might allow it to coexist with core journalism values such as credibility and expertise?

Marchionni found, not surprisingly, that haphazard implementation of community and crowdsourcing can mean a loss of perceived credibility, authority, and likeability. But organizations that do it well can create sustained interest and repeat engagement with their sites.

She began the panel by reiterating that conversational journalism is real. Anyone with Internet access and a few web tools can create and distribute news, collaborate with professional journalists in real time, and select which news stories and sources to follow. The gatekeeper no longer sits in the newsroom.

A theme that popped up throughout her research is perceived humanity and likeability of the journalist. She found that modern audiences are constantly sizing up authors, looking for similarities with themselves.

Marchionni presented tips for bringing the community into the news process, all based on her research:

- Add photos and bios of reporters and writers to a website. This is an easy way to give users the familiarity they're looking for.
- Put reporters and writers on video if possible. Marchionni found that video was a very powerful way to humanize the people behind the news. Audiences responded extremely well when reporters talked about themselves and how they covered a story in a short video clip.
- Write with voice. Users in her study trusted a reporter with a distinctive voice over a reporter who wrote straight AP-style inverted pyramid stories.
- Voice is good, informality is not. Too much informality, especially in hard news stories, became a problem. A balance between a journalist's and organization's credibility along with a conversational tone helped create and maintain a community.
- Use social media tools to crowdsource stories. This probably wouldn't have been true even five years ago, but now audiences expect it. Be explicit if a story was crowdsourced: audiences appreciate the candor.
- Don't use Twitter only to broadcast a message, use it to engage the audience.

161. In Marchionni's research, an unsuccessful attempt to bring conversational journalism to the masses can result in a loss of all of the following except for which selection?

    (A) Originality
    (B) Credibility
    (C) Likeability
    (D) Authority

162. When discussing that conversational journalism is real, Marchionni states that anyone can do it. She goes on to say that "the gatekeeper no longer sits in the newsroom." Relative to news outlets of the past versus conveyors of newsworthy items today, which of the following would best summarize her intended message?

    (A) You can do the news from your bedroom; you don't have to be in a studio.
    (B) News editors no longer decide what news is broadcast to the masses.
    (C) Technology exists to allow anyone to share news items.
    (D) Contemporary news is for the populus and is now being disseminated by them through modern technology.

163. Crowdsourcing is a tool mentioned in the recommendations made by Marchionni. Within the context of the passage, which of the following would represent the best definition of crowdsourcing in the news?

(A) Having several writers and reporters producing a new story
(B) News items that were consolidated from several sources into a cohesive news item
(C) Allowing citizens to use social media to add content to an existing news story
(D) Live interviews with individuals (i.e., the crowd) who are actually at the scene of a particular event where they give first-hand accounts and their own perspective of the event

164. From Marchionni's research, she developed recommendations which may assist in bringing more conversational journalism to the general public in a successful way. Of the following, which is NOT one of those recommendations?

(A) Provide the audience personal information about the reporters
(B) Limit the time reporters are seen in video; stick to the story
(C) Only use twitter to engage, not inform
(D) Balance between informality and credibility

165. News, especially on television, was very different 40 years ago when there were only three networks and the news was presented for 30 minutes to an hour each evening. In light of the continual supply of sensationalized news today, which statement about anchors from decades ago would be most accurate?

(A) Anchors in the 70s were seen as honest, dependable, and trusted to give you the most important news of the day.
(B) Four decades ago, anchors were viewed by a larger population than today and they had more authority and conveyed more confidence than news persons today.
(C) News is such a customized genre today that you can find a news source that tells you the news in a way that you want to hear (i.e., political or social preference).
(D) News in the 70s was only seen as trustworthy if it was more detailed and in printed form.

network and cable news programs, conversational news does not
ave a centralized person or board dictating what news a viewer receives
and when. In the modern era of crowdsourcing and mass news, which of
the following would the author agree decides what news is "newsworthy"?

(A) The reader
(B) The blogger
(C) The affiliated news agency
(D) The owner of the website

Hunting the Spark of Creativity

In his 1937 book, *"Think and Grow Rich,"* author Napoleon Hill identified 13 steps
to success, one of which was the power of the mastermind. "No two minds ever
come together without thereby creating a third, invisible, intangible force, which
may be likened to a third mind," Hill wrote.

He included the step to explain a principle of achievement—the standard idea
that two heads, or a group of heads, are better than one at creating innovations.
More than 75 years later, new research aims to put Hill's mastermind idea on
steroids.

Until recently, decision makers could only effectively harness shared creativity
from relatively small mastermind groups such as boards, panels or committees. Data
from these could be placed in pre-organized, well-structured, and well-categorized
"buckets" to extract creative knowledge.

The relatively recent growth and development of the Internet, however, along
with social network technology, provides an opportunity to expand the mastermind
concept to hundreds, or thousands, or even hundreds of thousands of geographi-
cally distant people.

University of Cincinnati complex systems scientist Ali Minai and a team of
researchers funded by the National Science Foundation (NSF) are attempting to do
just that—to develop computer-based tools to mine the Internet and communities
of social media for creative insights.

But first, the researchers must clearly define the highly personal subject of creativity by types, kinds, and categories to successfully identify it online. In addition,
they must find a way to organize large amounts of unstructured, creative data—
intermixed collections of text, video, images, and other information.

To do that, the researchers are examining creativity in neural networks in the
human brain; social networks related to interactions among people; and networks
of knowledge that develop in groups. And according to some observers, if successful, the project could be a game changer.

"It could be a huge, big deal," said Penn State University's Jack Matson, author
of the book *Innovate or Die: A Personal Perspective on the Art of Innovation*.

"Basically, cultures are innovation driven," he said noting the market intercon-
nectivity of nations like China and the United States. "Now that we're virtually
connected, the ability to innovate is going to make or break countries and societies."

"The future of societies will depend more than ever on their innovativeness, and this will be enabled by connectivity," said Minai. "I think that Professor Matson's statement is absolutely correct. The issue is how we can exploit the immense amount of knowledge that is latent in the networks that connect us and which is growing every minute."

Social Networks: A Better Understanding

"Being able to extract ideas from social networks is very much the ultimate goal of our research, but a major issue is which real-world networks we can access for this purpose," said Minai.

In recent years, social media networks have been increasingly difficult to access. Because of structural and privacy concerns, accessing Facebook content for research purposes is extremely challenging. While Twitter is more accessible, only a fraction of the data stream can be collected and even then a lot of the data is just "noise."

These noisy data streams make the goals of the project harder to achieve. But Minai already has a group of University of Cincinnati graduate students, funded by a previous NSF grant, working to mine meaningful information from Twitter and other online sources.

He anticipates the two projects eventually will help open vast possibilities for shared creativity and innovation among the millions that use social media. He also anticipates the research could help many modern institutions, including elections, parliaments, governing boards, free markets, and businesses. This is especially true of institutions that innovate using online presences.

167. The author of the passage quotes Napoleon Hill when he refers to a "mastermind." Which of the following statements best reflects the meaning of the word used here.

(A) A product that is greater than the sum of its parts
(B) An individual with great creativity
(C) Someone who can organize and lead others
(D) Shared ideas are always the best

168. When considering creativity, productivity, and group work as described in the passage, what evidence would most WEAKEN the argument of the passage?

(A) Congress trying to pass a budget
(B) Executives who rely on a board for decisions
(C) Large committees that rarely accomplish a task or goal
(D) Stock brokers deciding on a spending strategy

169. By harnessing the tremendous information flow of the Internet to create a pool of creativity, the author describes the organization of information into networks. All of the networks below were described in the passage except:

    (A) Neural network
    (B) Social network
    (C) Innovation network
    (D) Knowledge network

170. Which of the following would best reflect the author's main intent in writing this passage?

    (A) Human innovation can be expanded from the human resources of the world.
    (B) The Internet is the ultimate mastermind.
    (C) Creativity is exponentially on the increase due to the connectivity of the world.
    (D) Innovation is the engine that drives cultures and societies.

171. Social networks can be a valuable conduit through which information can be easily obtained. However, the author describes much of the data on social networks such as Facebook and Twitter as "noise." Which of the adjectives below best defines noise as used here?

    (A) Rude
    (B) Obnoxious
    (C) Juvenile
    (D) Meaningless

172. In the passage, the author quotes Jack Matson who suggested a driving force which keeps cultures alive. Which of the following is that driving force mentioned in the passage?

    (A) Technology
    (B) Ideology
    (C) Government
    (D) Innovation

Pure Expression: Lady Pink and the Evolution of Street Art

When I first started graffiti I was only 15 and there was already a long history of folktales in the subculture. There were heroes and villains and great epic deeds. By the mid-1970s some of the guys had already achieved whole trains—those are ten whole cars—top to bottom, painting the entire train . . . and we all had to try to achieve the greatness that was already shown. Very quickly it got good. The tourists thought that the subway trains came like that. They thought it was quite charming—they loved it.

[Street art] is a broad term for all the vandalism, but we specifically went for the trains. We didn't do street tagging. We didn't write on people's buildings. Our generation of graffiti writers, of the early 80s, specifically went for the subway trains.

Seeing your work rolling by on a massive train, roaring and making noise and dirty and gigantic, and it's rolling with all that energy—there is no other thrill and rush and excitement that you get by seeing your name roll by knowing that you were naughty and you got away with it.

But it quickly got out of hand. It was the 70s. New York City was in chaos economically and physically. Crime was rampant. By the early 80s, the city started to pick itself up and recover, and by the mid-80s, the graffiti had already been destroyed off the subway trains. They erased the graffiti with an acid, but it also destroyed the trains themselves, so they had to combat it in a different way. They developed the vandal squad, the graffiti police . . . [Graffiti] is very elaborate and stylized lettering—you have to study it and be schooled in order to read it. The police not only learned how to run the train tracks, but they learned how to read the stuff and they learned who's who. By 1989 the subway trains were completely clean, and they wiped the graffiti off the face of the Earth.

There [also] were infamous people underground that would destroy others' work. They couldn't do any artwork themselves. So if they destroyed something nice, everyone was talking about them . . . It was internal strife. It was no longer just fun and games and playing cops and robbers. Folks dropped out left and right. People grew up, got to earn a living. The shelf-life of a graffiti writer is only about two to five years, before you grow up and you have to join the real grown-up life by getting a job.

Graffiti as Folk Art

We need rebellion in our society. We need someone to question the status quo. Otherwise, our society will be stagnant. Our country is based on rebellion. If not, we'd still be speaking in a nice British accent. The free thinkers, our forefathers, were the ones that set us free, and we still need it in our society.

What we have been saying for the last quarter of a century is that the art world has become elitist . . . That you have to study in college in order to be authenticated as an artist and for your work to be valid is nonsense. We are all capable of doing art and creating art. You don't necessarily have to go to art school to be an artist. You can be an outside artist. You can be a folk artist. That's what we are—technically we are folk art.

If you are to define what folk art is, it's a grassroots movement. The young people who started the graffiti movement were teenagers, literally 13-, 15-, 16-year-olds making stuff up as they went along. The other street artists were also making stuff up—the beginning street artists like Keith Haring and [Jean-Michel] Basquiat and Jenny Holzer and John Specter and Richard Hamilton. All of these cats were the very first street artists. They were working in different mediums . . . stencils and posters and bucket paint, brush paint. Certainly not with letters or subway trains and spray paint the way we did. They were the first street artists . . .

Street Art Today

Early on, rock-and-roll was outlawed and feared and all of that, banished from society and the people who did it were outcasts. Now we see where rock-and-roll has gone. There's punk rock, metal, pop, and even hip-hop. There are many different levels of it but it's still all rock-and-roll. And I believe that's where graffiti has gone. It's being labeled in general as street art, but the street artists work in so many different mediums that have nothing to do with one another.

Today, street artists are working outside of spray paint, with knitting, wood, rubber bands, pencils and stickers and bucket paint—they're working with every medium possible . . . . For so long we have been given these urban landscapes that are dull and boring and utilitarian and gray. And then the street artists come along and we add some life and color and some urban love to our surroundings.

They're creating art for art's sake and not for profit. It's the purest form of expression you can imagine.

173. Graffiti has long been a problem in urban settings. However, the author says that tourists see graffiti in a very specific way. Which of the following best depicts how tourists are said to view this type of art?

    (A) Vandalous
    (B) Charming
    (C) Dirty
    (D) Rebellious

174. In the final paragraph of the passage, Lady Pink states that street art was done for "art's sake and not for profit." Which of the following was a statement made in the passage that most weakens this assertion?

    (A) Street art is vandalism.
    (B) Some street artists sought to destroy others' art.
    (C) There is a broad range of street art medium and types.
    (D) Street artists are typically teenagers.

175. Several street artists are listed in the passage as among the first of their genre. Of the list below, which was NOT among those first artists?

    (A) Jennifer Kreizman
    (B) Keith Haring
    (C) Jenny Holzer
    (D) Richard Hamilton

176. Many young adults are submerged in the culture of street art around the world. Based on the passage, which of the following would the author most likely agree is the driving force behind the continued efforts of these artists to exhibit their work?

    (A) Placing their art where as many people as possible will see
    (B) Making something plain look beautiful
    (C) Making their community a better place
    (D) The thrill of doing something illegal

177. Lady Pink makes an impassioned argument that rebellion is required for society to not grow stagnant. She further compares this hypothesis to the American Revolution. Which of the following statements would most weaken her hypothesis?

    (A) War resulted from the American Revolution.
    (B) The American Revolution was not simply for the sake of change.
    (C) The King of England forced the Americans into actions.
    (D) Americans didn't feel they were represented in the actions of Britain.

178. Which of the following would be the best description of how the "Elitist" art world most differs from the artistic work of street artists in this passage and thus influences how both are viewed?

    (A) Street art has a different medium than most accepted art of the day.
    (B) Famous artists are sought to display their work while street artists display their art for all.
    (C) The art world has a universally accepted venue within which to display its art.
    (D) Street art is vandalism, a criminal activity.

179. Many mediums and settings may be considered street art. In fact, the passage lists the materials that street artists of today may use. Of the following, which is NOT one of those materials?

    (A) Lights
    (B) Wood
    (C) Stickers
    (D) Rubber bands

#2TweetorNot2Tweet: Sarah Bertness and Natalie V. Hall

A writer and lifelong lover of the arts, I'm always looking for new avenues to share my coveted cultural discoveries and find live tweeting a dynamic and direct approach to include others in the performing arts experience. Emerging from the intersection of arts and technology, cultural institutions and artists are utilizing Twitter to engage a broader audience and to enhance the experience for social-media savvy art patrons like myself.

Though tweeting in the theaters may seem untraditional, the willingness to break with tradition is exactly what drew me to the art world in the first place. Art is about creative expression, and Twitter is an innovative means both to share my own impressions, and to further explore the discussion points raised within a performance.

To address what live tweeting means in the theater setting, the idea is not to oversaturate Twitter with exclamations or give a play-by-play of the play in question. The goal instead is to complement the performance with a well-researched, full-bodied, and engaging dialogue. The live-time Twitter audience is outside of the theater. If fellow audience members leave the theater wanting more, the Twitter conversation becomes a way of revisiting the performance, and keeping the buzz going long after curtains have closed.

Providence Performing Arts Center's (PPAC) "tweet seat" initiative, an experiment in live tweeting within the theater, has been extremely successful by social-media standards, trending every time. An innovative and well-executed program, I think it is crucial that parameters are set and abided by in these early stages of developing the role of live tweeting. As an arts patron, my goal is to share my own enjoyment with others, while never distracting or detracting from their own experience. In fact the vast majority of fellow patrons haven't the slightest idea that "tweet seats" exist at PPAC. Our seats are at the far back of the theater, and phones are silent and dimmed. Live tweeting is not for everyone. But within a well-executed setting it doesn't bother others, and my own experiences at the theater become more immersive and enjoyable. By live-tweeting, I am able to process my thoughts in a new way, capturing the energy and emotion of the performing arts and translating that into inspiring writing.

So to tweet or not to tweet? I'll be in the tweet seats, silently sharing the performance by hashtag for a whole other audience over the Internet.

The common arguments against tweeting during performances are usually that it takes the patron out of the "present" and therefore diminishes the impact of the show and that it is disrespectful to the artists. Both of these arguments are valid, but more often than not the battle cries against integrating social media with performance seem to reek of fear: administrators shouting "TRADITION!" with index finger to the sky, beards shaking.

Audiences are sharing thoughts and images because they are excited about what they are experiencing and want everyone to know about it. Isn't that exactly what we want to happen? Designating "tweet seats" has been controversial, but there are other alternatives. Why not promote intermission review contests with show-specific hashtags? Hold pre-show lectures or post-show discussions with live tweet-in questions? Institute a "first five minutes" rule, as you would with the press? If we can provide structured outlets for discussion and interaction while audiences are in our buildings and engaged, we can tap into something very powerful.

We also need to consider context. Standing in the back of the theater, I would be more concerned to see someone noodling around on a phone during a production of Hamlet than say, a Crosby Stills & Nash concert. This is not because Shakespeare Is A Sacred Experience (although it can be), it's more because Shakespeare moves quickly and requires a certain level of attention that is too easily disrupted by tweeting "Person next to me thinks Pompey is the volcano, LOL."* Or not. If you have an audience of students live-tweeting the assassination of Caesar, what might you discover?

When audiences come to us, particularly patrons who are young or new to more formalized arts participation, they are vulnerable. The experiences they have in our facilities can set the tone for future arts participation. By maintaining an air of outraged condescension regarding antiquated theater etiquette, we do not help our own cause. Refusal to adapt is not a brilliant strategy in the war to build audiences and ensure the future of the live performing arts. On an organizational level we should seek creative ways to harness and channel patron impulses, not squash them with tired pre-show announcements and angry ushers. Take a real look at your "audience guidelines" and try something new. Who knows? It might even be fun.

*Which I may or may not have done.

180. In light of the passage, which of the following would describe the author's attitude about tweeting in the theater?

   (A) Opposed
   (B) Supportive
   (C) Enthusiastic
   (D) Hesitant

181. Longstanding theater etiquette has dictated cultured behavior in a live theater performance. However, the author speaks to how technology can enhance that experience without distracting the individual or others from their own enjoyment. How can this be related to the modern university classroom?

   (A) Students texting during class
   (B) The use of computers and tablets during a lecture
   (C) Small group discussion rather than lecture for learning
   (D) Podcasts rather than lectures for student learning

182. The author is clear that live tweeting can enhance the viewing experience in the theater. However, she goes on to say that "parameters should be set and abided by." Of the following, which do you think the author would least support as a guideline for tweeting in the theater?

    (A) Tweeting is only allowed at specified times during the performance.
    (B) Individuals tweeting should be seated in specified locations.
    (C) Tweeting should be confined to experiences and not play by play tweets.
    (D) Tweets should not be in the form of critical evaluations of the performance.

183. According to the passage, which group would benefit most from live tweeting in the theater?

    (A) Others tweeting at the same time
    (B) People unable to attend the live performance
    (C) Individuals who enjoy the specific play or writer
    (D) The performers who could use the tweets to evaluate their own performance

184. With live tweeting in the theater, much like the use of technology in the classroom, which of the following would the author most agree is a major caution when doing this form of multitasking?

    (A) Disrupting the environment for others
    (B) The temptation to be critical of the performer or lecturer online
    (C) Being unable to add to the performance/lecture based on what you learn online
    (D) Being distracted by technology and missing the play/lecture

185. The second section of the passage also mentions audience guidelines in directing appropriate theater behavior. Of the following, which would be among the most important guidelines for the theater and the modern classroom?

    (A) Remain in your seat for the entirety of the performance/lecture.
    (B) Use of technology should be minimal and unobtrusive.
    (C) Attendees should remain respectful of the performers or lecturer.
    (D) The audience should remain quiet for the duration of the performance/class.

Defining a Cyberbully

At minimum, researchers say cyberbullying is a subset of aggression that primarily occurs with adolescents. Aggression, as an academic and research construct, refers to intentional behavior that hurts or harms another person. Bullying, meanwhile, refers to aggression where there is also an imbalance of power and repetition of the act or a "systematic abuse of power."

"Cyber aggression and cyberbullying correspondingly refer to aggression and bullying carried out via electronic media—mobile phones and the Internet," says Peter Smith, a professor of psychology at Goldsmiths College, University of London. "As such, they are mainly phenomena of the 21st century."

In fact, a 2010 study of cyberbullying found more than 97 percent of young people in the United States have some sort of Internet connection, which is a different measure than owning the technology. The study found youth had access to instant messaging, chat rooms, email, blogs, texting, social networking, online gaming, and other media associated with the Internet boom.

Definitions of cyberbullying typically start with three concepts: intent to harm, imbalance of power, and usually a repeated action, although some experts replace "repeated action" with "specific targets." While traditional bullying uses these defining characteristics, there is controversy as to whether all these concepts apply to cyberbullying and in what capacity.

For example, the possibility of misunderstanding intent exists more with electronic communication than with traditional bullying because of reduced social cues, social scientists say. The inability to see a smile or a wink on the face of a friend who sent an electronic message could result in the communication being construed as cyberbullying.

"There are also problems with the imbalance of power criterion," says Smith, who led the NSF-sponsored International Cyber Bullying Think Tank's definition subcommittee last year. In traditional bullying, this is usually taken as being in terms of physical strength or psychological confidence in a face-to-face confrontation, or in terms of the number of bullies against one victim.

"These are not so clear in cyberbullying, which is not face-to-face," he says. "There may nevertheless be an imbalance of power either through the anonymity of those committing the act, or if the perpetrators are known by the victim to have relative physical, psychological, or numerical strength offline, then an imbalance of power may still be a factor in the victim's perception of the situation."

Smith says in some cases, greater technological expertise could also contribute to an imbalance of power, such as the ability of a bully to develop a website and post mean things about a classmate or a friend. "Although it is easy enough to send emails and text messages," he says, "more sophisticated attacks such as masquerading, or pretending to be someone else posting denigrating material on a website, require more skill."

In one notable example, a 13-year-old Missouri girl, Megan Meier, committed suicide after being harassed through a popular social networking website by a boy she liked. The cyberbully, it turns out, was not a boy at all, but instead was the mother of one of Megan's former friends, who created a false identity to correspond with and gain information about Megan. The mother later used that information to humiliate Megan for spreading rumors about her daughter.

The incident clearly involved issues of anonymity, masquerading, and the greater relationship skills possessed by the mother, not the fact that the mother was an adult, which traditionally creates a power imbalance with adolescents.

The third concept, repeated action, also gives some researchers pause. Due to the nature of cyberbullying, the act or behavior may repeat itself without the contribution of the cyberbully, they say.

For example, taking an abusive picture or video clip on a mobile phone may occur only once, but if the person receiving the image forwards it to anyone else, it could be argued that this falls under the category of repetition.

Additionally, if something abusive is uploaded onto a Web page, every hit on that page could count as a repetition. Consequently, the use of repetition as a criterion for traditional bullying may be less reliable for cyberbullying.

"At this point we don't have a standard definition of cyberbullying that is used in research," says Jina Yoon, an associate professor of educational psychology at Wayne State University in Detroit, Mich. She says studies of cyberbullying use different definitions—a situation that can lead to challenges when developing plans or policies that seek to prevent it.

186. Social interactions of the modern adolescent are much more complex than with previous generations. In fact, in the simplest of times it may have been difficult to distinguish bullying from other social interactions that may occur between young adults. Of the following, which is the most important criterion to label an act as bullying?

   (A) The act is hurtful to the victim.
   (B) The victim is smaller than the accused.
   (C) There is intent to do harm.
   (D) The event occurred more than once.

187. Cyberbullying, appearing early in the 21st century, can be by many means. Which of the following was NOT listed as a vehicle through which people access the Internet and can cyberbully?

   (A) Texting
   (B) Gaming
   (C) Video messaging
   (D) Social networks

188. After reading the description of cyberbullying and comparing and contrasting it with bullying, which of the following would most likely only apply to cyberbullying?

(A) Number of people against one
(B) Smarter individual as the bully
(C) Greater physical strength
(D) More confidence in the bully

189. Another factor of cyberbullying that differs from bullying is the anonymity enjoyed by the bully. This might lead to behaviors not likely acted out in real world settings. Of the following, which is another example through which anonymity emboldens individuals?

(A) Looters wearing masks
(B) Rioters protesting police
(C) Police being murdered
(D) Suicidal terrorists acting on innocent people

190. According to the author, there is the problem of misunderstanding when it comes to online communication over face-to-face interaction. Of the following, which would BEST help to eliminate this virtual problem?

(A) Eliminating online communication
(B) Video chatting
(C) Emoticons
(D) Clearly written English rather than the text-speak of today

191. While bullying and cyberbullying can be obvious in many cases, there has been much debate about the true definition of these activities. Of the following, which is NOT one of the three criterion most commonly accepted as included in bullying and cyberbullying?

(A) Abuser is anonymous.
(B) There is intent to do harm.
(C) The abuse is repetitive in nature.
(D) The victim is seen as weaker than the abuser.

CHAPTER 9

Religion

American Zenophilia

Buddhists in America are generally divided between ethnic Buddhists, often Asian-Americans who are descendants of immigrants, and convert Buddhists. Buddhism is often broken into four categories: Theravada, which emphasizes the difference between the monks' authority and the lay people (practiced mostly in South and Southeast Asia), Mahayana, which concentrates less on monks (practiced in countries like China, Japan, and Korea), Tibetan Buddhism, a form of Mahayana led by the Dalai Lama, and Zen Buddhism, which is best known in America and teaches that everyone can be a Buddha through meditation and mindfulness.

One of the ways Americans have dabbled in Buddhism directly or indirectly is through medicine. Jon Kabat-Zinn, director of a stress reduction clinic at the University of Massachusetts Medical School, is credited with mainstreaming mindfulness meditation as a way to help people deal with stress.

Americans have also been interested in "engaged Buddhism," a term popularized in the 1960s by the Vietnamese Buddhist monk and author Thich Nhat Hanh, for people who want to apply meditation and dharma teachings to social injustice.

"Engaged Buddhism is the cutting edge of Buddhism today," Queen says. These Buddhists want more than to "just study ancient texts or philosophy." As a result, many of today's Buddhists promote peace, conduct prison and homeless outreach, and do environmental advocacy. The Buddhist Peace Fellowship is one of the largest organizations to be involved in such work.

"Buddhism teaches the notion of the interconnectedness of all things; what we do is part of a web of relationships," says Paul Numrich, professor of religion and interreligious relations at Methodist Theological School in Ohio. "The welfare of animals and plants are affected by our own actions."

Americans are less prejudiced against Buddhists than other kinds of believers, a recent Gallup poll suggests. Forty-three percent of survey respondents acknowledged at least "a little" prejudice against Muslims, while 18 percent said they had some prejudice against Christians, compared with 14 percent against Buddhists. However, fewer Americans viewed Buddhism favorably when compared with Christianity and Judaism: 91 percent for Christianity, 71 percent for Judaism, 58 percent for Buddhism, and 42 percent for Islam.

"Many people have an image of a Buddhist as somebody in the lotus position," Numrich says. "Americans are worried about global Islam in a way they're not worried about global Buddhism."

Buddhism's roots began to form in the United States when Asian immigrants came to the country to mine gold in California in the mid-nineteenth century. More Buddhists immigrated after the 1965 Immigration Act, when Americans were taking an interest in Eastern religions, says Buddhist scholar Charles Prebish, who teaches at Utah State University.

"Hippies began to realize that perhaps Buddhism was safer than drugs," Prebish says. "There's a myriad of ways that people have wandered into Buddhism without intending to do so." Some might pick up a Zen book at a bookstore; others might attend a meditation session with a friend . . . .

But does Buddhism fit with all aspects of American life? "If you look at a lot of psychological therapies, they're based on a notion of a healthy sense of ego," Prebish says. "Buddhism says we should let go of ego altogether."

And technology has produced a culture of multitasking, which can make it difficult to meditate. "Meditation, sitting down in a quiet room, turning off your computer, getting away from television, creating quiet space in your life, is not simple," Prebish says. "There are a lot of things going against people who might say, 'Aha, this is for me.'"

Unlike Christianity, where important rites are performed in a church, the practice of Buddhist meditation can be removed from a strictly religious context, notes Scott A. Mitchell of the Institute of Buddhist Studies.

"For whatever reason, people feel like they can practice Buddhism without being in a community," Mitchell says. "Buddhism's teachings focus on the community aspect, an interrelationship, which challenges the American idea of the individual." Buddhism is welcomed in America because it appears to provide benefits to individuals without negative consequences. "People generally believe Buddhism is a more pacifistic religion," he says. "Buddhism provides a bridge for non-normal American religion but not so completely different that they're shunned."

192. Based on the passage, which of the following list of Buddhist types would be the one in which meditation and mindfulness is the way that anyone can become a Buddha?

(A) Tibetan
(B) Zen
(C) Theravada
(D) Mahayana

193. Which of the following would this author mostly likely agree is a rationale for why Americans view Buddhism in a more favorable way than Islam according to the Gallop poll information presented in the passage?

(A) There are more Buddhists in American than Muslims.
(B) Buddhists principally promote peace and the interconnection of all living things.
(C) Islam is portrayed negatively in the media.
(D) Buddhists are more evangelical than Muslims.

194. The author mentions that Americans often "dabble" in Buddhism indirectly. Which of the following would best define what the intent of the author was in this description?

(A) Using Buddhist techniques while practicing another religion
(B) Learning about the Buddhist religion without its practices being applied
(C) Applying Buddhist teachings to areas outside of religion
(D) Maintaining personal associations with Buddhists without becoming one yourself

195. Which of the following would the author agree is the most likely impediment for the typical American adopting and practicing Buddhism today?

(A) The stigma of a non-Christian religion
(B) The lack of a communal practice of religion in Buddhism
(C) The time it takes away from other activities
(D) The lack of knowledge about Buddhism in the U.S.

196. Of the following statements, which best describes the contrast between Engaged Buddhism and the other practiced forms of Buddhism mentioned in the passage?

(A) Engaged is more about affecting external change than the others.
(B) Engaged is about more strict adherence to the practices of Buddhism.
(C) Engaged requires a greater amount of self-reflection and meditation than the other forms.
(D) Engaged results in a deeper connection to the interconnected web of life on Earth.

197. After reading the passage, which of the following best represents the main theme?

(A) Buddhism in America
(B) Types of Buddhism
(C) Buddhist practices
(D) Religions in America

198. The title of the passage is American Zenophilia, yet the author never uses nor defines the word anywhere in the passage. Of the following, which would be the most logical use of this term as it relates to this passage?

(A) Anti-Buddhism in America

(B) Enjoying the peace of meditation

(C) Failure of Buddhism to become popular suggests a fear for the religion

(D) Other religions lead to distrust of other practices such as Buddhism

U.S. Policy and Programs in Support of Religious Freedom

Religious freedom is a human right knitted into the fabric of our founding and enshrined in our Constitution. As such, the U.S. government continues to prioritize the advancement of this freedom into its broader foreign policy objectives. The same law that mandated the International Religious Freedom Report and created the Office of International Religious Freedom also gave us a series of powerful mechanisms to promote the cause of religious freedom worldwide. This includes the ability to identify and sanction governments that engage in or tolerate "particularly severe" violations of religious freedom. It also includes the ability to deny entry to the United States of government officials who have themselves directly carried out or were responsible for "particularly severe violations of religious freedom".

As in years past, the 2013 report chronicles the efforts of senior U.S. officials and our diplomatic corps to help people throughout the world enjoy the rights enshrined in the Universal Declaration of Human Rights and the International Covenant on Civil and Political Rights. Our officials are charged with speaking truth to power, promoting accountability and redress for injustices, and helping the global community connect with and understand the plight of members of little-known groups in far-flung places. Every day and at every level, we are meeting with and pressing government officials to respect the human rights, including religious freedom, of all individuals. Through various programs and resources, speeches and statements, campaigns and multilateral resolutions, we are intervening on behalf of oppressed communities and individuals, speaking with average citizens, and providing comfort and support to victims of abuses.

Promoting religious freedom is a whole-of-government effort, and the President, the Secretary of State, our country Ambassadors, and other senior Department officials, including the Ambassador-at-Large for Religious Freedom and the Special Envoy to Monitor and Combat Anti-Semitism, regularly raise religious freedom concerns around the world. The President has raised cases regarding individuals imprisoned for their religious beliefs, such as that of imprisoned Iranian-American Saeed Abedini, publicly and privately with other governments. In Egypt, the President condemned sectarian violence, including attacks on churches. Secretary of State Kerry has also emphasized the importance of ensuring freedom of religion for all Egyptians, regardless of their faith, with equal rights and protections under the law.

Embassies around the world advocate for and support freedom of religion. Active engagement by Embassy officials in Armenia encouraged the passage of a law to protect conscientious objectors. This led to the release of 28 Jehovah's Witnesses in the fall of 2013. In Pakistan, we support victims of religion-based persecution, fund programs to promote peaceful coexistence between religious groups, and are working to develop curricula and training materials to promote religious tolerance and combat violent extremism. In Egypt, our programs are developing Arabic-language and English-language educational materials that encourage diversity and understanding of others. The U.S. Embassy in Albania organized a civic education and religious tolerance program that engaged over 7,000 students in discussions of common civic values shared across religions.

U.S. officials from the Department of Justice and the Department of Homeland Security, using foreign assistance funds provided by the State Department, are implementing a training program in various countries in all regions of the world to assist governments in training local officials on enforcing non-discrimination laws and in cultural awareness with religious minorities. The training includes topics such as legislative reform, best practice models, prosecuting violent crimes moti-vated by religious hatred, and combating discrimination in employment, housing and other areas. So far, successful training sessions have been held in Bosnia and Herzegovina, Hungary, and Indonesia.

Teachers in Estonia, funded by the U.S. Embassy, were trained on Holocaust education which was incorporated into their existing curricula. The U.S. Ambassador in Moldova worked closely with municipal authorities to encourage them to allow the Jewish community to display a menorah publicly for the first time in three years. In Niger, continuous U.S. Embassy involvement with the local interreligious council provided resources that allowed the council to mediate local religious-based disputes and opportunities for members to participate in exchange programs to increase their religious tolerance education and efforts.

These efforts underscore the U.S. government's commitment to religious free-dom. But creating a more free and tolerant world, is not a job reserved for any one government or institution. Rather, it is a global requirement incumbent on all of humanity. Whereas repression of religious freedom contributes to instability and economic stagnation, respect for it leads to more security and prosperity.

199. Which of the following would most WEAKEN the argument of the global advancement of religious freedom?

(A) Rise and spread of ISIS in Syria

(B) U.S. legislation for State Freedom of Religion Laws

(C) Christianity spreading throughout the far East

(D) Buddhists, Muslims, Christians, and people of other religious sects living peacefully in middle eastern countries

200. The author's attitude about the success of the U.S. in being a leader of religious freedom would best be described as which of the following?

(A) Neutral
(B) Enthusiastic
(C) Positive
(D) Negative

201. From the information in the passage, it is reasonable to conclude which of the following?

(A) The U.S. supports the UN's mission toward religious freedom.
(B) The U.S. demands religious freedom be practiced in countries who are our allies.
(C) The U.S. leads the world in support of religious freedom.
(D) The U.S. plays a vital role in the global move toward religious freedom.

202. From the passage, which of the following is a role of foreign embassies in the support of religious freedom?

(A) To release statements condemning religious persecution
(B) To provide aid to victims of religious persecution
(C) To assist with campaigns and resolutions to support religious freedom
(D) To deny entry into the U.S. of foreign officials guilty of religious persecution

203. Considering the impassioned beliefs associated with religious practices, which of the following mechanisms used by the U.S. to support religious freedom would the author MOST AGREE is beneficial?

(A) Economic sanctions
(B) Penalties for particularly severe violations of religious freedom
(C) Pressure on governments to pass better laws to protect and insure the religious freedoms of the people
(D) Education and training

204. With religious freedom as part of our heritage and integral in our constitution, we must continue to work toward global religious freedoms. However, in recent years, this does not appear to be the case. Which of the following most suggests that the U.S. is not using its full legal authority to press for religious freedoms?

(A) Other countries restrict certain religious practices.
(B) Countries that harbor religious terrorists are not fully sanctioned as directed by the office of international religious freedom.
(C) Peoples of certain faiths are denied entry into countries with which we are allies.
(D) All religions are not represented equally around the world.

Lord of the Dance

"The flaming circle in which he dances is the circle of creation and destruction. . . . The Lord holds in two of his hands the drum of creation and the fire of destruction. He displays his strength by crushing the bewildered demon underfoot. He shows his mercy by raising his palm to the worshiper in the "fear-not" gesture and, with another hand, by pointing at his upraised foot, where the worshiper may take refuge. It is a wild dance, for the coils of his ascetic's hair are flying in both directions, and yet the facial countenance of the Lord is utterly peaceful and his limbs in complete balance."

The words of religion scholar Diana Eck describe the Hindu god Shiva in one of his three incarnations: Nataraja, Lord of the Dance. This vision of Shiva first was made accessible to his worshipers through bronze sculptures created between the ninth and thirteenth centuries in southern India. The rulers were the Chola and their temples were the center of culture . . . .

In early temples devoted to Shiva and Vishnu, stone images of the deities were enshrined in a sanctum off-limits except to those of the privileged classes—monarchs, priests, and Brahmin. In the sanctum the worshiper received grace by darshan, the act of seeing and being seen by the god. Those who could not go inside the temple were unable to receive grace.

According to scholar Vidya Dehejia, it was "around the sixth century that the deity began to assume a public persona not unlike that of a human monarch. The deity was required to appear in public and to preside over a number of festivities. The large, heavy stone image in the sanctum could not be carried to fulfill these functions, so the production of smaller and lighter processional images of deities began." By the end of the eighth century, the images were being made in bronze.

The heyday of temple bronzes lasted four hundred years after the Cholas emerged as a significant ruling power around 850, when Vijayalaya Chola captured the town of Tanjavur and established a new line of monarchs. Under the Chola, bronze casting was perfected using the same lost-wax technique used today in India. The Cholas built enormous temples and commissioned hundreds of bronze deities that changed Hindu religious practice.

As portable bronze sculptures, the gods became accessible to the most lowly of worshipers. "Nandanar, one among the sixty-three saints of Shiva, was one such worshiper," writes Dehejia. "He came from an untouchable community that provided leather for drums and animal gut for musical instruments used in the temples." When he arrived from a pilgrimage to a famous temple, Nandanar was denied entry. As the story goes, Shiva commanded the priests to admit Nandanar into the sanctum where he disappeared under the raised foot of Shiva. "For the many devotees barred entry into the temple or stopped short of the main shrine, the portable image carried in procession through the streets of the town provided an outlet for joyous darshan."

205. The passage paints a beautiful picture of the Hindu "Lord of the Dance" and the practice of the Hindu people. Of the following, which is the name of the Lord of the Dance?

(A) Vishnu
(B) Nataraja
(C) Shiva
(D) Brahmin

206. Most Hindu worshipers had not seen this incarnation of Shiva until after the ninth century. Of the following, which would the author most agree was the reason that early worshipers (prior to the ninth century) had never seen Shiva?

(A) They had not attained nirvana.
(B) Shiva was only present in the temple.
(C) Only a select few were permitted to observe Shiva.
(D) Shiva did not come to Earth.

207. In the Hindu faith, what was the only means through which a worshiper could receive grace from Shiva?

(A) Meditation
(B) Sacrifice
(C) Self-denial
(D) Seeing Shiva

208. Around the sixth century, Shiva began a new practice that allowed more worshipers the opportunity to experience darshan. Of the following, which practice made this wider opportunity possible?

(A) The sanctum was opened to all.
(B) Shiva made public appearances.
(C) People could visit the temple.
(D) Statues of Shiva could be viewed in the temple.

209. To be allowed into the sanctum of the temple to commune with Shiva, the passage states that you must belong to one of three groups, including what is called the Brahmin. Based on the reading, which of the following would most likely represent this group of individuals?

(A) Monarchs
(B) Socially high ranking people
(C) Priests
(D) Elders

210. The passage states that in the eighth century images of Shiva were being made of bronze. Of the following, which is the most likely rationale for this choice of material for the statues of the god Shiva?

(A) It was easily produced.
(B) Technology enabled their mass production.
(C) Resources were readily available.
(D) It allowed for small, light statues.

Taoism: The Story of the Way

According to Chinese tradition, the Tao existed before the world was born out of chaos. The Tao brought forth the world, and all beings naturally belong to the Tao. At its most fundamental level, Taoism does not refer to a god or a founding figure, but to a universal principle. Nonetheless, the story of Taoism is inextricably linked to the figure called Laozi (Lao-Tsu), the sage who first revealed the Way.

There have been many discussions about when and where Laozi lived, and even whether he was a historical figure at all. Laozi is said to have been seen in this world at a time corresponding to the sixth century BC Laozi is reputed to have been born in Hu, in Anhui province. A later legend of his birth tells us that Laozi's mother was a virgin who conceived him spontaneously, through the radiance of the Pole Star in the center of the sky. She carried her child in her womb for eighty-one years (a cosmic period of nine times nine) before he was born through her left armpit while she was leaning against a plum tree.

At birth, the baby was of course already old, hence the name "Old Child," in addition to "Master Lao," or "Old Master." After giving birth, Laozi's mother died. In fact this was a phenomenon of transubstantiation, because mother and son were one and the same person. Alone in the world, the Old Child chose the plum tree, which had lent support to his mother, as his ancestor, and took its name, *Li,* as his family name.

Laozi is said to have been at one time the scholar in charge of the calendar and archives at the court of the Chou dynasty (c. 1050-256 BC). Confucius (551-479 BC) wanted to see the Old Master to question him about ritual, because Confucius believed that ritual decorum was the key to good governance. He thought that as long as everyone kept to his status and rank in society and acted according to the established custom, all would be in order. The story of the meeting has many versions, but the main idea is always the same: Laozi did not agree with Confucius's ideas, and told his noble visitor that naturalness, personal freedom, and happiness were more important than trying to conform to traditional standards.

After having lived in this world for a long time, the Old Master decided to retire in the far-off mountains of the western regions. When he crossed the mountain pass that marked the end of the world of men, he was halted by the guardian, who asked him for his teachings. Laozi then dictated to him the small book consisting of some five thousand Chinese characters that we call the *Classic of the Way and its Power* (*Tao Te Ching*).

Laozi . . .contributed to the worldview in which mutually opposed and complementary forces, *yin* and *yang,* evolve from the primordial chaos into the phenomenal world of Heaven and Earth, the "ten thousand beings." Each of these beings, or parts of creation, is shaped and nurtured by the cosmic energies of Heaven in earth in endless numbers and continuous transformation.

According to this cosmology, all beings are related to each other through elaborate systems of correspondence. The creative and destructive processes are thus considered to be natural and not linked to any divine will or destiny. This was a universe that was created and evolved spontaneously through the interplay of cosmic forces according to the universal principle of the Tao.

. . .Neither a polytheism nor a monotheism, Taoism lifts humans up to a level above particular gods and ancestors, to a heaven above heaven, to the one universal principle that allows the world to find unity in its endless diversity.

211. Of the following statements, which would the author most agree is the main theme of the passage?

   (A) The birth of the universe and Taoism
   (B) Laozi, the author of Taoism
   (C) The practice of Taoism
   (D) Taoism and other religions

212. As the author depicts Taoism in his writing, which of the following adjectives would best describe his attitude about Taoism?

   (A) Supportive
   (B) Neutral
   (C) Skeptical
   (D) Enthusiastic

213. The title of the passage is "Taoism: The Story of the Way." From the article, who in fact was the author of "the way"?

   (A) The Guardian
   (B) Confucius
   (C) Lao-Tsu
   (D) Tao Te Ching

214. Taoism is not among the most well-known religious practices in the U.S. Based on this passage, which of the following would the author most agree is the major difference between Taoism and Christianity?

   (A) Christianity is monotheistic; Taoism has no god.
   (B) Taoism recognizes several gods.
   (C) The universe was spontaneously created as understood by Taoism.
   (D) Humans relied on the Tao for salvation.

215. In the third paragraph, describing the birth of Laozi, the author mentions a phenomenon called transubstantiation. Which of the following would best define the use of that terminology here?

(A) The Tao came to reside in the body of Laozi.
(B) This was the unification of the Old Child with the Old Master.
(C) It was used to describe the virgin birth of Laozi.
(D) One entity could not exist in two bodies at the same time and was passed from the mother to the son, resulting in her death.

216. Tao teaches that the universe formed spontaneously out of chaos from opposing forces. It is from this principal that a commonly used term has gained popular use in U.S. culture. From the list, which would be that term?

(A) Good and evil
(B) Yin and yang
(C) Order and chaos
(D) Entropy and enthalpy

Confucianism, by Alfred Dwight Sheffield

The distinctive features of Confucian doctrine may be summarized as follows:

(1) Filial piety is the cardinal social virtue. A dutiful son will prove dutiful in all the five relationships: those of father and son, ruler and subject, husband and wife, elder brother and younger, and that of friend. Such a tenet was naturally acceptable to a social system like the Chinese, with its patriarchalism and insistence on the family rather than the individual as the unit of society. Loyalty to family it raises to a religious duty in the rite of ancestor worship. Here Confucius did no more than emphasize with his approval a national custom—mentioned in the earliest odes—of offering food and wine to departed spirits. How far this family cult is to be construed as actual worship is disputable: some would compare it merely with the French custom of adorning graves on All Souls' Day. But it effectively strengthens the family bond, impressing as it does the sense of family unity and perpetuity through the passing generations.

(2) Between man and man the rule of practice is "reciprocity." "What you do not want done to yourself, do not do to others." Benevolence—an extension of the love of son and brother—is the worthy attitude toward one's fellows, but it should not be pressed to fatuous lengths. When asked his opinion of Lao-tse's teaching that one should requite injury with good, Confucius replied: "With what, then, will you requite kindness? Return good for good; for injury return justice."

(3) The chief moral force in society is the example of the "superior man." By nature man is good, and the unrighteousness of society is due to faulty education and bad example. Virtue in superiors will call out virtue in common folk. The burden of Confucius's teaching is therefore "superior" character—character so disciplined to a moral tact and responsive propriety that in every situation it knows the right thing and does it, and so poised in its own integrity as to practice virtue for virtue's sake. "What the small man seeks is in others; what the superior man seeks is in himself."

(4) Toward the world of spiritual beings the Confucian attitude is one of reverent agnosticism. The sage would have nothing to say of death and the future state. "We know little enough of ourselves as men; what, then, can we know of ourselves as spirits?" In his habit of referring to "T'ien" or "Heaven," Confucius may not have deliberately avoided the more personal term "Shang-ti" (Supreme Lord), and expressions of his are not lacking which suggest a personal faith: but speculation on the nature of being and the destiny of the world he treated simply as a waste of time. On a report that two bereaved friends were comforting themselves with the doctrine that life is but dream and death the awakening, he remarked: "These men travel beyond the rule of life; I travel within it."

In summary one might say that Confucius did not found any religious system, but transmitted one with a renewed stress on its ethical bearings. His interest was in man as made for society. Religious rites he performed to the letter, but more from a sense of their efficacy for "social-mindedness" than from any glow of piety. His faith was a faith in right thinking. The "four things he seldom spoke of—wonders, feats of strength, rebellious disorder, spirits"—were simply the things not tractable to reason.

217. Of the tenants in which Confucius believed and taught, which in the passage was listed singularly and not with its counterpart?
    (A) Son
    (B) Husband
    (C) Brother
    (D) Friend

218. In the historical and social context of China, how would the author agree that today's American differs from the people described in Confucius's China?
    (A) Americans are all about the individual, family is less important.
    (B) Americans do not practice spirit worship.
    (C) Americans do not practice Confucian reciprocity.
    (D) Americans are less ethical than the ancient Chinese.

219. The author states that Confucianism is not a religion but was a set of teachings of an individual. However, one of the teachings of Confucius sounds very similar to a major tenant of many religions. Of the following, which was listed in the text that could easily be found in the Bible, the Quran, or the Talmud?

(A) Requite injury with justice.
(B) What you do not want done to you, do not do to others.
(C) Virtue in superiors will call out virtue in common folk.
(D) Family rather than individual is a duty.

220. According to Confucius, of the following, which is the major driving force for society?

(A) Morality
(B) Family
(C) Example
(D) Religion

221. While Americans have the security of religious freedom in our country, there is much we could learn from Confucius. From the following list, which would the author most agree is the one in which Americans have deviated most from Confucius's teachings?

(A) Do to others as you would have them do to you.
(B) Your duty is to all five relationships including friend.
(C) Focus on the real world, not the afterlife.
(D) Requite injury with justice.

222. Confucius was focused on moral and ethical disciplines that would make society and humans better. While his teachings were not precepts of a religion, which of the following would the author most agree was true of Confucius and his faith?

(A) He was an atheist.
(B) He was agnostic.
(C) He was areligious.
(D) He was religious but did not dwell on the afterlife.

CHAPTER 10

Theater

Nothing Glamorous At All: A Talk with a Working Actor

Jeri Lynn Cohen has been a working actor in the Bay Area for about 25 years, performing with companies such as the Jewish Theatre, Magic Theatre, and the San Francisco Mime Troupe. In a recent e-mail interview, Cohen commented on why she loves her job, the ups and downs of the actor's life, and the importance of the arts.

NEA:	What do you love about your job?
JERI LYNN COHEN:	I love the community I work with. I love surrounding myself with others that are as passionate about what they do as I am. I love working with people that have faith in me, challenge me, are smarter than me.
NEA:	What's the hardest part?
COHEN:	The hardest thing about being an actor is not having any job security. Figuring out what you are going to do in between gigs is challenging and exhausting. Finding the right part-time job that is going to give you the flexibility you need to go on auditions—or when you need to take time off for rehearsal—and that pays enough and doesn't run you down. I often feel that working in the theater is not conducive to family life. I am a single parent, and when I am in performance I am constantly patching together childcare, which, if you are doing six or seven or eight shows a week, can be trying.
NEA:	What do you think would surprise people about life as an actor?
COHEN:	That there is nothing glamorous about it at all. That it is hard work. That it's not just the work that can be difficult and challenging but the getting of the work that can be stressful. That you have to remain flexible and resourceful in all aspects of your life so that you can make a life in the theater.

NEA: Why do you think theater is important?

COHEN: [It's] more important than ever because it brings the community together to experience a live production. We become more and more removed from gathering together to witness a happening and rely more than ever on computers and technology to tell us the story in a solitary setting. Theater is by nature a community experience and, unlike film or television, it still asks you to use your imagination.

NEA: Overall, why are the arts important to you?

COHEN: In this age when school budgets are being slashed left and right, the arts are the first thing to go. This is so wrong because, for many kids, it's the only way into understanding who they are . . . . Relating to someone's story or a visual image or being moved by a piece of music or movement, responding to it and realizing that you have a story too, that you might want to paint or make music or theater. You can't know it unless you are exposed to it, and you can't be exposed to it unless there is money to bring the arts to the kids or the kids to the arts.

223. Jeri Lynn Cohen is an actress from which city in the U.S.?

(A) San Francisco
(B) Los Angeles
(C) New York
(D) San Diego

224. Which of the following was NOT stated as a negative aspect of a career in acting?

(A) Low pay early in your career
(B) Lack of job security
(C) Difficult on family life
(D) Hard work

225. Of the following activities, which would Cohen most likely feel also supports the same important aspect she mentions of theater?

(A) Being at a baseball game.
(B) Watching a movie at home with your family.
(C) Streaming live music on your mobile device.
(D) Chatting with friends on Facetime?

226. What does Cohen mean when she says that film and television do not ask you to use your imagination like theater does?

(A) The time frame for a play in a theater is shorter and provides less detail than does a longer movie or television program.
(B) Story lines are more detailed in television and movies.
(C) Visual effects are provided for you in movies and television.
(D) With digital media, the younger generation uses their imagination much less than in the past.

227. How does Cohen suggest that theater and the arts in general in public schools help young people?

(A) Nurture a passion for the arts
(B) Discover their self-identity
(C) Learn and develop a talent in acting or music
(D) Provide a sense of community of like-minded artists

228. Of the following, which is the only one in which Jeri Cohen did NOT perform?

(A) Bay Area Theatre
(B) Jewish Theatre
(C) Magic Theatre
(D) San Francisco Mime Troupe

Social Sciences

CHAPTER **11**

Anthropology

Scientists Find Earliest "New World" Writings in Mexico

Scientists have uncovered evidence of what is believed to be the earliest form of writing ever found in the New World. The discovery was based on glyphs carved on a cylindrical seal used to make imprints and on greenstone plaque fragments found near La Venta in Tabasco, Mexico, in the Gulf Coast region. The writings were produced by the Olmecs, a pre-Mayan civilization, and are estimated to date from 650 BC.

The artifacts, which push back the date for the first New World writings about 350 years, challenge previously held notions about the earliest of Mesoamerican peoples who developed the first system of written communication.

"It was generally accepted that Mayans were among the first Mesoamerican societies to use writing. But this find indicates that the Olmecs' form of written communication led to what became forms of writing for several other cultures," said John Yellen, an archaeologist and NSF's program manager for the research.

Excavations led by Mary E.D. Pohl of Florida State University, resulting in the discovery of the Olmec writings were conducted at San Andrés, near La Venta in 1997 and 1998. Her team included colleagues Kevin O. Pope of Geo Eco Arc Research, Christopher von Nagy of Tulane University and four students, three American and one Dutch. Pohl's team worked for several years beyond the initial excavations to analyze, refine, and confirm the estimated date of the Olmec writings.

"We knew we had found something important," said Pohl, whose research was funded primarily by NSF. "The motifs were glyph-like, but we weren't sure at first what we had until they were viewed more closely."

Scientists had previously discovered related hieroglyphic scripts and an associated "sacred 260-day calendar" among the people of the Mayan, Isthmian, and Oaxacan regions in the Late Formative period (400 BC to AD 200). These peoples came from areas around the Gulf Coast region across wide areas of eastern and southern Mexico surrounding the gulf.

Describing the findings in the journal *Science* in 2002, Pohl suggested that these writings and calendric systems "have close similarities, indicating that they probably came from a common ancestral script." These ancestors, the Olmecs, appear between 1300 BC and 400 BC, considered the Formative period of Mesoamerican history.

"The connection between writing, the calendar, and kingship within the Olmecs is indicated in these communications, dating to 650 BC, which makes sense, since the Olmecs were the first known peoples in Mesoamerica to have a state-level political structure, and writing is a way to communicate power and influence," Pohl said.

Pohl's group found one of the indicators of this political system as they excavated through a rare sampling of Olmec refuse debris that included human and animal bone, as well as objects such as food-serving vessels, hollow figurines, and the cylinder seal and greenstone plaque fragments containing the evidence of Olmec writings.

One of these writings contained the glyphic element determined to be close to early Mayan counterparts representing the day sign "ajaw," or "king." The scientists interpreted part of the glyphic inscription to contain the word "3 Ajaw," the name of a day on the 260-day calendar, which could also represent the personal name of a king. Whether or not the interpretation is entirely accurate, Pohl said that the evidence suggests association between writing and "rulership." The cylinder seal, for example, was probably used to imprint clothing with the King 3 Ajaw symbol. Clothing and jewelry were important items, Pohl said, to show rank and status in the Olmec society and the connection of minor nobility at San Andrés to the rulers at La Venta.

And what happened to the Olmecs?

"It is unclear, but at least in the lowland region of the Tabascan coastal plain where we conducted our research, flooding due to changing courses of rivers over time led to the abandonment of the Olmec settlement at San Andrés and probably other sites in this area," Pohl explained. "It is possible, too, that the Mayans increased their power and came to dominate, taking over trade routes, leading to the end of the Olmecs as we know it."

229. Which of the following would the author mostly likely use as a substitute for the term Mesoamerica?

(A) Early America
(B) South America
(C) Central America
(D) North America

230. Of the following, which people are suggested to be the ancestors of the others in the list?

(A) Mayan
(B) Oaxacan
(C) Isthmian
(D) Olmecs

231. Which of the following is NOT a stated link between the people groups in Mesoamerica?

(A) Writing style and language
(B) Kingship
(C) Funerary rituals
(D) Calendar usage and style

232. Of the following, which does the author provide as the most likely explanation for the disappearance of the Olmecs?

(A) Natural disaster
(B) Environmental changes
(C) Became the Mayans
(D) Changing river patterns and domination by the Mayans

233. How many days are present in the Olmec calendar?

(A) 365
(B) 260
(C) 180
(D) 400

234. The passage states that the Mayans were typically thought to be the first Mesoamerican culture to use writing. Of the following, which would the author most support as the rationale for this hypothesis?

(A) Mayan writings were the oldest writings found to date.
(B) Mayans used writing in their rituals and celebrations which helped them be widespread.
(C) All other Mesoamerican writing used a Mayan-based alphabet and syntax.
(D) Mayan was the first to be translated and understood.

Will Baby Crawl?

In much of the developed world, popular wisdom holds that crawling is universal. All infants go through a crawling stage to gain the strength and coordination they need to take their first steps, right?

Not necessarily, say a number of researchers including David Tracer, an associate professor of anthropology and health and behavioral sciences at the University of Colorado at Denver. Since 1988, Tracer has been conducting field research among the Au people of Papua New Guinea—a nation of 1,400 islands and 4 million people north of Australia. That's where he observed that Au children do not crawl, but learn to walk anyway.

Infant crawling rarely happens in indigenous cultures, says Tracer, a biocultural anthropologist. He has documented that Au babies are carried by their mothers or siblings 86 percent of the time placed in a sitting position, not on their stomachs. Instead of crawling, Au youngsters go through an upright "scooting" phase—pushing themselves along with their hands and scooting on their backsides.

The neuromuscular development of children is strongly conditioned by the cultural context in which they grow up and by the way the children are handled as infants, says Tracer. Au parents discourage crawling for good reason: In doing so they reduce the risk of their babies contracting parasites and diarrheal disease. Nutritional deficiencies also impact the development of Au children, who usually start walking a few months later than youngsters in the United States and Europe.

David Tracer didn't set out to study crawling. He was in New Guinea to explore the relationships between Au mothers and children, and to research child health issues such as nutrition, growth, and development—with the help of a grant from NSF's Directorate of Social, Behavioral, and Economic Sciences (Division of Behavioral and Cognitive Sciences). But his early observation that Au children don't crawl led him into deeper explorations of culture, biology, and child development.

Tracer, along with graduate student Sara Wyckoff, applied the most widely accepted standard for measuring early childhood neuromuscular development (the Bayley Scales of Motor Development) to a sample of 113 Au children. These tests measure an infant's ability to sit, stand, and perform in various ways that require the coordination of large muscles. The researchers conducted two series of tests on Au children, one in a horizontal posture and one in a vertical upright posture.

Tracer found that more than half of the Au children routinely failed the horizontal test, while more than half passed the vertical test. In contrast, children raised in developed countries excel when tested in horizontal postures, but have lower scores on vertical tests early in their development.

"These deviations from Western standards are conditioned by a cultural milieu in which children are carried more than 75 percent of the time and are discouraged from spending time in horizontal postures," says Tracer.

By contrast, most children in Western societies are encouraged to get plenty of tummy time. This remains true even though infants are often put on their backs to sleep in order to reduce the likelihood of Sudden Infant Death Syndrome (SIDS). Tracer suggests that crawling may have developed as recently as two centuries ago, as wooden floors and rugs replaced dirt floors, and parents began to feel that it was safe for their babies to crawl.

Tracer's work supports the idea that developmental milestones depend on opportunities, and opportunities vary with culture. In other words, babies are not hardwired for crawling: they may also scoot, roll, or slither their way to that universal goal—walking.

235. Would the author agree with the statement that crawling is a better means with which infants learn to walk since Au babies that scoot learn to walk later than Western babies who crawl?

(A) Yes, because the author clearly makes that statement in relationship to crawling versus scooting infants.

(B) No, the delay in walking is attributable to other factors in the society and not simply related to crawling versus walking.

(C) Yes, in safe and clean environments crawling is safer and better than scooting.

(D) No, since even delayed, the infants still learn to walk equally as well only a few months later.

236. Why was David Tracer researching the Au people of Papua New Guinea?

(A) Learning about the interaction between mothers and children in the region

(B) Studying the crawling versus scooting behavior of babies

(C) Researching the living conditions of the Au people and their families

(D) Examining the lifestyle including healthcare of the Au people

237. According to the passage, which of the following means of developing the muscle strength and confidence needed to start walking would have been the most recent in human evolutionary development?

(A) Crawling

(B) Scooting

(C) Roll

(D) Slither

238. Considering the statement of the author that "babies are not hardwired for crawling," which of the following statements would best represent the concept conveyed in that portion of the passage?

(A) Babies are not genetically instructed to crawl before they walk.

(B) Babies do not instinctively crawl before they walk.

(C) The nervous system of infants is not designed to crawl before walking.

(D) The muscular system can be strengthened by differing means to develop the control, strength, and confidence needed before an infant can walk.

239. Which of the following would the author most agree represents the main theme of the passage?

(A) Infants of different cultures learn to walk equally well using different learning opportunities which depend on the culture in which they grow.

(B) Crawling is the best means by which babies learn to walk in safe environments.

(C) Scooting is equally suited for babies to use as a means to achieve the ultimate goal of walking.

(D) The means with which an infant achieves the goal of walking is irrelevant.

240. Of the following statements, which would most weaken the author's argument in the passage?

(A) Babies from other cultures learn to walk before American babies.

(B) Au babies walk before babies from other tribes in Australia.

(C) Babies from cultures that do not allow their babies to crawl learn to walk much later than American babies.

(D) Babies from cold climates learn to walk at the same developmental stage as Au babies.

CHAPTER 12

Archeology

The Golden Hoard: An Ancient Afghan Treasure Is Recovered

A two-thousand-year-old Afghan treasure has come to light after a quarter century of rumors, legends, and speculation. Ibex figurines and jeweled scabbards and golden beasts—nearly 21,000 pieces in all—have been found again.

Precisely where the treasure is, Afghan officials aren't saying in the interests of security. The gold hoard from the ancient kingdom of Bactria has survived the years of chaos since it was discovered: the Soviet invasion, the warring among the *mujahaddin*, and the rise of the Taliban. Stories circulated that the golden objects had been carried off to Moscow, or sold on the black market, or melted down. In one account, just before the American forces arrived in 2001, the Taliban ran out of time trying to blow the central bank's vault. No one could say for sure what had happened.

Then in August of 2003, the government of Afghanistan announced that the Bactrian gold had been found and invited archaeologist Fred Hiebert to verify the fact. "I went over there to try and find out whether there was any truth to this rumor that the Bactrian gold was safe," says Hiebert, a specialist in ancient trade in Central Asia. "We were invited to inventory what collections they had, systematically, and do a verification."

Hiebert held the original field notes from the excavation by Russian archaeologist Viktor Sarianidi in the 1970s. With support from the National Endowment for the Humanities and the National Geographic Society, he and museum specialist Carla Grissmann were in Afghanistan last summer to conduct an inventory. The treasure, they determined, was intact.

The artifacts were uncovered in 1978 in the Mound of Gold, or Tillya Tepe, in a northern Afghan province that lies between the Hindu Kush Mountains and the Amu Darya River. The site was rumored to contain a golden man buried in a coffin of gold. Instead, Sarianidi's team found a four-thousand-year-old temple, and within its walls, the tombs of five women and one man. The archaeologists speculated that sometime during the first century CE, a tribe of Bactrian nomads had hidden the graves within the ruins of the abandoned temple.

Each person was interred with a dazzling array of jewelry, beads, buckles, coins, mirrors, and gold plaques that had trimmed their clothing—which, as was the nomadic tradition, the nobles had worn or carried with them in life. Four of the six nomads were buried with their heads facing north. Coins were placed in the mouths of two of the women: the toll for Charon to ferry them across the river Styx.

The necropolis dates from a time in Bactria about which little is known. "We call it a dark period in history, because it's very hard to find archaeological remains of these people," Hiebert says. "They have some dwellings, but they tend to be small. It's hard to get a handle on who the nomads were. So we can use this set of artifacts to help us understand what role they might have had in Silk Road trade, and what role they might have had in terms of the melding of cultures in this area."

241. Considering the passage, which of the following best reflects the author's main message she wished to convey to the reader?

(A) Golden artifacts found in Afghanistan
(B) Bactrian tombs and the treasure within
(C) The survival and rediscovery of the Bactrian Tomb
(D) The armies that sought the Bactrian gold

242. The Bactrian treasure survived many episodes of danger which could have stripped the tomb of its gold. Of all these dangers, which of the following was NOT one mentioned in the passage?

(A) Invasion from Russia
(B) Civil War
(C) Taliban looters
(D) Afghan tomb raiders

243. Of the bodies found in the tomb site, many had early possessions near them. However, what item was found placed in their mouths?

(A) Coins
(B) Ibex figurines
(C) Gold
(D) Beads

244. According to the author, which of the following is the MOST likely reason for the treasure being preserved from the most recent threat?

(A) American Military
(B) Afghan Government
(C) United Nations forces
(D) Russian Troops

245. Based on the passage, what adjective most reflects the sentiment of the author toward the Bactrian treasure and its preservation?

(A) Supportive
(B) Neutral
(C) Enthusiastic
(D) Judgmental

246. Throughout the passage, the author mentions various threats to the Afghan treasure, one of which was the Taliban. Of the following, which would the author agree is the most likely reason the Taliban was interested in obtaining this treasure?

(A) They wanted to secure their heritage and keep it safe.
(B) It represented an aspect of their deeply held religious beliefs.
(C) It would finance their terrorist activities.
(D) It could be used to extort money or prisoners from countries like the U.S.

From the Rainforest: Rescuing an Altar from Looters

The ruins at Cancuén were considered of minor interest until 1999, when archaeologist Arthur Demarest stumbled through a tangle of trees and vines at the site and sank to his armpits. He realized that the hilltop was in fact the top story of an enormous building. His team uncovered a three-story palace whose dimensions are comparable to that of six football fields. In the latest chapter of his adventures, Demarest helped reclaim a limestone altar looted from the ancient ball court at Cancuén last year. While conducting an NEH-funded excavation in the region, he aided villagers and the Guatemalan authorities in recovering the six-hundred-pound artifact.

"This region has been much neglected because it doesn't have any temples," says Demarest. "Instead, there are hills with caves in them, which were used as natural temples. It turns out these caves are filled with all sorts of treasures. And we have one of the largest palaces in the ancient Maya world, with a buried palace underneath it."

Cancuén, which means "Place of Serpents," is in one of the most remote tropical rainforests in the Petén region—the cradle of Preclassic Maya civilization, where howler monkeys, woolly anteaters, and rare birds reside, and trees span sixteen feet in diameter. At its peak, its royal palace housed more than a thousand residents and several thousand people lived on the surrounding lands. It rivals Tikal's central acropolis in size, and is better preserved than other ancient Maya ruins because it was constructed out of limestone instead of concrete and mud.

"I learned early on that when you dig in a place where there hasn't been much work done before, you make big discoveries—it's pretty straightforward," Demarest says. "However I also have learned that there are always good reasons why nobody ever worked there before: they are remote, there are health issues, they are in swamps and jungles far from everything, and they're often in zones of war and conflict."

The site was first documented in 1905 and 1908, but archaeologists reported that it was of little interest; in 1967 Harvard graduate students mapped 5 percent of the area, but were dissuaded from exploring further by the dense vegetation.

Archaeologists now know that the steep karst towers at Cancuén were the model for the temples of the northern rainforests. "The name for temple in ancient Maya means sacred mountain," Demarest says. "Where we are, in the jungle, there are remnants of karst towers—very eroded limestone honeycombed with caves, which were considered the entrance to Xibalbá, the underworld."

King Taj Chan Ahk ruled Cancuén in the second half of the eighth century, expanding his kingdom at a time when most others in the region were collapsing. According to Demarest, what distinguished the king's rule was a Machiavellian focus on promoting commerce and establishing blood ties. "He took advantage of the situation," says Demarest. "He made alliances with other rulers and married off his daughters. Q'eqchi' schoolchildren call him the *gran suegro*, the great father-in-law." The king made the most of Cancuén's position as a mercantile port city on the Pasión River. The river was the main channel for redistributing jade, quetzal feathers, cacao, obsidian for blades, and pyrite for mirrors. The city's inhabitants were wealthier than the norm: even artisans were buried with jade inlays in their teeth and elaborate ceramic figurines, a custom reserved for royalty elsewhere.

When the western region of the Maya world began to collapse in 750, its wealthier inhabitants began to flee. "Cancuén received the upper-status refugees. Taj Chan Ahk's boom was between 757 and 800, just as the dissolution was occurring elsewhere. He built his boom on the collapse," Demarest says. "He thrived because his in-law rivals were coming to visit—previously affluent houses moved greater distances." In contrast to most other Classical Maya kingdoms, no evidence of Cancuén's involvement in a major war has been found to date.

"Taj Chan Ahk took advantage of the situation," Demarest says. "But eventually Cancuén, a powerful epicenter, was destroyed too. The population was reoriented and the cult of divine kingship ended, which was the core of what generated tablets, monuments, and treasures—these legitimating monuments."

Demarest, a professor of archaeology at Vanderbilt University, has been conducting excavations in Latin America since 1976, and in the Petexbatœn region of Guatemala since 1989. In the Petexbatœn records he found mention of a marriage between a prince from Dos Pilas and a princess from Cancuén, and set out to explore.

Since Demarest initiated the first formal study of the ruins at Cancuén four years ago, he and his team have uncovered the royal palace's buried plazas, rooms, benches, staircases, walls, and stucco fragments from cornices and doorways. The stucco ornamentation depicts hieroglyphs, zoomorphic designs, deities, and larger-than-life portraits of kings. By examining the designs' cosmology and accompanying epigraphs, researchers are learning about the civilization that flourished in the region more than 1,200 years ago.

"We have recovered dozens and dozens of masterpieces of Maya art," Demarest says. "This is an atypical case, because usually the stucco melts like chalk in rain. But at Cancuén the monuments and stuccos fell in, were covered with rubble, preserved, and sealed." The jungle helped preserve the palace, with vegetation shoring up the inner walls.

247. Which of the following names was used in Mayan culture to refer to the "Place of Serpents"?

(A) Xibalbá
(B) Q'eqchi'
(C) Cancuén
(D) Petexbatœn

248. Which of the following was NOT given as a possible reason for the site at Cancuén being undisturbed for so long?

(A) It is in a politically dangerous place.
(B) The sight is in a remote jungle region.
(C) With swamps and jungle, there are disease bearing insects.
(D) Money for such an excavation had not been readily available.

249. Which of the following would the author most likely substitute for his use of the term Machiavellian in reference to the King's focus on commerce?

(A) Ruthless
(B) Calculated
(C) Political
(D) Ethical

250. According to the author, what sets Cancuén apart from other Mayan cities?

(A) Cancuén was built in a jungle.
(B) Cancuén was never in a war.
(C) Cancuén's king was more ruthless than other leaders in Mayan culture.
(D) Cancuén was far removed from other Mayan cities, which were closer together.

251. Although first discovered in the early 1900s, the site wasn't excavated until the turn of the century. What rationale does the author provide for this delay in the interest in the site?

(A) It is in a politically dangerous place.

(B) With swamps and jungle, there are disease bearing insects.

(C) Funding for such an excavation was unavailable.

(D) Extremely dense vegetation created intolerable burdens for archaeologists.

252. Much of the sight at Cancuén was protected from looters and remained unexplored due to the remoteness and thickness of the jungle. In the final paragraph, the author states that the jungle helped preserve the walls of the palace; yet, she also mentions that the stucco artwork fell inward. Which of the following would most likely explain this apparent discrepancy?

(A) The walls consisting of artwork fell but the outer support walls did not.

(B) The jungle only grew on walls without artwork.

(C) The artwork was only placed on the interior walls that were not built well.

(D) The walls remained but the stucco layer detached and fell off the wall intact.

CHAPTER 13

Cultural Studies

Four Bands Community Fund Kick-Starts Small Businesses

Four Bands Community Fund is a Native American community development financial institution based in South Dakota. Founded in 2000, it has grown to be the leading organization on the Cheyenne River Indian Reservation in the areas of small business training and lending, entrepreneurship education, and financial literacy. It encourages the economic development and quality of life for all communities and residents on the reservation.

From Sept. 2010 to Sept. 2012 Four Bands implemented a Social and Economic Development Strategies project designed to prepare local entrepreneurs to start or diversify 20 businesses. The basis for this project was a report Four Bands commissioned in 2008 called "Business Opportunities in the Cheyenne River Reservation Market." This report examined the local business marketplace, consumer demand, possibilities for start-ups, and expansion of existing businesses. This report informed the organization's development of strategies to increase business growth on the Cheyenne River Reservation.

Four Bands recruited interested entrepreneurs and paired them with business mentors. This mentor-entrepreneur relationship allowed entrepreneurs to research, develop and write business plans with the assistance of experienced local business leaders and the Four Bands business development manager. Participants in the program were assisted in achieving concrete, specific, and meaningful goals towards starting or expanding their business. Such milestones included applying for and receiving financing; depositing savings into an Individual Development Account to acquire owner's equity; creating marketing budgets; and securing leases or purchasing sites for their businesses.

Many of the entrepreneurs did not have access to traditional means of business financing through banks and Four Bands provided participants with capital through the Four Bands Community Fund Revolving Loan Fund. This gave access to essential start-up or expansion capital to some businesses. Some went on to secure loans from local banks to expand. Four Bands also supplied 12 businesses with $2,000 in marketing materials and three businesses received

$5,000 packages. Through the work of Four Bands, 20 businesses were created or expanded during the project period. These businesses included:

- Certified public accountant firm
- General construction, roofing, and dry wall companies
- Quilt-making business
- Maid service
- Life insurance broker

Many businesses were able to increase their size from one or two employees to six, eight, and more. These businesses were able to succeed because Four Bands did extensive planning and market research beforehand to determine the level of support and ability for certain businesses to flourish in the community. Since these businesses were in demand by Tribal and community members, they easily attracted customers. The owner of Diamond D Construction said he had to turn away clients because he was booked for months.

Seeing this growth in private ownership and economic development, more Tribal members are motivated to start their own businesses. Four Bands will continue to provide business-related training services and strengthen its partnership with Tribal leadership to bring greater economic security to the Cheyenne River Reservation.

253. Based on the information provided in the passage, the role of the Four Bands Community Fund is most significantly which of the following?

    (A) To enhance the economic diversity of the reservation
    (B) To enable all small businesses to prosper on the reservation
    (C) To assist individuals to enhance their personal standing in the community
    (D) To provide needed services for the people living on the reservation

254. Which of the following conclusions about people living on the reservation not having access to funding from traditional sources can be inferred from the passage?

    (A) Individuals didn't have sufficient capital to start new businesses.
    (B) People didn't know how to obtain funding for their business ideas.
    (C) There were too few banks on the reservation to loan money to small business entrepreneurs.
    (D) Traditional banks didn't think the business plans would be successful.

255. Which of the following statements, if true, would most weaken the argument that the Four Bands Community Fund benefits economic development of small businesses on the reservation?

(A) One of the ten supported businesses failed within the first year.
(B) Five of the ten businesses funded did not provide essential services to the community.
(C) A third of the businesses were owned by people not living on the reservation.
(D) Other businesses made more money than the supported businesses on the reservation.

256. The business model detailed in the passages appears successful for small businesses on the reservation; however, which element from the passage would most likely be important for this model to be successful for small businesses outside of the reservation?

(A) Financial backing of the business owner
(B) Experience of the proposed small business manager
(C) Type of business/services that will be rendered to the community
(D) What training and mentoring will be available to the business owner

257. When the ideas of the passage are considered, which of the following small business ideas would be less likely to survive and grow?

(A) Automotive repair
(B) Restaurant
(C) Housekeeping service
(D) Health insurance company

258. Which of the following best represents the main theme of this passage?

(A) Small business benefits from loans and advising.
(B) Reservation businesses are essential to reservation life.
(C) Four Bands Fund invests resources both financial and advisory in reservation businesses and people.
(D) The small business model developed works for reservations.

Can Anyone Be Creative?

To start with the obvious, creativity is a good thing. Creative people tend to be happier and more successful than less creative people. They are funnier and sexier and they can use their creativity to cope with stress and heal more quickly after trauma. Obvious negative stereotypes still persist. Some are true: creative people are more anxious. Others are simply false: your average creative person is *not* more likely to be severely mentally ill. There are hidden biases as well. Teachers and bosses alike say they value creativity, but they may still unconsciously dislike creative people.

This disconnect between what we say versus what we think may come from the many half-truths and bits of misinformation about creativity. Despite the cliché that no one agrees on what creativity is, there's a pretty strong consensus among researchers on how to define it. Creativity can be a person, a process, a product, or a place, and it should be both new and task appropriate or relevant. Of course, this definition tells us everything and nothing.

With Ronald Beghetto, I've proposed a Four-C Model of Creativity. Mini-c is personal insights: Ideas which are new and meaningful to you, even if others have gone there first. It could be the spark that gets you to add nutmeg to your hot chocolate, or the first time you use duct tape to solve a problem. Little-c is everyday creativity, recognized by others—perhaps a song played at a coffeehouse or a birdhouse sold at a craft fair. Pro-c takes you to the level of the expert, typically reflecting a decade of practice. It might be a biology professor who studies animal communication or the latest Saints Row video game. Big-C is genius: Mozart, Martin Luther King, Mark Twain, or Frida Kahlo. Big-C takes time. Is Jason Robert Brown an immortal Broadway composer? He's certainly a current superstar (and one of my favorites), but we need another hundred years to see if he's entered the repertoire alongside Gershwin, Rodgers and Hammerstein, and Cole Porter.

So: Can Anyone Be Creative?

Anyone can be mini-c. Most people can be little-c. Several can be pro-c. A scattered few can be Big-C.

How?

Lists of suggestions on how to be more creative have begun popping up everywhere, from Buzzfeed to *Newsweek*. They are usually rooted in some fact and will rarely do harm. They tend to make things a bit simple and overlook important details. Does brainstorming work? Sometimes (better to write down ideas instead of shouting them out all at once, and the boss should wait outside the room). Does spending time in a different country make you creative? Well, it's a start—assuming you take the time and effort to experience and absorb the culture around you; the people who go to China and eat at McDonalds aren't going to necessarily see a boost. Regardless of the nuances, however, there is a broad research basis for understanding the traits, abilities, and behaviors that can make you more creative.

Being open is a major component. You might try new foods, have intense conversations, take (sensible) risks, go to museums, play with ideas, let yourself daydream a little, appreciate beauty, and generally enjoy all the different experiences that life has to offer. Yet being creative also requires follow-through and tremendous amounts of work and knowledge. An aspiring novelist must read, write, rewrite, and then repeat. Getting ideas (divergent thinking, or generation) is easy. Picking our best ideas and executing them (convergent thinking, or evaluation) is hard. Insight and inspiration are sexy; midnight revisions and weekend afternoons in the library are not.

259. Creative people are said to be valued in their places of business but disliked by their bosses. How can this apparent discrepancy be understandable?

(A) Bosses love their business approach but dislike their social skills.
(B) Creativity often produces greater profit yet the individuals do not relate well to their bosses who have different personalities.
(C) People who are creative do not get along with people who are inherently not creative.
(D) Individuals in positions of authority are not creative people and fail to understand and associate with them.

260. Considering many of the professors whose classes you have attended and whose lectures you've heard, which of the "C" groups would you place them into?

(A) Mini
(B) Little
(C) Pro
(D) Big

261. After reading this passage, in order to enhance creativity which behavior would be most beneficial for many individuals to adopt and practice?

(A) Being focused on one thing for many years
(B) Being open to new ideas and opportunities
(C) Study in your area of interest the works of those pro-c and Big-C individuals
(D) Expose your mind to a vast array of topics and ideas

262. Considering the passage, from the people of our generation, who would most likely be considered in the Big-C classification?

(A) Stephen Hawking
(B) Bill Gates
(C) Donald Trump
(D) Neil Armstrong

263. The passage suggests that creative people more easily deal with stress yet are more anxious than non-creative people. How can you reconcile this apparent discord in the description of creative people and the lives they live?

    (A) We all experience anxiety yet creative people are less stressed because of their ability to cope and thus experience more frequent bouts of anxiety with lessened severity.
    (B) Stress and anxiety are two separate issues.
    (C) Just because they can deal with stress better, it doesn't mean they do deal with stress enough and are thus more anxious.
    (D) Coping with the stress makes creative people more anxious.

264. There are many character traits that set creative people apart from the rest of the population. Of the following, which is NOT a trait listed that distinguishes creative people from others?

    (A) Relaxed
    (B) Happier
    (C) Sexier
    (D) Funnier

Towards Life in the Fast Lane

"O public road . . .
You express me better than I can express myself"

—Walt Whitman

Poets have written for generations about the restlessness of American life, about an ingredient in the American psyche that keeps people looking beyond the next rise in the hill.

A little more than forty years ago, that restlessness took concrete form, in a federal law creating the Interstate Highway System. Before it was finished, it would become the country's largest public works project, crisscrossing 42,000 miles and altering the physical and cultural landscape forever.

The highways are emblems of our desires, Gertrude Stein says. "Think of anything—of cowboys, of movies, of detective stories, of anybody who goes anywhere—or stays at home—and you will realize that it is something strictly American to conceive a space that is filled with moving. That is filled, always filled, with moving."

A new film looks at the effects of this grand highway project: the towns it opened up to prosperity and commerce, the neighborhoods it split, the boom it gave to the steel industry in the 1950s, the car culture it spawned, and the price it paid in oil shortages in the 1970s.

"The highways are divided, and our feelings about them are divided as well," said Larry Hott, producer and director of *Divided Highways: The Interstates and the Transformation of American Life*. The ninety-minute documentary, supported by the National Endowment for the Humanities and by the state humanities councils of Texas and Oregon, is scheduled to air on PBS October 29.

Divided Highways captures the blur of cars flashing down the interstates, the jam into the malls, the fleeting images of a passing roadside. Superimposed over the visual hustle are sociologists, engineers, activists, and philosophers describing the profound impact the Interstate Highway System has had on our culture and commerce, on cityscapes and landscapes.

The story resonates on many levels. The documentary reminds Americans what an encompassing role the car and the highway play. There is a light-hearted moment as columnist Molly Ivins recreates the scene of a mother breaking up a backseat battle between her children. And humorist Dave Barry recollects family trips with Dad at the wheel: "'There's the Grand Canyon,' he would say as we passed at forty or fifty miles per hour. We saw a lot of the country. We didn't actually touch any of it or get out. But we saw a lot of the country, thanks to the Interstate Highway System."

For Michelle Grijalva, a Yaqui Indian/Mexican American who studies Indian peoples and their interaction with American technology, the speed is a sadness: that at seventy-five miles per hour, we do not see the simple things in life, like watching a cactus bloom, nor do we see the land that the highways are designed to bring us closer to. "On the highways, destination becomes everything," Grijalva observes.

Highways were destiny and without enough roads to take us somewhere, there was gridlock. A commercial from the 1960s addresses the annoyance: "What's a citizen gonna do?" asks the narrator. "Don't honk your horn, raise your voice. Ask for better highways," comes the answer.

The answer was to come at a price, and the price was sometimes paid by poorer neighborhoods. The Overtown neighborhood of Miami is an example used in the film. Footage from the 1950s shows a vibrant community, and local attorney Jesse McCrary describes a neighborhood with churches, night clubs, restaurants, hotels, lawyers' offices and doctors' offices. Modern footage shows I-95 running over the center of what is now only empty lots, vacant buildings, and boarded businesses.

"The neighborhood could not continue to thrive because the highway came right into the heart of the neighborhood," says McCrary on camera. "There are as many sixteen-wheelers at this intersection twenty-four hours a day as you have taxis in New York City. You cannot run a business of any kind with that kind of vehicular traffic over your head all day, every day, twenty-four hours a day."

265. The U.S. interstate highway system is credited for facilitating many changes in our country since its creation over 50 years ago. Of the following, which was NOT listed in the passage as owing its cause to the highways?

(A) Spike in oil and gasoline prices
(B) Rapid growth of towns
(C) Increased steel stocks
(D) Importance and social standing of car ownership

266. Among those things created by the highway system, the author states that it altered the "cultural landscape" of the U.S. forever. Which of the following would the author most agree is the foundation for her statement?

(A) Highways divided communities and further segregated populations into the haves and have nots.
(B) The cities owing their genesis to the highways created great cultural opportunities.
(C) Jobs needed to create and maintain the highways have led to greater prosperity for more people.
(D) Highways brought diverse people together more easily for blended cultural experiences.

267. Fifty years ago, the highway system changed the culture of American life profoundly. Of the following, which would the author most agree has made a similar impact on American life and culture?

(A) Cell phones
(B) Internet
(C) Airlines
(D) Bullet trains

268. While the interstate system opened the country to almost everyone, there are some who see its use as a negative. Of the following, which would the author agree has had the most negative impact on the American culture?

(A) The cost of maintenance detracts from other valuable social programs.
(B) Only people with cars (affluent people) experience the world. Thus there is still division.
(C) Travel is from point A to point B and little is experienced between.
(D) Cultural clashes are more frequent because of the blending of diverse people.

269. The documentary *Divided Highways*, as described in the passage, includes statements from many stakeholders that include all of the following except for which choice?

(A) Engineers
(B) Car manufacturers
(C) Activists
(D) Philosophers

270. The highway system profoundly altered the physical landscape of the U.S. Native Americans certainly can attest to the relationship of the people with the land and are thus perfect advisors to listen to about the landscape and the cultures. Of the following, which would Michelle Grijalya suggest that Native Americans believe has been the most negative impact of the highways on the U.S.?

(A) Disruption of animals and nature
(B) Visual loss of the beauty of the land
(C) The pollution of the environment caused by so many vehicles
(D) People focusing on moving and not the land around them

Planned Paradise: Making the Florida Dream

The scene was basic training, but the backdrop was strictly palm trees and orange groves for millions of American soldiers preparing to fight in World War II.

"Imagine you've spent your youth in Fargo, North Dakota," says Gary Mormino, professor of history at the University of South Florida. "You come to Miami Beach and what you see is all these troops training on golf courses. And the barracks is the Black Stone Hotel in the Art Deco District of Miami Beach." This, Mormino says, is how the Sunshine State cast its spell on a generation. "They all pledged to return. And they would, as transplants, as retirees, as tourists."

Over the next fifty years, the population boom that began with World War II transformed the southern state from a sleepy backwater of three million to an international mecca of more than eighteen million . . . .

The Florida that Mother Nature provided was not quite tenant-ready when millions of returning soldiers prepared to finance new homes through the GI Bill. Air conditioning, exhaustive dredging of the coasts, and savvy marketing would be needed to transform Florida from a tropical wild into a picture of postwar domesticity.

"The heat was pretty unbearable," recalls Thomas C. Wilcox, a former Army Air Corps private who attended gunnery school in Fort Myers in 1943. "We did a lot of perspiring." Initially viewed as a luxury, air conditioning became a competitive necessity for hotels in Miami by 1955. Wilcox says he would not have considered vacationing in Florida until AC came along, but he did so afterward, finally retiring there in 1980.

The city Wilcox chose for retirement, Cape Coral, did not exist in 1950. It had to be invented. An "instant city," Cape Coral was envisioned as a sprawling matrix of canals that would make the dream of waterfront property come true even for those living miles inland. It was the brainchild of developers Leonard and Julius Rosen, who used aggressive salesmanship and the image-making power of the national media to turn an uninhabited peninsula on the Gulf Coast into the largest city in southwest Florida at that time.

Before the first model homes were built, the Rosens began a massive advertising blitz. They took out ads on TV and in tabloids, gave away imaginary homes on *The Price Is Right*, and flew in prospective buyers for free getaways. Here, boiler-room tactics took over. Salesmen bugged rooms to spy on clients and, in the event that a buyer "forgot" his checkbook, kept blank checks from every bank in the nation on hand.

For all the marketing schemes and development bravado that went into making the Florida Dream, the deciding factor was price. Although Florida had long been an icon of easy living, it was a lifestyle accessible only to the middle and upper classes. In the burst of upward mobility after World War II, however, a car, house, and vacation were suddenly within reach. "A retired mailman could move here from Chicago and live on the water," Mormino says. "Florida was a dream state for the working class."

271. To make the Florida Dream come true for developers, many salesmen in the early days employed what the author terms as "boiler-room tactics." Based on the passage, which of the following would most likely be the definition of this terminology?

(A) Tireless efforts
(B) Telemarketing
(C) Long difficult hours
(D) Dishonest or illegal activities

272. According to the passage, which of the following was the most likely driving force behind the mass migration of people into Florida?

(A) Cheap real estate
(B) Training in Florida during WWII
(C) Warm climate
(D) Adventure of something different

273. For the move to Florida, there was much excitement, hope, and dreams of the people as they traveled to their new homes. However, there were drawbacks to living in Florida. Which of the following did the author state as a major deterrent and disadvantage of living in Florida?

(A) Heat
(B) Water
(C) Insects
(D) Limited housing

274. In the discussion of housing and land in Florida, the author mentions one particular development: Cape Coral. Which of the following would the author most agree sets this city apart from many others in the South?

(A) It is crossed by many canals so all can have waterfront.
(B) It is one of the few cities in southwest Florida.
(C) It is the largest city in Florida.
(D) It has only existed since 1950.

275. Even with all the marketing schemes used to attract buyers to Florida, the author states that there was one simple element that all considered as the final factor in moving to Florida. Which of the following was that criterion stated by the author?

(A) Location
(B) Price
(C) Air conditioning
(D) Water-front property

276. Florida is often seen as the playground and retirement location for celebrities and the wealthy. Which of the following groups would the author agree most benefited from the availability of real estate in Florida?

(A) Veterans
(B) Middle class
(C) Upper class
(D) Celebrities

Of Poets, Prophets, and Politics

In the town of Al-Basrah in Iraq, poets gather every year for a poetry festival, just as they did fourteen centuries ago.

In Cairo every Friday, people come together at the shrine of Ibn al-Farid, a thirteenth-century Sufi poet, to hear his poems read. And in Yemen, poetry is still vital for negotiating and settling tribal disputes.

While Westerners may be surprised by the notion that poetry is an effective way to convey a political message, Bassam Frangieh says it is an integral part of Arab culture.

"In every Arab country every day, poets appear on television, on the radio, or in the newspaper. Every single newspaper in the Arab world every day has poetry—this is nothing new," says Frangieh, who is professor of Arabic at Yale University. "Poetry is the essence of Arab culture."

The tradition extends back hundreds of years before the advent of Islam. Frangieh describes an ancient practice: "Once a year, all the tribes would meet in a place next to Mecca called Souk Ukaz, or the market of Ukaz. Poets from all over Arabia would come to compete and recite their poems in front of judges. These judges were either poets themselves or critics. Each year the festival's winning poem would be transcribed in golden letters and hung on the door of Ka'bah in Mecca for the whole year. It was like the Nobel Prize of ancient Arabia."

From Algeria to Yemen, Arabic is the official language of more than two dozen nations with disparate histories and peoples. "An Arabic poet is a poet who writes in Arabic, whatever his race or nation may be in contemporary terms," says Roger Allen, who taught an NEH summer seminar on Arabic literature at the University of Pennsylvania. He notes that Westerners often see "Arab" and "Muslim" as the same term. "To be sure, the majority of Arabs are Muslims, but there are significant communities of Arabs who are not—the Maronites of Lebanon and the Copts of Egypt, for example." Arabs make up less than 10 percent of the population of one billion Muslims worldwide.

An affinity for poetic language is deeply rooted in Arab culture, and historically, the poet has held a position of high esteem. "The Arab poet was the voice of his tribe, its defender and representative—above all, its provocative force," says Frangieh. The tribes took their name from the camel-herding Bedouins who called themselves 'arab, or people from the land of Arbi in the Syrian desert.

Nomadic tribes relied on poets to recount news and offer political commentary, and to keep an oral record of tribal history—triumphs, defeats, marriages, and deaths were recorded in verse. "The poem itself reflects the history of the tribe—the principles, the values, the customs, the traditions," Frangieh explains. "You want to know anything about the Arabic people—about their history, tradition, genealogy, battles, love affairs—you turn to poetry."

277. Poetry is a beautiful literary vehicle in which people for centuries have expressed themselves and found pleasure in the reading and hearing of poems. In the passage, the author directs our attention to poetry as used in everyday life in the Arab world and how it is used differently than we have grown accustomed to in the western world. Of the following, which is a means in which poetry is used in the country of Yemen as described in the passage?

(A) For political debate
(B) To contract materials and goods
(C) To settle arguments
(D) In religious celebrations

278. The idea of poetry for use in everyday life as well as in the political arena seems a far cry from what is portrayed in the media as to how the Arab world communicates and solves problems today. Of the following, which best represents the contrasts this passage presents in the context of the media's view of the Arab world today?

(A) Poetry is peaceful and unites people, the Arab world appears in the media to solve their disputes through violence and death.
(B) The media only sensationalize their feeds and do not paint the real picture.
(C) Poetry is not as widespread today as it was in past generations.
(D) Political turmoil is more easily approached through violence than poetry.

279. For the annual poetry festival in Souk Ukaz, those poets attended and recited their poetry in the hopes of receiving the highest of awards. Which of the following was awarded to the winner of this poetry festival?

(A) Large monetary award
(B) Their poem was placed on a door at Mecca.
(C) Contract for publishing more poetry
(D) Attendance to the office of the highest government official, much like the Super Bowl teams going to the White House

280. Other than for artistic enjoyment and expression, how can the poetry in the Arab world compare to subcultures and populations in America? Of the following, which might most resemble that common cultural usage between our worlds?

(A) Poetry used to commemorate important events
(B) Rap artists having a rap-off to settle who is the best
(C) Satirical poetry in the form of memes which are widespread on the Internet
(D) Poetry used to convey deep emotion and dissatisfaction with society and the government

281. As people moved from place to place as nomadic tribes, oral communication and poetry were important for many reasons in the present and to pass information down through the generations. Of the following, which was NOT a means in which poetry was said to be used by these nomadic Arabs?

    (A) Relay news stories
    (B) Business contracts
    (C) Political editorials
    (D) Tribal history

282. Poets in the Arab world are held in high esteem and serve important roles for their cultures and communities. Based on what you have read in the passage, which of the following would the author most agree holds a similar place in American culture as the poets do in the Arab world?

    (A) Journalists
    (B) Comedians
    (C) Actors
    (D) Singers

CHAPTER 14

Economics

Value of U.S. Mineral Production Decreased in 2013

Last year, the estimated value of mineral production in the U.S. was $74.3 billion, a slight decrease from $75.8 billion in 2012. According to the U.S. Geological Survey's annual Mineral Commodity Summaries 2014 report, the 2013 decrease follows three consecutive years of increases. Net U.S. exports of mineral raw materials and old scrap contributed an additional $15.8 billion to the U.S. economy.

"To put this in context, the $90.1 billion value of combined mined, exported, and recycled raw materials is more than five times greater than the 2013 combined net revenues of Internet titans: Amazon, Facebook, Google, and Yahoo. This illustrates the fundamental importance of mineral resources to the nation's economy, technology, and national security," said Larry Meinert, USGS Mineral Resources Program Coordinator.

Minerals remain fundamental to the U.S. economy, contributing to the real gross domestic product at several levels, including mining, processing, and manufacturing finished products. The U.S. continues to rely on foreign sources for raw and processed mineral materials. This annual USGS report is the original source of mineral production data for the world. It includes statistics on about 90 mineral commodities essential to the U.S. economy and national security, and addresses events, trends, and issues in the domestic and international minerals industries.

"Decision makers and policy makers in the private and public sectors rely on the Mineral Commodity Summaries and other USGS minerals information publications as unbiased sources of information to make business decisions and national policy," said Michael J. Magyar, Acting Director of the USGS National Minerals Information Center.

Production increased for most industrial mineral commodities mined in the U.S., and prices remained stable. Industrial mineral commodities include cement, clays, crushed stone, phosphate rock, salt, sand and gravel, and soda ash, which are used in industrial applications such as building and road construction and chemical manufacturing.

Production of most metals was relatively unchanged compared with that of 2012, but reduced prices resulted in an overall reduction in the value of metals produced. Domestically produced metals include copper, gold, iron, molybdenum, and zinc, which are used in a wide variety of products including consumer goods, electronic devices, industrial equipment, and transportation systems.

Domestic raw materials and domestically recycled materials were used to process mineral materials worth $665 billion. These mineral materials, including aluminum, brick, copper, fertilizers, and steel, and net imports of processed materials (worth about $24 billion) were, in turn, consumed by downstream industries with a value added of an estimated $2.4 trillion in 2013.

The construction industry began to show signs of improvement in 2012, and those trends continued in 2013, with increased production and consumption of cement, construction sand and gravel, crushed stone, and gypsum, mineral commodities that are used almost exclusively in construction.

Mine production of 14 mineral commodities was worth more than $1 billion each in the U.S. in 2013. These were, in decreasing order of value, crushed stone, gold, copper, cement, construction sand and gravel, iron ore (shipped), molybdenum concentrates, phosphate rock, industrial sand and gravel, lime, soda ash, salt, zinc, and clays (all types).

In 2013, 12 states each produced more than $2 billion worth of nonfuel mineral commodities. These states were, in descending order of value—Nevada, Arizona, Minnesota, Florida, Texas, Alaska, Utah, California, Wyoming, Missouri, Michigan, and Colorado. The mineral production of these states accounted for 64% of the U.S. total output value.

283. Which of the following most closely represents the main theme of this passage?

 (A) Explanation for the decline in mineral production in 2013
 (B) Description of all minerals produced in the U.S.
 (C) The importance of minerals to the U.S. economy
 (D) How minerals and their economics affect policies

284. According to the article, why is U.S. mineral production important for the technology sector?

 (A) Better economies are more advanced technologically.
 (B) Minerals are used to construct factories and buildings for the production of technology.
 (C) Mineral materials are used to increase the transportation of essential technology components.
 (D) Metals are used in electronic devices.

285. Which of the following explanations would be most accurate in understanding why domestic and international mineral production would be important for government policy makers.

(A) Many U.S. businesses rely on minerals as their raw materials.
(B) Minerals are a large part of the gross domestic product of the U.S.
(C) New construction for the housing market relies on minerals.
(D) Combined value of minerals in the U.S. is just under $100 billion annually.

286. The author states that mineral prices remained stable while domestic production increased (paragraph five). Of the following, which scenario would most likely explain the unchanging prices?

(A) U.S. mineral exports increased to foreign countries.
(B) International mineral production also increased parallel with that of the U.S.
(C) Demand for minerals declined while production increased.
(D) The global use of minerals and mineral materials grew at the same rate as its production.

287. Considering the availability of mineral materials as stated in the passage, which of the following changes would most affect the economy of the U.S.?

(A) Increase in clean or green energy production
(B) Decline in new housing
(C) Halt to new road construction or road improvements
(D) Development of new technology infrastructure

288. Twelve states are listed that, combined, produce 64 percent of the U.S. total output. Which of the following produces the MOST of all the states?

(A) Alaska
(B) Minnesota
(C) Nevada
(D) Texas

New Orleans Nonprofit, The Idea Village

The sign posted at an event sponsored by New Orleans nonprofit, The Idea Village, should give a clue to anyone looking to find out more about the organization and its approach: "Crazy Ideas." It's the kind of spirit that the entrepreneurs who founded The Idea Village harnessed in their quest to reverse the economic decline of the Crescent City. Their success over the past 13 years has helped make New Orleans an entrepreneurial magnet: *Forbes* magazine named New Orleans the "Biggest Brain Magnet" of 2011 as well as the No. 2 "Best City for Jobs." And a July 2010 Brookings Institution report, "Katrina After 5," found that New Orleans' entrepreneurial activity was 40 percent above the national average, while *Inc.* magazine called New Orleans the "Coolest Startup City in America."

Those are heady accolades—both for a city that was battered by ferocious storms in the 2000s and for a region that saw a significant brain drain of its talented younger people during that time. But the achievements of today didn't come without a lot of hard work, and some savvy investments, to get the ball rolling.

Among those investors in New Orleans' turn-around was EDA. In 2009, in the wake of Hurricanes Katrina and Rita, EDA invested $800,000 with The Idea Village to help the city protect itself from further economic catastrophe, by encouraging economic diversification and the creation of a base of disaster-resilient industries, such as healthcare, information technology, and web design.

In order to develop a critical mass of such knowledge-intensive industries, New Orleans needed to expand its intellectual capital. EDA's investment funded the IDEAcorps program, which matched visiting MBA students from top-tier business programs of such institutions as the University of Chicago, the Massachusetts Institute of Technology, and Tulane University with local entrepreneurs and start-up companies.

These newly-minted business professionals helped provide technical assistance and business assistance to entrepreneurs, focusing on such fields as green technology, medical distribution and production, information technology, web development, and digital media production.

To date, 586 MBAs from 14 different universities have participated in IDEAcorps. In the 2012 Idea Village Entrepreneur Season, a six-month-long business assistance and education program that provides opportunities and support to entrepreneurs, 697 entrepreneurs received direct support, $2.2 million in resources were allocated, 14,405 hours of strategic consultation were delivered, and 75 events produced.

"Since its inception in 2000, The Idea Village has recognized that New Orleans has the assets needed to become an authentic self-sustaining entrepreneurial community," said Tim Williamson, cofounder and CEO of The Idea Village. "[The] investment and partnership from the Department of Commerce's Economic Development Administration is great validation that a movement has become a model—creating jobs, opportunities, choices, and a new generation of leaders for our community."

EDA's involvement with The Idea Village and New Orleans' community of entrepreneurs didn't end in 2009. In 2011, the agency awarded a second grant to The Idea Village, for $400,000, to further build on its programs that support entrepreneurship and to scale up New Orleans Entrepreneurial Week into a regional innovation challenge.

On August 28 of that year, during a visit to New Orleans, U.S. Secretary of Commerce Penny Pritzker visited The Idea Village and announced a new $600,000 EDA investment to continue this model public-private partnership. The latest grant will support technical assistance to an additional 300 local businesses in high-growth industries through programs such as IDEAcorps, and it will build upon the successful track record of The Idea Village's Entrepreneur Season. The grant will also help ensure the long-term sustainability of these efforts by underwriting the creation of a five-year strategic plan to guide future efforts to support New Orleans' entrepreneurial ecosystem and promote small businesses throughout the region.

The benefits of investments like this are clear. As EDA and Idea Village join forces, they are helping a once battered New Orleans economy to transform itself into a more resilient, innovative, and entrepreneurial place to do business.

289. Which of the following is the nickname used to refer to New Orleans in the passage?

(A) Bourbon Street City
(B) Mardi Gras City
(C) Capital of Louisiana
(D) Crescent City

290. Which of the following list would be the most disaster-resilient industry in which to invest for New Orleans and the Idea Village?

(A) Restaurant
(B) Hospital
(C) Retail
(D) Agriculture

291. Which of the following rationales is the most likely explanation of why a program such as the Idea village would receive a second grant of half as much in financial resources as the first award?

(A) Federal money was spread more evenly to other programs.
(B) Less money was requested by the Idea Village Project.
(C) New Orleans had begun to self-sustain its own job growth.
(D) Slower economy decreased available funds.

292. As New Orleans leads the way as among the best cities in the U.S. for jobs, which of the following categories of businesses has been the most responsible for the surge in job growth of the city?

(A) Disaster-resilient industries
(B) Knowledge-intensive industries
(C) Retail-based services
(D) Real estate businesses

293. With which of the following explanations for the rapid growth of the New Orleans business community and economy would the author most agree?

    (A) Injection of outside resources into large businesses spurned the growth and recovery of New Orleans.
    (B) The federal government will always produce more rapid growth by the utilization of federal grants.
    (C) Local and regional resources and "crazy ideas" lead the way for the recovery of New Orleans and should be a model for other communities in financial and economic difficulty.
    (D) Investment and nurturing of entrepreneurs and small businesses can lead to large scale growth.

294. As part of the restoration efforts for New Orleans, the process involved what the author terms an expansion of its "intellectual capital." Of the following, which would best define what was meant by the use of this term?

    (A) More business schools in the city
    (B) Money for small business loans
    (C) People with wisdom and experience
    (D) Successful businesses coming to New Orleans

How to Estimate the Cost of Starting a Business from Scratch

How much does it cost to start your own business?

Of course, the answer depends on your business model and your chosen industry. However, a useful estimate based on a 2009 study conducted by the Ewing Marion Kauffman Foundation puts the average cost of starting a new business from scratch at just over $30,000.

Many small businesses, particularly freelance, online, and home-based businesses come in a lot lower than this, often needing only a few thousand to get started.

But averages aside, what can you do to calculate your specific startup costs? Read on.

Understand the Types of Costs a Startup Will Incur

Before you do any estimating it's important to understand how startup costs are categorized. All startup costs (meaning the period before you start generating income) include two kinds of spending: expenses and assets.

1. Expenses—These are the costs for operations that occur during the startup phase, although they will continue throughout the life of the business. Startup expenses include deductible items such as travel, payroll, rent, office supplies, marketing materials, etc. Expenses also include initial organizational costs like legal fees, state incorporation fees, etc. You can write

off up to $5,000 in business startup costs and another $5,000 in organizational expenses in the year that you start a business.
2. Assets—Also known as capital expenses or expenditures, these are the one-time costs of buying assets such as inventory, property, vehicles, or equipment as well as making upfront payments for security deposits. These startup assets don't usually qualify for deduction, however, some can be written off through depreciation at tax time.

Define What You Need to Spend Money On

To estimate your startup costs, start by creating two lists—one for your startup expenses and one for your assets. Your list should be informed by the aspects of your business that will have costs associated during the startup phase, such as facility improvements or the equipment and inventory you need. But don't forget to consider items such as brochures, business cards, and website development costs or any security deposits you need to make. Do you need the help of a consultant, tax advisor, or lawyer to help you get started?

Next, categorize these items as essential or optional—do you really need to spend money on these before you start making any kind of income?

Assign Costs

Now we come to crunch time—assigning costs to your startup "to do" list. This process is always going to be a best guess, but be realistic and use past experience, research, and advice from other entrepreneurs to guide your cost estimates. Organizations such as SCORE and your local Small Business Development Center can provide free and valuable advice about how to calculate your startup costs.

Whatever you do, don't underestimate your costs, or try to force your costs to fit the amount of money you have available. If the costs are too high, consider another approach to starting a business.

- Could you run a home-based business?
- Instead of buying inventory upfront could you have manufacturers drop ship?
- Could you subcontract rather than hire employees?
- What about buying surplus office equipment and furniture from the government at or below cost?

It's All in the Timing

Remember, as mentioned above, startup costs are accrued before you have income to supplement your business. So develop your budget with this in mind. For example, startup expenses such as rent and payroll are only that until your business is operational, once you reach that point they become running expenses that you take out of your profits as deductible against your taxable income. So you may want to delay some of your depreciable costs until your business is up and running.

295. Although the article is about the steps and considerations of starting a business, there may also be a time to consider alternatives. Of the following, which was NOT one of the listed alternatives to starting from scratch?

(A) Buy supplies in bulk
(B) Home-based business
(C) Subcontract the workforce
(D) Ship from manufactures to customers

296. Many suggestions are given on how to estimate and even save costs when starting a new business. Of the following that were not listed in the passage, which would the author most agree would be an additional important consideration before starting the process of opening a business?

(A) Rent versus buying the building
(B) Where to establish the business since some states and cities have different tax codes and incorporation fees.
(C) Risk versus reward assessment of your product
(D) Physical location of the building within the community

297. There are many considerations one faces prior to establishing a new business. In the passage, one area is expenses. Of the following, which could NOT be classified as an expense in your start up process?

(A) Rent
(B) Equipment
(C) Payroll
(D) Supplies

298. Expenses and assets are two of the many fiscal requirements for a startup of a new business. Of the following, which would the author most agree is the definition of what are considered assets?

(A) Materials and fees that are revolving and recurring
(B) Deductible items for taxes
(C) Fees that are paid for legal or incorporation purposes
(D) Budget items that, after the initial payment, you own

299. The author seems very knowledgeable about small business practices as well as the pitfalls that may occur during the startup period. Included in the passage were ways in which you may start a small business with much lower startup costs incurred. Of the following, which was NOT one of those listed options?

(A) Do freelance work
(B) Franchise
(C) Have an online business
(D) Utilize a home-based business

300. In the modern technological age, there is a wide range of products and items that can assist a business owner in the startup and operation of their business. Of the following list, which would the author MOST agree would be an optional item rather than an essential one for a new business owner?

(A) Smart phone
(B) Website
(C) Accounting software
(D) Wide-screen monitor

301. Not all new business owners will have the business wisdom to be successful in the startup period and will seek advice and assistance from several groups or individuals. Of the following, which was NOT listed among those who may be sought for their advice or assistance?

(A) Accountant
(B) Lawyer
(C) Consultant
(D) Tax advisor

Sourcing Strategies and Innovation—Diversity and Inclusion Create Big and Strong Organizations

We mostly think of diversity and inclusion issues as it relates to people and organizations. The benefit of thinking in this dimension comes from bringing in groups of people with a broad range of experiences, styles, and approaches to solve organizational problems in creative ways.

The same applies to sourcing strategies for plugging in outside organizations with our own. This is relevant to contracting, partnerships, and strategic alliances. Sourcing strategies give us the opportunity to reflect on the strengths and challenges of our organizations and be intentional about what kind of outside company can provide the biggest advantage. These successful strategies are key to building an organization that is constantly learning and organically innovative.

Clayton Christensen in "Innovator's Dilemma: When New Technologies Cause Great Firms to Fail" talks about the factors that affect an organization's ability to be creative and innovative. These three factors which ". . . affect what an organization can and cannot do [are] its resources, its process, and its values." He goes on to say that large companies usually reject promising opportunities because smaller companies are better positioned financially, culturally, and process-wise to pursue them.

Many of us spend a lot of time bemoaning the fact that it is so difficult to innovate or leverage technology in government because of how we budget, procure, and bureaucratize. But is it really that bad?

The Office of Management and Budget (OMB) put out an intriguing memo. For those non-bureaucrats, we live and die by OMB memos—we even give them names and numbers. It's sort of like when your mother tells you to do something—always listen to your Mom. This memo is commonly known as Myth-busters. Here, myth #10 tells that tells us that getting broad participation from a variety of vendors is good for us. If we do this, we'll grow up to be big and strong—Mom, uh . . . I mean OMB has a point here. Here's the fact:

"The government loses when we limit ourselves to the companies we already work with. Instead, we need to look for opportunities to increase competition and ensure that all vendors, including small businesses, get fair consideration."

Successful leaders will create an ecosystem where strategic partnerships exist in which each partner or vendor has an important role to play. Consider a shipping analogy—after all, for those who know me, it's all about cruising.

Large ships tend to be slow and difficult to maneuver. They are like agencies or large companies with entrenched cultural traditions and a heritage of processes. These ships need the help of pilot boats or tug boats to help them maneuver tight channels or clear reefs in order to have a successful journey. These smaller ships are like smaller agencies or small businesses that are able to go into places the big guys can't fit and are nimble, quick, and flexible. Finally, we have yachts and other small pleasure boats that can run circles around everyone—like the tender boats that ferry people back and forth to shore much more effectively and safely than the big guys can.

Whether you're a Harvard Business School professor, a Mom, or a frequent cruiser, the value of the variety and capabilities that we apply to sourcing work in organizations is a key to success.

302. Throughout the passage and included in the title, the author makes use of the term "sourcing strategies." While in the business world this may be a commonly understood term, for most laypersons it is not. Based on the passage, which of the following would best fit the definition of that termi-nology as used by the author?

   (A) Out-competing other businesses
   (B) Buying other companies to increase your business assets
   (C) Partnering with other businesses that can enhance your business
   (D) Increasing cash flow through increased infusion of capital investors

303. Using sourcing in your business may include all but which of the following selections?

   (A) Contracting
   (B) Incorporating
   (C) Partnerships
   (D) Strategic alliances

304. The author creatively uses business terminology as well as words most often included in science passages. One of those examples occurs in paragraph two where she mentions an organization that needs to be "organically innovative." Of the following list, which would be the best definition of that term used here?

(A) Blending of like companies
(B) A natural process; not contrived or manipulated
(C) Utilizing the best businesses to enhance your own
(D) Using human innovation and not industrial or technological

305. The author refers to the work of Clayton Christensen who wrote about the "Innovator's Dilemma." In this work he describes three factors that "affect what an organization can and cannot do." Of the following, which is not included in his list?

(A) Products
(B) Resources
(C) Processes
(D) Values

306. As with a previous question, the author uses another biological term in the passage. In paragraph seven she states that "successful leaders will create an ecosystem . . . ." While she uses a shipping analogy, which of the following biological illustrations would the author most agree matches her idea of the ecosystem in business?

(A) Parasitic organisms and the host
(B) Lion and hyenas
(C) Predator and prey
(D) Dog and owner

307. In this passage about business practices, sourcing strategies, and success, the author notes that "the government loses when we limit ourselves...." This occurs in paragraph six. Based on the passage, in what way would the author most agree these principals can also help the government?

(A) Bigger business will increase the tax revenue for the government.
(B) Better businesses will increase the GDP by increasing exports to other countries.
(C) More competitive and successful businesses increase the economy of the country.
(D) More business partnerships bring financial gain to the government as stated in the OMB Myth #10 memo.

308. In the author's shipping analogy of sourcing, small ships are characterized as providing greater services and diversity to the larger ships because of three of their characteristics. Of the following, which is NOT a characteristic of the small business that can innovate the larger business?

(A) Nimble
(B) Flexible
(C) Quick
(D) Diverse

One-Woman Juice Empire

In the early 1980's, Marie Muque Kigoma began a juice business in her back yard by hand squeezing passion fruit into juice. She poured that juice into recycled bottles, which she sold to neighborhood families, restaurants, and supermarkets in Burundi's capital, Bujumbura. Working as a full-time nurse and raising her three children, Kigoma needed the extra income to make ends meet.

Today, she runs FRUITO, Burundi's most successful juice company, which employs 50 full-time workers and buys from more than 1,800 small scale farmers. With her "never give up" attitude and support from the United States African Development Foundation (USADF), Kigoma epitomizes the truth that success is possible despite overwhelming odds and circumstances.

Kigoma encountered and overcame an onslaught of obstacles along her road to prosperity. Early on, a bottle shortage in Burundi left her without a means of packaging her juice. On the verge of quitting her start-up business, Kigoma's husband encouraged her to persevere. But Burundi's four-month dry season continued to plague FRUITO. Without a proper refrigeration container, Kigoma's business couldn't store enough juice to continue sales during the dry season. As a result, she had to annually downsize her company, forcing her hard-working employees to scramble to find alternative sources of income.

And then in 1993 came the Burundi Civil War, a 12-year ethnic conflict that claimed 300,000 lives and forced many private businesses, including FRUITO, to shut down. But Kigoma was not ready to give up. After three years, FRUITO reopened, but still confronted historic setbacks of inadequate equipment, untrained staff, unreliable electric power, and an inability to buy and store enough fruit during the dry season. The ensuing financial crisis took on a more personal form when Kigoma lost her husband to malaria several years later.

But things began to change in 2008 when FRUITO entered into a partnership with USADF. It was just the catalyst Kigoma needed to jumpstart her business. FRUITO used the USADF grant to purchase farming tools for fruit growers to increase their production levels during the growing season. FRUITO also invested in a cold room needed to preserve juice concentrate during the dry season. Now, FRUITO can make sales throughout the year. This was good news for the rural farmers as the new demand for their produce has increased their income levels too.

The USADF grant was also designed to empower the rural farmers by setting up a more cost effective distribution channel for their produce. In the past, the farmers lost profit because they were too dependent on middlemen to transport their crops directly to FRUITO. FRUITO now has their own trucks available to pick up farmers' fruit directly for a lower cost and in turn pay the farmers a better market value for their produce.

After nearly 30 years, Kigoma proves that profitable businesses can be built at the community level—to benefit both the passion fruit farmer and the nurse with the dream of a successful company.

309. Overcoming obstacles was essential in the success of FRUITO and for Marie Kigoma. Of the following, which was NOT an obstacle faced by this determined woman?

    (A) Death of her husband
    (B) Civil War
    (C) Lack of refrigeration
    (D) Inadequate supply of fruit during the dry season

310. Although the war lasted 12 years, FRUITO was not operational for only three years. How does this timing reflect upon the character of Marie Kigoma as reflected in the passage?

    (A) Even faced with war, she was going to make a profit at any cost.
    (B) It was only one of many obstacles she had to overcome to be successful.
    (C) She closed only during the time of the war when fighting was close to the business.
    (D) FRUITO closed only when there were no available employees who were not fighting in the war.

311. Of the following statements, which is most accurate about the role the USADF grant played in the growth of FRUITO?

    (A) It provided the refrigeration and processing equipment needed to assist FRUITO produce more juice year round.
    (B) The grant provided for more efficient farming equipment to increase production.
    (C) The grant assisted in increasing farming efficiency and productivity as well as provided a means for storage of more product.
    (D) The grant enabled the building of new production facilities in other parts of the country.

312. For farmers, reducing cost and increasing productivity is key to success. How were the farmers helped to do both of these?

    (A) They obtained new equipment.

    (B) They purchased land near the factory to minimize transportation.

    (C) They formed a new transportation company to distribute produce to more businesses more quickly.

    (D) They eliminated transportation cost by FRUITO transporting the produce thus allowing the famers the cost savings to increase productivity.

313. Of the following statements, which would most closely represent the theme of this passage?

    (A) How to make a living in the fruit juice business

    (B) A never give up attitude leading to success

    (C) Communities working together to provide lasting services even in difficult times

    (D) The success of one woman with a dream, determination, and passion (fruit)

314. Marie Kigoma was not a juice worker and owner her entire life. In fact she began producing juice in her backyard to make additional money for her family. What was her occupation when she began making the juice?

    (A) Janitor

    (B) Nurse

    (C) Teacher

    (D) Waitress

CHAPTER 15

Education

Historically Black Colleges and Universities and Higher Education Desegregation

The U.S. Supreme Court's 1896 decision in Plessy v. Ferguson established a "separate but equal" doctrine in public education. In validating racially dual public elementary and secondary school systems, Plessy also encouraged black colleges to focus on teacher training to provide a pool of instructors for segregated schools. At the same time, the expansion of black secondary schools reduced the need for black colleges to provide college preparatory instruction.

By 1953, more than 32,000 students were enrolled in such well known private black institutions as Fisk University, Hampton Institute, Howard University, Meharry Medical College, Morehouse College, Spelman College, and Tuskegee Institute, as well as a host of smaller black colleges located in southern and border states. In the same year, over 43,000 students were enrolled in public black colleges. HBCUs enrolled 3,200 students in graduate programs. These private and public institutions mutually served the important mission of providing education for teachers, ministers, lawyers, and doctors for the black population in a racially segregated society.

The addition of graduate programs, mostly at public HBCUs, reflected three Supreme Court decisions in which the "separate but equal" principle of Plessy was applied to graduate and professional education. The decisions stipulated: (1) a state must offer schooling for blacks as soon as it provided it for whites (Sinuel v. Board of Regents of University of Oklahoma, 1948); (2) black students must receive the same treatment as white students (MacLaurin v. Oklahoma State Regents, 1950); and (3) a state must provide facilities of comparable quality for black and white students (Sweatt v. Painter, 1950). Black students increasingly were admitted to traditionally white graduate and professional schools if their program of study was unavailable at HBCUs. In effect, desegregation in higher education began at the post-baccalaureate level.

In 1954, the U.S. Supreme Court decision in Brown v. Board of Education rejected the "separate but equal" doctrine and held that racially segregated public schools deprive black children of equal protection guaranteed by the Fourteenth Amendment of the United States Constitution. The Plessy decision, which had governed public education policy for more than a half-century, was overturned.

Despite the landmark Supreme Court decision in Brown, most HBCUs remained segregated with poorer facilities and budgets compared with traditionally white institutions. Lack of adequate libraries and scientific and research equipment and capabilities placed a serious handicap on many. Many of the public HBCUs closed or merged with traditionally white institutions. However, most black college students continued to attend HBCUs years after the decision was rendered.

Soon after the Brown decision, Congress passed Title VI of the Civil Rights Act of 1964 to provide a mechanism for ensuring equal opportunity in federally assisted programs and activities. In enacting Title VI, Congress also reflected its concern with the slow progress in desegregating educational institutions following the Supreme Court's Brown decision. Title VI protects individuals from discrimination based on race, color, or national origin in programs or activities receiving federal financial assistance. Passage of the law led to the establishment of the Office for Civil Rights (OCR).

315. The "separate but equal" doctrine in the U.S. was the driving force behind the creation of several historically black colleges and universities. Of the following list, which is the ONLY one that was not mentioned in the passage?

   (A) Lincoln University
   (B) Howard University
   (C) Morehouse College
   (D) Spelman College

316. In paragraph four, after the desegregation of public schools, most black college students chose to attend HBCUs in spite of their poorer facilities when compared to predominantly white universities. Which of the following statements would the author most agree was the rationale behind their selection of a college?

   (A) Black students remained in the mindset of segregation and preferred to stay with what was familiar.
   (B) While the courts dictated desegregation, society was not fully accepting the principal.
   (C) Black students felt safer in HBCUs.
   (D) There was actually little difference between the black and white universities relative to resources.

317. While the separate but equal doctrine may have seemed acceptable on paper, it was not achieved in practice. In fact, three supreme court decisions further defined the equality that must be achieved. Of the following selections, which was NOT one of those decisions directing separate but equal practices discussed in the passage?

(A) Schooling must be offered for black students as soon as it is for whites.
(B) Black students must receive the same treatment as whites.
(C) States must appropriate the same money to black and white colleges.
(D) Facilities must be equal on black and white campuses.

318. Based on the failure of separate but equal to in fact make education equal for black students, of the following, which would the author most agree would be a similar situation regarding same sex marriages today?

(A) Marriage for one should be the same for all.
(B) Marriage should be reserved for man and woman and civil unions for same gender partners.
(C) Since genders are distinct for heterosexual couples, there already exists a difference.
(D) Marriage for same sex couples would degrade what it means for heterosexual marriages.

319. Black colleges played a major role in the education and training of black Americans. The author lists several predominant careers in which black students were trained. Of the following, which was NOT one of those listed?

(A) Doctor
(B) Accountant
(C) Teacher
(D) Minister

320. The establishment of black secondary schools is said to have drastically reduced the need for college preparatory instruction among black students. Today, students of all races attend junior colleges and take college remedial course work following their secondary education. Of the following, which would the author most agree is the explanation for this increase?

(A) The black secondary schools were better than the schools of today.
(B) Today's secondary students don't learn information, they learn how to pass standardized exams.
(C) Students are less interested in college in modern times.
(D) American students go into the workplace rather than college.

The Value of a College Degree

The escalating cost of higher education is causing many to question the value of continuing education beyond high school. Many wonder whether the high cost of tuition, the opportunity cost of choosing college over full-time employment, and the accumulation of thousands of dollars of debt is, in the long run, worth the investment. The risk is especially large for low-income families who have a difficult time making ends meet without the additional burden of college tuition and fees.

In order to determine whether higher education is worth the investment, it is useful to examine what is known about the value of higher education and the rates of return on investment to both the individual and to society.

The Economic Value of Higher Education

There is considerable support for the notion that the rate of return on investment in higher education is high enough to warrant the financial burden associated with pursuing a college degree. Though the earnings differential between college and high school graduates varies over time, college graduates, on average, earn more than high school graduates. According to the Census Bureau, over an adult's working life, high school graduates earn an average of $1.2 million; associate's degree holders earn about $1.6 million; and bachelor's degree holders earn about $2.1 million (Day and Newburger, 2002).

These sizeable differences in lifetime earnings put the costs of college study in realistic perspective. Most students today—about 80 percent of all students—enroll either in public 4-year colleges or in public 2-year colleges. According to the U.S. Department of Education report, Think College Early, a full-time student at a public 4-year college pays an average of $8,655 per year for in-state tuition, room and board (U.S. Dept. of Education, 2002). A full-time student in a public 2-year college pays an average of $1,359 per year in tuition (U.S. Dept. of Education, 2002). These statistics support the contention that, though the cost of higher education is significant, given the earnings disparity that exists between those who earn a bachelor's degree and those who do not, the individual rate of return on investment in higher education is sufficiently high to warrant the cost.

Other Benefits of Higher Education

College graduates also enjoy benefits beyond increased income. A 1998 report published by the Institute for Higher Education Policy reviews the individual benefits that college graduates enjoy, including higher levels of saving, increased personal/professional mobility, improved quality of life for their offspring, better consumer decision making, and more hobbies and leisure activities (Institute for Higher Education Policy, 1998). According to a report published by the Carnegie Foundation, non-monetary individual benefits of higher education include the tendency for postsecondary students to become more open-minded, more cultured, more rational, more consistent and less authoritarian; these benefits are also passed along to succeeding generations (Rowley and Hurtado, 2002). Additionally, college attendance has been shown to "decrease prejudice, enhance knowledge of world affairs, and enhance social status" while increasing economic and job security for those who earn bachelor's degrees (Ibid.)

Research has also consistently shown a positive correlation between completion of higher education and good health, not only for oneself, but also for one's children. In fact, "parental schooling levels (after controlling for differences in earnings) are positively correlated with the health status of their children" and "increased schooling (and higher relative income) are correlated with lower mortality rates for given age brackets" (Cohn and Geske, 1992).

The Social Value of Higher Education

A number of studies have shown a high correlation between higher education and cultural and family values, and economic growth. According to Elchanan Cohn and Terry Geske (1992), there is the tendency for more highly educated women to spend more time with their children; these women tend to use this time to better prepare their children for the future. Cohn and Geske (1992) report that "college graduates appear to have a more optimistic view of their past and future personal progress."

Public benefits of attending college include increased tax revenues, greater workplace productivity, increased consumption, increased workforce flexibility, and decreased reliance on government financial support (Institute for Higher Education Policy, 1998).

321. Rapidly rising costs for higher education tuition and fees have been highly publicized and debated in the media and in many legislatures. All things considered, which of the following would be most responsible for this increased cost over simply inflation?

(A) More students seeking higher education than ever before requires greater overhead cost to the university that is passed along to the student.

(B) State and federal subsidies to universities has stopped, requiring institutions to make up the difference yet maintain quality programs.

(C) Cost of books, materials, faculty salaries, and utilities has increased resulting in the increase in tuition.

(D) Fewer universities are accepting students than 30 or 40 years ago.

322. In the passage, many benefits and pitfalls of higher education were discussed. In the list below, which of the following was NOT presented as a benefit of pursuing a degree?

(A) Better living conditions for their children

(B) More leisure activities

(C) Making better decisions on purchases

(D) Decreased job mobility through job security

323. Much of the passage compares and contrasts a college education versus full time employment as the next step after high school. The author states that one consideration is ". . .the opportunity cost of choosing college over full-time employment." Which of the following best mirrors the sentiment of the author from this segment of the passage?

(A) Individuals may bypass an opportunity for full-time employment that would have been more beneficial than would result from going to college.

(B) By going to college you limit your occupational opportunities later.

(C) Just because you have a college degree doesn't mean you wouldn't have had a lucrative and enjoyable career in full time employment otherwise.

(D) Finding and applying to universities does cost more than finding a job.

324. The passage discusses the cost and benefits of a college education in the preparation for a career. Here, the author makes a statement that highly educated women spend more time with their children. Of the situations below, which would the author most agree can explain for this apparent discrepancy in the data?

(A) Educated women are more likely to postpone their career advancement by staying home and raising children until they are older and in school.

(B) They realize the value of being an example and nurturing their children thus they make more time with them outside of their time at work.

(C) Because of their higher incomes, they are able to spend more time with their children.

(D) Educated women have children later in life when their careers are established and their incomes higher thus enabling them to take more time off of work to be with the family.

325. College educated individuals are also a benefit to their communities, not only to themselves. In the passage, several of these social benefits are listed. Which of the following was NOT stated in this passage?

(A) Increased productivity

(B) Increased tax revenues

(C) Increased spending

(D) Increased job mobility

326. The author details and discusses a wide range of considerations about a college education. Of the following, which best represents the main message of the passage?

(A) While a college education is valuable, it can't be measured in dollars alone.

(B) Students should attend college rather than take a job.

(C) The value of a college education depends on your intended career.

(D) Only those who can afford college can understand its investment value.

Refugee and Displaced Children: Back to School—or Not?

The end of summer is when children here head back to school. But what about refugee and displaced children? Do they get to go to school too?

Children whose lives have been disrupted by conflict and crises need special care. In times of crisis, experts say, attending school can give children a sense of stability, safety, and hope. Education is also a basic human right.

Educating uprooted children is a challenge. According to the latest figures from UNICEF, nearly 30 million children worldwide are not in school because their countries are embroiled in conflicts or have suffered other disasters. These children account for fully half of all school-aged children world-wide who are not attending school.

After more than three years of warfare, three million children in Syria are no longer in school. More than half a million Syrian refugee children in neighboring countries face the same predicament. This includes half of all registered refugee children in Jordan and most (80 percent) in Lebanon. Many communities hosting Syrian refugees have tried to make space in overcrowded schools by resorting to double- and even triple-shifts. Syrian children in Turkey and Northern Iraq also struggle because they do not understand Turkish or Kurdish.

In Iraq, education is also under siege. Throughout much of the country, school will be delayed for months, in part because more than 2,000 schools now house families forced to flee the mayhem unleashed by ISIL extremists.

In Gaza, schools now shelter more than a quarter of the civilians displaced by recent fighting. And many school buildings are damaged or destroyed, including those run by the United Nations Relief and Works Agency for Palestine Refugees in the Near East. When they do reopen, nine out of ten UNRWA schools will need to run on double-shifts.

The Middle East is just one region facing this issue. In Guinea, Liberia and Sierra Leone, the Ebola outbreak has closed schools that were serving at least 3 million primary school children.

In Nigeria, the militant Islamic group Boko Haram has waged a terror campaign against schools, murdering or kidnapping hundreds of teachers and students, including more than 200 school girls who have yet to be released.

In the conflict-ravaged Central African Republic, more than two thirds of children are out of school. UNICEF estimates that a third of schools have been struck by bullets, set on fire, looted or occupied by armed groups.

As time passes, risks mount, including the risk that refugee children will never catch up or will never return to school at all.

Attending school can help children heal and shield them from adults who might harm them, exploit them, or recruit them to fight. Schools can promote reconciliation by teaching tolerance, human rights, and conflict resolution.

Humanitarian programs often focus on the life-saving essentials such as providing clean water, food, medical care, and shelter. But teachers, schools, even classes held under a tree, in a tent or via video can also save lives. The U.S. Government supports the UN refugee agency, UNICEF, UNRWA, and other organizations that work to educate children caught in conflicts and crises around the world. As our own children flock back to school, we must remember those whose lives and dreams have been put on hold, and do our best to help them.

327. For refugee children, attending school is much more than about education. Of the following, which is NOT a benefit of school mentioned in the passage for refugee children?

(A) Stability
(B) Happiness
(C) Security
(D) Hope

328. In the passage, the author makes the strong statement that "Education... is a basic human right." As one of thousands of animals species on the planet, which of the following would most reflect the urgency in the author's words as it may relate to the animal kingdom?

(A) Adult herd animals protect their young from predators.
(B) Mothers teach their young how to survive.
(C) Survival of the fittest and smartest means the smartest will survive to pass on their genes.
(D) Those animals who fail to learn the lessons will not survive.

329. In order to express the dire need to consider assisting refugee children with their education, the author gives a statistic of the percentage of refugee children who represent those not in school. Of the following, which was that number given by the author?

(A) 40%
(B) 50%
(C) 60%
(D) 75%

330. Wars and natural disasters are credited for the direct or indirect displacement of children from their schools. Of the following, which is one where an Ebola outbreak disrupted education?

(A) Gaza
(B) Syria
(C) Nigeria
(D) Liberia

331. The author states that even classes held under a tree can save lives. Which of the following would the author most agree is the philosophy behind this statement?

(A) By educating children they have a greater chance of a longer, happier life.
(B) Staying together in groups deters radical terrorists from kidnapping children, enslaving them or forcing them into their military.
(C) Schools teach the children how to avoid the military or terror groups.
(D) A sense of belonging to anything positive gives the children hope for a better life.

332. Lessons learned in foreign countries in turmoil or ravaged by disease can be applied in our own country in situations such as the displacement of people during hurricane Katrina. Of the following, which might the author most support in areas dealing with educating so many new incoming students?

(A) Increase funding for state education in those regions with overcrowding.
(B) Break the year into three semesters (including summer) and allow the students to rotate through two of the three to provide space to accommodate them all.
(C) Construct temporary new school classrooms until those individuals can return to their homes.
(D) Send some of the children and families to other areas where overcrowding is not as much of a problem.

CHAPTER 16

Geography

The Global View

When TVA [Tennessee Valley Authority] set out to reclaim the environmentally devastated Copper Basin, the results could be seen from outer space.

While folks in the Valley are proud of TVA and what it has done for our corner of the South, we don't generally think of it as making a global difference. But some of TVA's achievements have literally changed the way our planet looks from outer space. Beginning in the 1930s and continuing in the present day, TVA has been slowly erasing an old planetary scar that you could have seen if you were in a spaceship orbiting the earth.

Many people may not have heard of the Copper Basin. It's hard to imagine that in moist, fertile southeastern Tennessee there was an area of more than 50 square miles—bigger than many cities—that was described in the national magazine *Discover* as "the only bona fide desert east of the Mississippi."

It has been compared to the Dakota Badlands, the Gobi, and the moon. But the Copper Basin wasn't a natural desert. During the time of Jackson and Crockett, it was a dense green forest drained by the Ocoee River, near where the states of Georgia and North Carolina meet Tennessee.

Then, in 1843, copper was discovered here. By the 1850s, this patch of Polk County supported one of the biggest copper mines in America. It wasn't the mining itself that changed the land so much as what they did to the copper ore after they brought it up.

By a process known as heap roasting, they burned away the ore's impurities, mostly sulfur, before shipping it out. The area was too remote for the delivery of fuel by train, so they cut down the trees. Over the next few decades, they felled every tree in sight. Then they dug up the stumps and burned them, too.

An Eternal Fog

Worse, sulfuric smoke hung over the basin like an eternal fog. Mules wore bells to keep from running into one another. Though they didn't talk about acid rain in the 19th century, they definitely had it. Almost all the rain that fell in Polk County was acid rain, and soon the soil was too acidic to grow anything.

At one time, about 35,000 acres of land was utterly bare. Fifty inches of rain per year not only infused the ground with acid but washed it away altogether.

The basin lost as much as five feet of topsoil. Birds and other wildlife disappeared. Long stretches of the Ocoee, filled with acidic sediment, died.

By the time TVA officials got their first look at the Copper Basin in the 1930s, the destruction had been proceeding for 90 years and looked irreversible. TVA established a Civilian Conservation Corps camp in the Copper Basin, and millions of seedlings were dutifully planted, but most of them didn't take. The soil was still too acidic, where there was soil at all. Not even kudzu, the Japanese vine that was to run riot in other parts of the South, could be made to grow in the Copper Basin.

After 30 years of replanting, Apollo astronauts in the 1960s could still use the scar in the Appalachians as a navigational aid. The three man-made marks on the planet that were visible from space were said to be the Great Wall of China, the pyramids of Egypt, and the Copper Basin in Tennessee.

Songbirds Return

Today more than 90 percent of this former desert is reforested. Government fishery experts have reintroduced native fish to once-strangled stretches of the Ocoee. And after an absence of more than a century, songbirds have returned on their own.

In five years or so, planners say, the restoration will be complete. But TVA intends to leave about 100 denuded acres in the vicinity of the historic Burra Burra mine—just to remind people what the earth looks like when we don't take care of it.

333. Based on the passage, who is the most likely person to have authored this work?

(A) TVA administrator
(B) Local journalist
(C) Writer for a national newspaper
(D) Foreign correspondent

334. Why does the author quote the phrase "the only bona fide desert east of the Mississippi" when referring to this region of Tennessee?

(A) Deserts by definition can be places other than hot arid environments.
(B) The destruction of the environment had turned it into a region resembling a desert.
(C) The natural geology and geography of the region allowed comparison to a sandy desert.
(D) The remoteness and isolation of the area was compared to an uninhabitable dessert.

335. Of the following list, which was the Copper Basin NOT compared to?

(A) Sahara desert
(B) Gobi Desert
(C) Badlands of Dakota
(D) The moon

336. Evidence of the restoration of the Copper Basin, which demonstrates a natural return to the former ecology and environment which existed before copper mining began, would best be seen in which of the following?

(A) Reforestation from seedlings planted by the TVA.
(B) Increase in native fish populations as introduced by local fisheries.
(C) Decrease in the amount of acid rainfall per year.
(D) Songbirds being observed in the Copper Basin.

337. Of the following list of man-made objects, which is NOT listed as viewable from space by the Apollo Astronauts?

(A) Great Wall of China
(B) Copper Basin
(C) Pyramids of Egypt
(D) Panama Canal

338. The author states in the restoration efforts for the Copper Basin that the songbirds returned "on their own." Of the following, which would the author most agree was the reason for their return?

(A) Introduction of a food supply as the native fish were reintroduced.
(B) As the toxins were removed, the area was no longer dangerous.
(C) Proper habitat for the birds returned through reforestation.
(D) Natural predators had been eliminated during the desert period of the Copper Basin.

California's Restless Giant—The Long Valley Caldera

In the 1850s, Gold Fever brought the first waves of European settlers through the Long Valley area of eastern California. Today, thousands of visitors are attracted to the area year round by the spectacular mountain scenery of the eastern Sierra Nevada, a landscape sculpted over the past 4 million years by glaciers, earthquakes, and volcanic eruptions. About 760,000 years ago a cataclysmic volcanic eruption in the area blew out 150 cubic miles—600 cubic kilometers (km3)—of magma (molten rock) from a depth of about 4 miles (6 km) beneath the Earth's surface. Rapid flows of glowing hot ash (pyroclastic flows) covered much of east central California, and airborne ash fell as far east as Nebraska. The Earth's surface sank more than 1 mile (1.6 km) into the space vacated by the erupted magma, forming a large volcanic depression that geologists call a caldera.

Today, broad and flat Long Valley, through which the Owens River lazily meanders on its way south, occupies the eastern half of this caldera, which is 10 miles (16 km) by 20 miles (32 km) in extent. Magma still underlies the caldera and heats underground water, feeding local hot springs and steam vents. The underground heat now drives three geothermal power plants, producing a combined 40 megawatts of electricity.

Long Valley Caldera is part of a large volcanic system in eastern California that also includes the Mono-Inyo Craters chain. This chain extends from Mammoth Mountain at the southwest rim of the caldera northward 25 miles (40 km) to Mono Lake. Eruptions along this chain began 400,000 years ago, and Mammoth Mountain was formed by a series of eruptions ending 58,000 years ago. The volcanic system is still active—eruptions occurred in both the Inyo Craters and Mono Craters parts of the volcanic chain as recently as 600 years ago, and small eruptions occurred in Mono Lake sometime between the mid-1700s and mid-1800s.

Although no volcanic eruptions are known to have occurred in eastern California since those in Mono Lake, earthquakes occur frequently. These are caused by movement along faults and by the pressure of magma rising beneath the surface, two closely related geologic processes. In 1872, a magnitude 7.4 earthquake centered 80 miles (125 km) south of Long Valley was felt throughout most of California, and moderate (magnitude 5 to 6) earthquakes have shaken the Long Valley area since 1978.

In 1978 a magnitude 5.4 earthquake struck 6 miles southeast of the caldera, heralding a period of geologic unrest in the Long Valley area that is still ongoing. That temblor ended two decades of low quake activity in eastern California. The area has since experienced numerous swarms of earthquakes, especially in the southern part of the caldera and the adjacent Sierra Nevada. The most intense of these swarms began in May 1980 and included four strong magnitude 6 shocks, three on the same day. Following these shocks, scientists from the U.S. Geological Survey (USGS) began a reexamination of the Long Valley area, and they soon detected other evidence of unrest—a dome-like uplift within the caldera. Measurements showed that the center of the caldera had risen almost a foot (30 centimeters) since the summer of 1979—after decades of stability. This swelling, which by 2014 totaled more than 2.5 feet (75 centimeters) and affected more than 100 square miles (250 km2), is caused by new magma rising beneath the caldera.

339. Historical documents are filled with accounts of the Gold Rush as well as Gold Fever. This is a term that this author also uses in the first sentence of the passage. Which of the following would best define this term as intended by the author?

(A) Overcrowding by gold seekers always lead to diseases spreading through their populations.

(B) As people often act irrationally when they have a high temperature, the quest for gold also lead people to act irrationally.

(C) When people would find gold, their sympathetic nervous system would mimic the same symptoms as illness and fever.

(D) Gold as found in the ore in many regions contained toxins that would spawn illnesses in the region.

340. The area of California described in the passage is the eastern portion of the Sierra Nevada. Geologically, this area has been shaped and modified over hundreds of thousands of years. Of the following, which geological event was NOT listed as a cause if its formation and shaping over the years.

(A) Eruptions

(B) Erosion

(C) Glaciers

(D) Earthquakes

341. Often associated with a volcanic eruption is a geological formation called a caldera. Of the following, which would visibly most resemble a caldera?

(A) The ridge of a glacial mountain

(B) Eroded river valley

(C) Crater on the moon

(D) A sink hole

342. Which of the following statements best represents the main theme of the passage?

(A) Volcanic activity created and is continuing to shape the Long Valley Caldera.

(B) Geologic forces are ever present in reshaping the earth.

(C) Volcanoes may lay dormant for hundreds of years, but that does not mean they are safe.

(D) California is an active source of geological activity that is reshaping the region.

343. The author states that in the genesis of the caldera, the surface sank more than one mile. However, over the past few years, geologists are monitoring the caldera closely because it has risen 2.5 feet. How does such a small geological movement generate such interest in many and alarm in some?

    (A) Any movement, no matter how small, suggests new volcanic activity.
    (B) Although just a few feet in elevation, over 100 square miles a huge surface area raised.
    (C) The one mile drop initially was over a much smaller area.
    (D) The rise in elevation is coupled with increased heating of the area suggesting new lava beneath.

344. In much the same way that geologists observe for even the slightest change in geological features to suggest any level of new or changing geological forces, the human body is also highly dynamic. Of the following, which would most be synonymous with the caution geologists are taking with these new signs from the volcano?

    (A) Elevated temperature in a patient
    (B) Area of skin that grows larger, is dark, or changes color or shape
    (C) Pain in any area of the body
    (D) Elevated blood pressure like the increase in elevation of the volcano

Ocean Warming Affecting Florida Reefs

Late-summer water temperatures near the Florida Keys were warmer by nearly two degrees Fahrenheit in the last several decades compared to a century earlier, according to a new study by the U.S. Geological Survey.

Researchers indicate that the warmer water temperatures are stressing corals and increasing the number of bleaching events, where corals become white resulting from a loss of their symbiotic algae. The corals can starve to death if the condition is prolonged.

"Our analysis shows that corals in the study areas are now regularly experiencing temperatures above 84°F during July, August, and September; average temperatures that were seldom reached 120 years ago," said Ilsa Kuffner, a USGS research marine biologist and the study's lead author. "When corals are exposed to water temperatures above 84°F they grow more slowly and, during extended exposure periods, can stop growing altogether or die."

The new analysis compares water temperatures during two time periods a century apart at two of Florida's historic offshore lighthouses—Fowey Rocks Lighthouse, off Miami, and Carysfort Reef Lighthouse, off Key Largo, Florida. The first period included data from 1879 to 1912, while the second period spanned from 1991 to 2012. Temperatures at a third area, a reef off Islamorada, Florida, were also monitored from 1975 to 2007.

"What's interesting is that the temperature increase observed during this recent 32-year period was as large as that measured at the lighthouses spanning 120 years," said Kuffner. "This makes it likely the warming observed at the lighthouses has actually occurred since the 1970s."

The study indicates that August is consistently the month when Florida's ocean temperatures peak. In the analysis of recent decades, average temperatures for August have been at or very close to 86°F. At Fowey Lighthouse from 1879 to 1912, the average August temperature was just 84.2°F. Temperatures this August at the same location, though not included in the study, averaged 87°F.

Coral bleaching is currently underway in the Florida Keys, highlighting the real-time impact that warmer ocean temperatures are having on reefs. Corals can recover from bleaching if the waters cool down within a few weeks, but mortality usually ensues if corals remain bleached longer than a month or two.

345. Evidence for ocean warming as an underlying cause of coral bleaching is presented as water temperature data taken around 1900 compared to those measures taken around 2000. Of the following, which would most weaken the argument for higher temperatures being the cause of coral death?

   (A) The earlier temperature recordings were taken on fewer days than the modern data.
   (B) Thermometers used in the 1879-1912 study were much less accurate than the measures today.
   (C) Meteorological events were not recorded along with the temperature.
   (D) The location and depth of the temperature readings cannot be verified to be the same.

346. The author suggests that the higher temperatures eliminate the algae upon which the coral rely for their growth and survival. If in fact, these temperatures did not kill the algae, which of the following most likely will account for their absence from the coral bed?

   (A) Metabolic processes of the coral beneficial to the algae slow and stop in higher temps, forcing the algae to find a better, more reliable food source.
   (B) Algae prefer cooler water and will abandon the coral for cooler and deeper water and an alternative food supply.
   (C) In times of limited food supply, algae will go dormant until the raw materials are again available. This is why the coral can recover in a few weeks if temperatures moderate.
   (D) Other algae predators increase their predation in higher temperatures and strip the algae from the coral faster than the algae can grow.

347. Of the following, which best represents the main theme of this passage?

    (A) Global warming is leading to the death of ocean dwellers such as coral.
    (B) Coral reef bleaching is caused by higher temperatures that destroy the symbiotic algae.
    (C) Higher water temperatures lead to coral bleaching and in time coral death.
    (D) Symbiotic coral algae are sensitive to increased temperatures resulting in their loss and subsequent coral death.

348. The author of this article most likely has written it for what audience?

    (A) Journalist
    (B) Teacher
    (C) Lobbyist
    (D) Oceanographer

349. Ilsa Kuffner states in the passage that corals in water temperatures above 84°F grow more slowly. Which evidence below would most directly support this assertion.

    (A) At higher temperatures the algae also grows more slowly.
    (B) Higher water temperatures result in slower mitotic activity of coral cells.
    (C) At higher temps the salinity of the water increases and could explain the slower growth.
    (D) At 84 degrees the algae remains, yet the corals grow more slowly.

350. Which of the following was NOT a temperature measure sight described in the passage?

    (A) Pensacola
    (B) Miami
    (C) Key Largo
    (D) Islamorada

CHAPTER **17**

History

"A Most Magnificent Ruin": The Burning of the Capitol during the War of 1812

Around 8 p.m., on the evening of August 24, 1814, British troops under the command of Vice Admiral Sir Alexander Cockburn and Major General Robert Ross marched into Washington, D.C., after a victory over American forces at Bladensburg, Maryland, earlier in the day. The nation was in the midst of war. Word of the approaching forces sent most of the population fleeing, leaving the capital vulnerable. Meeting little to no resistance, British troops set fire to much of the city, in retaliation for the Americans' burning of the Canadian capital at York on April 27, 1813. Those who remained on the evening of August 24, 1814, were witness to a horrifying spectacle. The British torched major rooms in the Capitol, which then housed the Library of Congress, as well as the House, the Senate, and the Supreme Court. The White House, the navy yard and several American warships were also burned; however, most private property was spared.

At the time, the U.S. Capitol was still being constructed and consisted of only the north and south wings connected by a wooden walkway spanning the area intended for the center building. Damage to parts of the wings was severe, but the building was not completely destroyed. Fortunately, architect Benjamin Henry Latrobe had used fire-proof building materials, such as sheet iron, marble, sandstone, zinc, and copper. His extensive use of masonry vaulting also proved to be practical as well as aesthetic. As a result, the exterior structure survived and many of the interior spaces remained intact.

The British focused their destructive work on the principal rooms, foregoing the lobbies, halls and staircases, thus securing their escape route. In the south wing, soldiers ignited a giant bonfire of furniture slathered with gunpowder paste in the Hall of the House of Representatives (now National Statuary Hall). The heat from the fire grew so intense that it melted the glass skylights and destroyed much of the carved stone in the room, including Guiseppe Franzoni's life-size marble Statue of Liberty seated on a pedestal, located above the Speaker's rostrum. Downstairs, the Clerk's office was transformed into an inferno of burning documents and furniture; this fire produced a heat so great it forced the British to retreat from the south wing, leaving half of the rooms on the first floor unscathed.

In the Supreme Court Chamber, on the first floor of the north wing, troops piled furniture from nearby rooms to create another great bonfire, severely damaging the Doric stone columns. Upstairs, a large room that then housed the Library of Congress' collection of over 3,000 books served as a ready stockpile of fuel. The space burned so fiercely that it endangered a portion of the exterior stone wall. From the library, winds spread the flames to the Senate Chamber, where the damage to the art and architecture was also severe. Upon seeing the flames of the Capitol from his temporary residence at the Octagon House, French minister Louis Sérurier remarked, "I have never beheld a spectacle more terrible and at the same time more magnificent."

351. Which of the following most likely explains why private property in Washington, D.C. was spared while the Capitol was burned?

(A) The act was retaliation for the burning of the Canadian capital.
(B) They did not wish to incite the citizens to war as had happened in the Revolutionary War.
(C) They were sending a message to the U.S. government.
(D) The Capitol burning was an attempt to disrupt the government, not to destroy the country.

352. Henry Latrobe used fire proof materials in the building of the Capitol (paragraph two). Of the following, which most likely explains his choice of building materials?

(A) They were the most visually attractive building materials of the day.
(B) He anticipated another British attack.
(C) It was an attempt to insure the longevity of the building and its contents.
(D) It was to preserve the government and record of its activities in the safest of buildings.

353. What was meant by the French minister when he said of the fire, "I have never beheld a spectacle more terrible and at the same time more magnificent"?

(A) He had never seen a larger, more amazing fire.
(B) He didn't like the Americans, and while the destruction was terrible he was glad it happened.
(C) Since the French were American allies, he knew that the Americans would ask the French for more help.
(D) He preferred a different architectural design and after the fire he would exert his personal style to the building.

354. Why does the Capitol today not house all of the offices which were housed in the Capitol building as detailed in the passage?

(A) The separation of powers required the branches to be in separate buildings.

(B) The staff of each office and the holdings of the Library of Congress became too large to accommodate them all.

(C) With more states, there are more congressmen and thus less room for anything else.

(D) The Capitol was only meant to house Congress and before more buildings could be produced, the library and supreme court were temporarily housed there.

355. According to the passage, why were more than half of the rooms on the first floor spared?

(A) The British ran out of time.

(B) Americans counterattacked and drove them out before they could finish.

(C) The conditions became too dangerous for the troops to complete the burning.

(D) There were no important documents in those rooms.

356. Based on the passage, which of the following most likely explains why the British attempted to burn the American Capitol.

(A) Capitols are a sign of power and authority and burning them demonstrates who has won the battle.

(B) Americans had burned the Canadian Capitol the year before.

(C) They hoped to further render the American government incapable of recovery.

(D) The burning was revenge for the American Revolution.

Abraham Lincoln's "Blind Memorandum"

Could George B. McClellan have become the seventeenth President of the United States? It certainly appeared to be a possibility as Abraham Lincoln assessed the military and political landscape of the United States in the summer of 1864.

President Lincoln understood that his chances of reelection in November hinged on military success in a war now in its fourth year. By the summer of 1864, Gen. Ulysses S. Grant had settled in for a prolonged siege against the Confederates near Petersburg, Va., and Gen. William T. Sherman made slow progress toward Atlanta. Confederate Gen. Jubal A. Early, meanwhile, had led his troops to the very gates of Washington, D.C. in July. The war effort seemed to have stalled for the Union, and the public blamed President Lincoln.

The political news for Lincoln was no brighter. Republican insider Thurlow Weed told Lincoln in mid-August 1864 that "his re-election was an impossibility." Republican party chairman Henry J. Raymond expressed much the same sentiment to Lincoln on Aug. 22, urging him to consider sending a commission to meet with Confederate President Jefferson Davis to offer peace terms "on the sole condition of acknowledging the supremacy of the Constitution," leaving the question of slavery to be resolved later.

It was in this context that Abraham Lincoln wrote the following memorandum on Aug. 23, 1864: *This morning, as for some days past, it seems exceedingly probable that this Administration will not be re-elected. Then it will be my duty to so co-operate with the President elect, as to save the Union between the election and the inaugura- tion, as he will have secured his election on such ground that he cannot possibly save it afterwards.—A. Lincoln*

Lincoln folded the memorandum and pasted it closed, so that the text inside could not be read. He took it to a cabinet meeting and instructed his cabinet members to sign the outside of the memo, sight unseen, which they did. Historians now refer to this document variously as the "Blind Memo" or "Blind Memorandum" because the cabinet signed it "blind." In so doing the Lincoln administration pledged itself to accept the verdict of the people in November and to help save the Union should Lincoln not be re-elected.

As if on cue, Lincoln's fortunes began to change. As expected, the Democrats nominated George B. McClellan for president on August 30 but saddled him with a "Copperhead" peace Democrat, Representative George H. Pendleton, as a running mate. The Democratic platform declared the war a failure and urged that "immediate efforts be made for a cessation of hostilities," which even McClellan could not fully support. Then General Sherman scored a tremendous victory when Atlanta fell to the Union on Sept. 2, 1864.

The brighter military outlook, expert political maneuvering by Lincoln and his reinvigorated party (running in 1864 as the National Union Party), and the nega- tives associated with McClellan and the Democrats spelled victory at the polls for the Republicans. Safely re-elected, Lincoln brought the memorandum with him to the next cabinet meeting on November 11. He finally read its contents to the cabinet, reminding them it was written "when as yet we had no adversary, and seemed to have no friends."

357. According to the passage, who was blamed the most for the lack of Union progress in the Civil War?

   (A)   Ulysses S. Grant
   (B)   William T. Sherman
   (C)   George McClellan
   (D)   Abraham Lincoln

358. To which political party did Abraham Lincoln belong?

(A) National Union
(B) Republican
(C) Democratic
(D) Wigg

359. Based on the passage, which of the following would the author MOST AGREE was Lincoln's rationale for his decision not to petition the Confederacy for peace?

(A) It would have been unconstitutional.
(B) He felt he would have conceded slavery to the South.
(C) He wanted to unify the United States during his presidency.
(D) He would not have the support of Congress.

360. During his re-election bid, Lincoln faced Democrat George McClellon and his vice presidential running mate who the author terms as a "Copperhead" peace Democrat. What did the author mean by that statement?

(A) Tenacious
(B) Crafty
(C) Dangerous
(D) Stealthy

361. Which of the following would the author agree Lincoln meant when he reminded his cabinet in the last paragraph "when as yet we had no adversary, and seemed to have no friends"?

(A) The South was not seen as the enemy, but also not as friend.
(B) No one agreed with Lincoln and his platform, even within his own party.
(C) Prior to the election, the Republicans were blamed for everything.
(D) A political adversary gave Americans an alternative to Lincoln and his policies.

362. Of the following statements, which best describes the likely role of the author of this passage?

(A) Journalist
(B) Historian
(C) Politician
(D) Editorial writer

Civility in the Senate

Henry Clay is best remembered as "the Great Compromiser." Beginning with the admission of Missouri into the Union in 1820, and lasting through the monumental Compromise of 1850 that staved off civil war for another decade, Clay served as a unifier, repeatedly bringing the competing interests of North and South, abolitionists and slaveholders, to the bargaining table of the U.S. Senate. Clay's longest period of service in the Senate ended in 1842. At that time, he resigned his Senate seat with the intention of mounting a new presidential campaign. On March 31, 1842, with tears in his eyes, Clay bid the Senate "a long, a last, a friendly farewell." It proved to be a premature valedictory, but it went as follows:

> **Henry Clay's Valedictory to the Senate, March 31, 1842**
>
> . . . [D]uring my long and arduous services in the public councils, and especially . . . in the Senate, the same ardor of temperament has characterized my actions, and has no doubt led me, in the heat of debate . . . to use language offensive and susceptible of ungracious interpretation towards my brother senators.
>
> If there be any who entertain a feeling of dissatisfaction resulting from any circumstance of this kind, I beg to assure them that I now make the amplest apology . . . . I assure the Senate, one and all, without exception and without reserve, that I leave the Senate Chamber without carrying with me to my retirement a single feeling of dissatisfaction towards the Senate itself or any one of its members. I go from it under the hope that we shall mutually consign to perpetual oblivion whatever of personal animosities or jealousies may have arisen between us during the repeated collisions of mind with mind.
>
> . . . I beg leave to deposit with [the Senate] my fervent wishes, that all the great and patriotic objects for which it was instituted, may be accomplished—that the destiny designed for it by the framers of the Constitution may be fulfilled—that the deliberations now and hereafter, in which it may engage for the good of our common country, may eventuate in the restoration of its prosperity, and in the preservation and maintenance of her honor abroad, and her best interests at home . . . . May the blessings of Heaven rest upon the heads of the whole Senate, and every member of it; . . . and when they shall retire to the bosoms of their respective constituencies, may they all meet there that most joyous and grateful of all human rewards, the exclamation of their countrymen, "well done thou good and faithful servants."

Denied the presidency again in 1844, he returned to the Senate for three tumultuous and pivotal years, 1849 to 1852. Those final years proved to be Clay's greatest challenge of all, as a statesman, an orator, and compromiser. In the last great effort by the Great Triumvirate to shape the destiny of the nation, Clay presented the Senate with a series of resolutions designed to calm the argument over slavery, settle the dispute over westward expansion, and hopefully avoid the secession of southern states and preserve the Union. His "omnibus bill" went down to defeat in 1850, but individually each resolution was passed, and civil war was once again avoided.

Clay enjoyed a national reputation as a western orator who colored his speech with entertaining stories tailored for a wide audience. He adopted a deliberative style that made effective use of calculated pauses, well-timed body gestures, and simple arguments. As Clay himself admitted on several occasions, the heat of debate often led him to harsh criticism of his opponents, and certainly placed him among the best-loved but also most-hated men in American politics. When he decided to resign from the Senate in 1842 to once again pursue the presidency, one contemporary likened it to "the soul's quitting the body."

In a fitting tribute to Clay and to the nature of the Senate, his colleague and strongest opponent, John C. Calhoun, commented: "I don't like Clay. He is a bad man, an imposter, a creator of wicked schemes. I wouldn't speak to him, but, by God, I love him!"

363. In modern graduation ceremonies, the valedictorian is often the person with the highest grade point average in the class. In the passage, Henry Clay's speech is called the valedictory. Of the following, which statement best reconciles these terms?

(A) Henry Clay was the highest ranking member of the Senate when he gave his speech.
(B) The valedictory is a farewell speech traditionally given by the student with the highest GPA in graduation ceremonies.
(C) The highest ranking individual of a group will be the valedictorian and give a speech.
(D) They are separate terms with no relationship to each other.

364. Credited as the author of the great Compromise of 1850 that delayed the Civil War for 10 years, Clay introduced the compromise that the northern states had to return runaway slaves to the South as part of the Fugitive Slave Law and as a concession for obtaining California as a free state. Of the following, which best reflects how this was actually a victory for the northern free states?

(A) California gave the northern states additional votes in the Senate.
(B) The compromise delayed the cessation of southern states at least 10 years.
(C) Although a law, it was never enforced in the northern states, and thus it was as if it never existed.
(D) More Americans moved to the free states of the north to escape the oppression of slavery.

365. Although the Compromise delayed the Civil War, it did not prevent it from occurring. Of the following, which most likely explains why the compromise was only one in the political sense?

(A) Slavery and freedom for blacks were ideologies that simply could never exist at the same time in the same country.

(B) Neither side was prepared to actually compromise.

(C) The South was only accepting the legislation as a stall tactic until the resources of war were sufficient.

(D) The northern political powers were slowly eroding the doctrine of slavery in order to prevent the southern states from leaving the union.

366. In his valedictory, Clay states that his hope is the heated debates in which he played a role may ". . . engage for the good of our common country . . . ." From the following, which statement best reflects how this is almost impossible in modern politics?

(A) The government never compromises today.

(B) Executive orders to not need debating.

(C) Liberal and conservative ideologies seem as far apart as slave and freemen.

(D) Today's media stirs debate into hate and fighting.

367. The author states that for the final years of his role in the Senate Clay was challenged the most of his career in three areas. Of the following, which is NOT one of those listed challenges faced by Clay?

(A) As a statesman

(B) As a southerner

(C) As an orator

(D) As a compromiser

368. Toward the end of his valedictory, Clay says "May the blessings of heaven . . . ." and he closes with a quote from the bible "well done thou good and faithful servant." If that had been given today, how might the great compromiser have been met in the media and social media?

(A) Chastised for being a bigot and intolerant

(B) Demonized as a religious radical or zealot

(C) Ridiculed for holding to antiquated ideals

(D) All of the above

369. For the Compromise of 1850 and the following omnibus bill, there were three critical areas of disagreement that Clay sought to reconcile between the states. Of the following, which was of the least of the difficult political areas?

(A) New statehood
(B) Slavery
(C) Westward expansion
(D) Southern secession

CHAPTER 18

Linguistics

Language Change

In some ways, it is surprising that languages change. After all, they are passed down through the generations reliably enough for parents and children to communicate with each other. Yet linguists find that all languages change over time—albeit at different rates. For example, while Japanese has changed relatively little over 1,000 years, English evolved rapidly in just a few centuries. Many present-day speakers find Shakespeare's sixteenth century texts difficult and Chaucer's fourteenth century Canterbury Tales nearly impossible to read.

Why They Change

Languages change for a variety of reasons. Large-scale shifts often occur in response to social, economic, and political pressures. History records many examples of language change fueled by invasions, colonization, and migration. Even without these kinds of influences, a language can change dramatically if enough users alter the way they speak it.

Frequently, the needs of speakers drive language change. New technologies, industries, products, and experiences simply require new words. Plastic, cell phones, and the Internet didn't exist in Shakespeare's time, for example. By using new and emerging terms, we all drive language change. But the unique way that individuals speak also fuels language change. That's because no two individuals use a language in exactly the same way. The vocabulary and phrases people use depend on where they live, their age, education level, social status, and other factors. Through our interactions, we pick up new words and sayings and integrate them into our speech. Teens and young adults for example, often use different words and phrases from their parents. Some of them spread through the population and slowly change the language.

Types of Change

Three main aspects of language change over time: vocabulary, sentence structure, and pronunciations. Vocabulary can change quickly as new words are borrowed from other languages, or as words get combined or shortened. Some words are even created by mistake. As noted in the Linguistic Society of America's publication *Is English Changing?*, *pea* is one such example. Up until about 400 years ago, *pease* referred to either a single pea or many peas. At some point, people mistakenly assumed that the word *pease* was the plural form of pea, and a new word was born. While vocabulary can change quickly, sentence structure—the order of words in a sentence—changes more slowly. Yet it's clear that today's English speakers construct sentences very differently from Chaucer and Shakespeare's contemporaries . . . . Changes in sound are somewhat harder to document, but at least as interesting. For example, during the so-called "Great Vowel Shift" 500 years ago, English speakers modified their vowel pronunciation dramatically. This shift represents the biggest difference between the pronunciations of so called Middle and Modern English.

Agents of Change

Before a language can change, speakers must adopt new words, sentence structures, and sounds, spread them through the community and transmit them to the next generation. According to many linguists—including David Lightfoot, NSF assistant director for social, behavioral, and economic sciences—children serve as agents for language change when, in the process of learning the language of previous generations, they internalize it differently and propagate a different variation of that language.

Linguists study language change by addressing questions such as these:

- Can we trace the evolutionary path of a language?
- How do language changes spread through communities?
- How do historical circumstances influence language change?
- What is the relationship between language learning and change?

370. The author clearly illustrates the many ways in which languages have changed through the centuries. From early Egyptian hieroglyphs through the Greek and Latin to the English most know today. Which of the following would best illustrate how, in some ways, communication has come full circle today?

   (A) Coded messages for secret groups
   (B) Use of different fonts in documents
   (C) Digital images sent via the Internet
   (D) Emoji characters in text messages conveying meaning

371. Languages change and that is a simple fact of human communication. However, the driving forces behind those changes are listed in the text. Of the following, which is NOT a suggested pressure that leads to language changes?

   (A) Geographical differences
   (B) Social responses
   (C) Economic status
   (D) Political agendas

372. Of the following statements, which best represents the main theme of the passage?

(A) The dynamics of language are driven by few pressures.
(B) Languages are fluid and evolve over time.
(C) Little change in language allows reliability between generations.
(D) Young people primarily lead to language changes.

373. The author states that as languages change there are three main aspects where this change can most easily be seen. Of the following, which is NOT one of those three?

(A) Pronunciation
(B) Context
(C) Vocabulary
(D) Sentence structure

374. New words may enter into a language due to different pressures or occurrences. Twenty years ago, there was no such word as "blog" in the English language. Of the following, which would the author most agree is the reason for the creation of this word?

(A) Creativity
(B) Technology
(C) Accessibility
(D) Mobility

375. Language is that vehicle through which all humans communicate. Through the generations, it must be a reliable means of doing so. However, as languages are taught and learned, the changes occur. In the passage, what group does the author credit as being the agents of change?

(A) Parents
(B) Teachers
(C) Adults
(D) Children

376. To understand and observe how languages change, linguists address several pertinent questions. Of the following, which is NOT one of the questions addressed in the passage?

(A) Are words used in multiple languages at the same time?
(B) Does language change while being taught?
(C) Do events in history lead to language change?
(D) Does a language have a distinct evolution?

How Did Cool Become Such a Big Deal?

It is generally believed that it is not until the sixties that "cool" goes viral, as we would say. But before it does, Leroi Jones (aka Amiri Baraka) takes up its meaning in his 1963 history of blues and jazz, *Blues People*. For Jones, the obvious context for a discussion of cool is the recent history of cool jazz and the longer history of African-American inequality. More or less a beatnik at the time, Jones was already a provocateur, although his take on cool could be described as conventional by today's standards.

Cool jazz began with Miles Davis, who, Jones points out, "went into a virtual eclipse of popularity during the high point of the cool style's success." Perhaps Davis's personal problems were to blame, but Jones complains that more than once he has read articles calling Miles Davis "a bad imitation" of the white West Coast trumpeter Chet Baker, the embodiment of cool jazz success. If anything, Jones said, it was the other way around.

The greater irony, however, for Jones was that cool jazz "seemed to represent almost exactly the opposite of what cool as a term of social philosophy had been given to mean." For black people, to be cool was to be "calm, even unimpressed, by what horror the world might daily propose." Cool was a quietly rebellious response to the history of slavery and post-Civil War injustices. "The term was never meant to connote the tepid new popular music of the white middle-brow middle class. On the contrary, it was exactly this America that one was supposed to 'be cool' in the face of."

By this point, however, cool was well-noticed and recorded. In 1961, *Webster's Third New International Dictionary of the English Language, Unabridged*, mentioned cool jazz and added a new sense to its old definition of cool: "mastery of the latest in approved technique and style." A few years later, according to Robert L. Moore, cool outpaces swell, until then the most prominent slang term of approval going back to the teens and twenties.

As I walked through the exhibition [at the National Portrait Gallery called "American Cool"], the images of cool increasingly came from areas of American life far removed from jazz. And more and more of the cool faces were not black: Lauren Bacall, James Dean, Bruce Springsteen, Steve Jobs. In retrospect, of course, they're all cool. Even Woody Guthrie, who in the 1940s was everything cool was not: white, rural, and folksy.

Linguists have a term for insisting that a word must always mean what it once meant. It's called the etymological fallacy. It's a fallacy because meanings change over time, just as cool has gone from referring to a certain temperature to a word my eight-year-old son uses to describe his new BMX bike. And yet words also come bearing history, emitting scents picked up on the roads they've traveled. Cool in its slang form is certainly an example of this, carrying an invisible statement of origins, reminding us of the treasures of jazz, black culture generally, and the difficult history of integration.

It also reminds us of another function of slang, one elucidated recently by Michael Adams in his book *Slang: The People's Poetry*. Slang is creative, aesthetically interesting, and rich in meta-commentary, some of which becomes hard to discern just a few years later, less so perhaps in the case of a word like cool, which is still readily used and readily understood, but at times can be a little hard to nail down.

377. Within the passage, the author describes an "etymological fallacy." Considering his example, which would he most agree is a current example of such a word?

(A) Genesis

(B) Gay

(C) Juice

(D) Tight

378. The author mentions that before the use of the word "cool" an earlier term in American culture was used to mean the same thing.

(A) Sweet

(B) Awesome

(C) Swell

(D) Right-on

379. As the author describes the use of slang in society, he suggests that slang is rich in "meta-commentary." From the tone of his writing and of known slang, which of the following would the author agree is the best definition of that terminology?

(A) Terms that have significance in a specific social setting.

(B) Individual words that additionally emphasize the message of a statement as a whole.

(C) Rebellious communication.

(D) Secretive language interpretable by only a select few.

380. In the passage, the author details the career of Miles Davis. While doing so, he mentions a "virtual eclipse of popularity." Of the following, which do you think the author meant by the statement?

(A) Miles Davis retired, but made a comeback.

(B) His career slowly decreased until it ended.

(C) His music temporarily lost its public appeal but it returned in time.

(D) Chet Baker's popularity overshadowed that of Miles Davis.

381. The author mentions the role of different cultures and races in the evolution of "cool." However, of the following, which would the author most agree was the contribution of African American Musicians to "cool"?

(A) Miles Davis was the godfather of cool.
(B) Black musicians created cool.
(C) Whites imitated the cool of black musicians.
(D) Cool spans all musical genres and decades.

382. Of the following statements, which would the author most agree represents the meaning of the passage?

(A) Society determines the usage of words such as cool, not limited to a simple definition in a dictionary.
(B) The evolution of cool is an amazing journey.
(C) Cool is a nebulous word that no one can define but everyone knows it when they feel it.
(D) Cool is an example of the etymological fallacy.

Trüth, Beaüty, and Volapük

Johann Schleyer was a German priest whose irrational passion for umlauts may have been his undoing. During one sleepless night in 1879, he felt a Divine presence telling him to create a universal language. The result was Volapük. It was designed to be easy to learn, with a system of simple roots derived from European languages, and regular affixes which attached to the roots to make new words. Volapük was the first invented language to gain widespread success. By the end of the 1880s there were more than 200 Volapük societies and clubs around the world and 25 Volapük journals. Over 1500 diplomas in Volapük had been awarded. In 1889, when the third international Volapük congress was held in Paris, the proceedings were entirely in Volapük. Everyone had at least heard of it. President Grover Cleveland's wife even named her dog Volapük.

Though Schleyer was German, a large part of the Volapük vocabulary was based on English. "Volapük" was a compound formed from two roots, vol (from "world") and pük (from "speak"). However, it was often hard to spot the source of a Volapük word because of the way Schleyer had set up the sound system of the language. "Paper" was pöp, "beer" bil, "proof" blöf and "love" löf. He had rational reasons for most of the phonological choices he made. For simplicity, he tried to limit all word roots to one syllable. He avoided the 'r' sound, "for the sake of children and old people, also for some Asiatic nations." The umlauts, however, were there for löf.

"A language without umlauts," he wrote, "sounds monotonous, harsh, and boring." He decried the "endlessly gloomy u and o," the "broad a" and the "sharp i" of umlautless languages. Though many members of the growing Volapük community may have agreed with his aesthetic judgment, many others thought that for Volapük to have a serious chance at being a world language, the umlauts had to go.

Indeed, in the United States especially, those umlauts added a threatening and/or ridiculous air of foreignness to the language. Much fun was had at the expense of Volapük on account of those umlauts in local papers such as the *Milkaukee Sentinel*:

> A charming young student of Grük
> Once tried to acquire Volapük
> But it sounded so bad
> That her friends called her mad,
> And she quit it in less than a wük.

By 1890 the Volapük movement was falling apart due to arguments about umlauts and other reforms. Schleyer left the Volapük Academy and formed his own academy of loyalists. Other Volapükists created their own versions of the language— Nal Bino, Balta, Bopal, Spelin, Dil, Orba—all of which immediately fell into the obscurity that soon swallowed Volapük itself.

383. Johann Schleyer, the creator of Volapük, was a linguist in his spare time. What was his original occupation?

(A) Scholar
(B) Politician
(C) Doctor
(D) Priest

384. One of the difficulties for Schleyer, as the author notes in the passage, is his love and fascination for the umlaut. Which of the following statements best describes the meaning of this word?

(A) Emphasis placed only on certain vowel sounds in the sentence
(B) Changing vowel sound based on other sounds and letters in a word
(C) A glottal sound given to certain vowels as heard in many languages
(D) A syllabic structure that governed the formation and pronunciation of words

385. Of all the human languages upon which Schleyer could base his new language, which of the following did he choose as the foundation of Volapük?

(A) English
(B) German
(C) Latin
(D) French

386. In the formation of Volapük, Schleyer avoided the use of the "r" sound for children, elderly, and Asian speakers. In America, which group could easily be added to that group and would understand and easily accept the lack of the "r" sound in their language?

(A) Southerners
(B) Bostonians
(C) Midwesterners
(D) Texans

387. Volapük eventually went the way of the dodo and faded into obscurity after spawning many modified versions of the language. Of the following, which was NOT a spin-off of Volapük?

(A) Balta
(B) Grük
(C) Orba
(D) Nal Bino

388. Volapük lost favor over time as spin-off languages were created and people found their own "flavor" of a universal language to speak. Of the following statements, which may the author most agree is the explanation for this abandonment of Volapük in favor of the creation of so many new languages?

(A) Just as people like different foods, they will prefer different languages.
(B) Language is a social institution as much as a means for communication.
(C) People become comfortable with their socially accepted language and that is the reason for so many languages worldwide.
(D) People wanted the notoriety of creating their own language that they felt was better.

"Toad-stranglers," "Whoopensockers" and Other Findings from the *Dictionary of American Regional English*

A good number of office workers in Washington, D.C., are *slugs*. On a rainy day in Baltimore you'll catch a lot of folks carrying what they jokingly call *bombazines*. And in states along the Gulf, talk about the weather could be all about the last *toad-strangler*. As Christina Pazzanese of the *Harvard Gazette*, in a review of the NEH-funded *Dictionary of American Regional English*—or *DARE* for short—points out, words like "slug" (a commuter who hitches a ride), "bombazine" (umbrella), and "toad-strangler" (a drenching rain) challenge "the conventional wisdom that the gumbo of American English has lost much of its local tang."

The fifth volume of *DARE*—covering words starting with "sl" and ending with "zydeco"—was published in the spring of 2012 by Harvard University Press and is the culmination of more than fifty years of lexicographical efforts at the University of Wisconsin. Michael Montgomery writes in *American Speech* that the regional labels for terms and sources one encounters in *DARE* are among its many strengths and are rarely found in other dictionaries. Montgomery should know: He's an editor of a regional dictionary—*DSME*, or The *Dictionary of Smoky Mountain English*. As a lexicographer, Montgomery knows firsthand the challenges of attributing regional labels. He writes, "It usually makes sense to indicate the locale of a citation from any work by Mark Twain to be where the work was set, not his native Missouri. After all, the gentleman moved about right smart and even so, he was conceived in Fentress County, Tennessee, on the western edge of Appalachia, so he may have imbibed a tad of mountain ways to talking while in the womb."

There is even a volume six, an index, which, Montgomery notes, lists fifty-eight terms that originated in Algonquian languages. Among other attributes of the ultimate volume are contrastive maps that, as one reviewer puts it, are "not areal but populational." This is cartography in which "speech drives geography, rather than the other way around."

DARE's primary strength might be, as John McWhorter writing in the *New Republic* has it, "charting the under-the-radar regional language nationwide. . . . There is a delightful muchness in it." McWhorter goes on to note that from 1965 to 1970, the editor, Frederic Cassidy, and his staff covered 1,002 communities, asking 2,777 people about which words they used for 1,847 various items. The finished dictionary contains 60,000 entries and 2,985 maps. Among the sixty thousand words in the regional lexicon is a Georgia term for firefly—"a third-shift mosquito."

The blog of the *Paris Review* notices something shocking—three ways to tell a woman that her slip is showing: "it's snowing down south"; "your father likes you better than your mother"; or "Whitey's out of jail."

The staff at *The Week* cite a number of their favorite entries, including Wisconsin's "whoopensocker," meaning "anything extraordinary of its kind—from a sweet dance to a knee-melting kiss"; Virginia's "jabble," a verb, for "shake up or mix"; and Nantucket's "slatchy," describing "the sky during a fleeting moment of sunshine or blue sky in the middle of a storm."

389. As the author writes about the regional colorful terms within the English language, he mentions the ". . . gumbo of American English." Of the following, which statement most likely reflects his meaning in choosing this term?

(A) Spicy
(B) Rich with many different ingredients
(C) Satisfying
(D) Hearty and flavorful

390. Several volumes of DARE have been publish in an attempt to capture many of the regionally specific terms used for common items and activities in America. Of the following, which is the title from which DARE was derived?

    (A) Dictionary of American Regional English
    (B) Dictionary of Anglicized Revised English
    (C) Dictionary of American Relative English
    (D) Dictionary of Alternative Regional English

391. Within the volumes of DARE are what the author terms as "contrastive maps." Of the following descriptions, which best reflects the information contained within these maps?

    (A) They show all terms used for a specific location.
    (B) They illustrate each state and the terms used for specific items and activities.
    (C) They position multiple terms over regions in which they are used.
    (D) They define imaginary borders within the United States by the most commonly used term for an item.

392. An example of what one may find listed in DARE would be the description of the appearance of blue sky in the midst of a storm. Of the following, which would be the term used to describe this in the New England states?

    (A) Jabbly
    (B) Slatchy
    (C) Blomby
    (D) Gleetchy

393. In our world, there are items, foods, and beverages that have only existed for a few decades and that the founders of our English language could never have dreamed. Those include the multitude of carbonated soft drinks available today. The terms for these most likely exist on a contrastive map within the DARE volumes as well as on social media pages and memes. Of the following, which would you least expect to be listed under a regional map for soft drink?

    (A) Soda
    (B) Coke
    (C) Polypop
    (D) Pop

394. From information presented in the passage, which of the following terms would be applicable to the phrase "third-shift mosquito"?

(A) Butterfly
(B) Firefly
(C) Dragonfly
(D) Horsefly

Navajo Code Talkers: World War II Fact Sheet

Guadalcanal, Tarawa, Peleliu, Iwo Jima: the Navajo code talkers took part in every assault the U.S. Marines conducted in the Pacific from 1942 to 1945. They served in all six Marine divisions, Marine Raider battalions, and Marine parachute units, transmitting messages by telephone and radio in their native language—a code that the Japanese never broke.

The idea to use Navajo for secure communications came from Philip Johnston, the son of a missionary to the Navajos and one of the few non-Navajos who spoke their language fluently. Johnston, reared on the Navajo reservation, was a World War I veteran who knew of the military's search for a code that would withstand all attempts to decipher it. He also knew that Native American languages, notably Choctaw, had been used in World War I to encode messages.

Johnston believed Navajo answered the military requirement for an undecipherable code because Navajo is an unwritten language of extreme complexity. Its syntax and tonal qualities, not to mention dialects, make it unintelligible to anyone without extensive exposure and training. It has no alphabet or symbols, and is spoken only on the Navajo lands of the American Southwest. One estimate indicates that less than 30 non-Navajos, none of them Japanese, could understand the language at the outbreak of World War II.

Early in 1942, Johnston met with Major General Clayton B. Vogel, the commanding general of Amphibious Corps, Pacific Fleet, and his staff to convince them of the Navajo language's value as code. Johnston staged tests under simulated combat conditions, demonstrating that Navajos could encode, transmit, and decode a three-line English message in 20 seconds. Machines of the time required 30 minutes to perform the same job. Convinced, Vogel recommended to the Commandant of the Marine Corps that the Marines recruit 200 Navajos.

In May 1942, the first 29 Navajo recruits attended boot camp. Then, at Camp Pendleton, Oceanside, California, this first group created the Navajo code. They developed a dictionary and numerous words for military terms. The dictionary and all code words had to be memorized during training.

Once a Navajo code talker completed his training, he was sent to a Marine unit deployed in the Pacific theater. The code talkers' primary job was to talk, transmitting information on tactics and troop movements, orders and other vital battlefield communications over telephones and radios. They also acted as messengers, and performed general Marine duties.

Praise for their skill, speed and accuracy accrued throughout the war. At Iwo Jima, Major Howard Connor, 5th Marine Division signal officer, declared, "Were it not for the Navajos, the Marines would never have taken Iwo Jima." Connor had six Navajo code talkers working around the clock during the first two days of the battle. Those six sent and received over 800 messages, all without error.

The Japanese, who were skilled code breakers, remained baffled by the Navajo language. The Japanese chief of intelligence, Lieutenant General Seizo Arisue, said that while they were able to decipher the codes used by the U.S. Army and Army Air Corps, they never cracked the code used by the Marines. The Navajo code talkers even stymied a Navajo soldier taken prisoner at Bataan. (About 20 Navajos served in the U.S. Army in the Philippines.) The Navajo soldier, forced to listen to the jumbled words of talker transmissions, said to a code talker after the war, "I never figured out what you guys who got me into all that trouble were saying."

In 1942, there were about 50,000 Navajo tribe members. As of 1945, about 540 Navajos served as Marines. From 375 to 420 of those trained as code talkers; the rest served in other capacities. Navajo remained potentially valuable as code even after the war. For that reason, the code talkers, whose skill and courage saved both American lives and military engagements, only recently earned recognition from the Government and the public.

The Navajo Code Talker's Dictionary

When a Navajo code talker received a message, what he heard was a string of seemingly unrelated Navajo words. The code talker first had to translate each Navajo word into its English equivalent. Then he used only the first letter of the English equivalent in spelling an English word. Thus, the Navajo words "wol-la-chee" (ant), "be-la-sana" (apple) and "tse-nill" (axe) all stood for the letter "a." One way to say the word "Navy" in Navajo code would be "tsah (needle) wol-la-chee (ant) ah-keh-di- glini (victor) tsah-ah-dzoh (yucca)."

Most letters had more than one Navajo word representing them. Not all words had to be spelled out letter by letter. The developers of the original code assigned Navajo words to represent about 450 frequently used military terms that did not exist in the Navajo language. Several examples: "besh- lo" (iron fish) meant "submarine," "dah-he- tih-hi" (hummingbird) meant "fighter plane" and "debeh-li-zine" (black street) meant "squad."

395. The Navajo code talkers were part of what branch of the military in World War II?

(A) Army
(B) Navy
(C) Air Force
(D) Marines

396. Based on the passage, which of the following would be the most likely occupation of the author?

(A) Journalist
(B) Historian
(C) Novelist
(D) Educator

397. The Navajo codes have yet to be broken even today. This was one of the many beneficial elements of this code that military professionals enjoyed and protected. Of the following, which would the author most agree was a major benefit to the troops of the code talkers?

(A) They had confidence the code wouldn't be broken.
(B) Theirs was the fastest of the codes to be transmitted and interpreted.
(C) Colorful words were used in the code.
(D) A talker was with every company of troops.

398. Although the war ended in 1945, the Navajo code has only recently been made known to the public. Of the following, what is the most likely rationale for the delay in this release of information to the public?

(A) The Freedom of Information Act requiring its release only recently passed.
(B) The code was still in use by the military and remains unbroken.
(C) It was only a small part of the much larger operation of World War II.
(D) It was so complex that it was impossible to adequately tell novices of its significance.

399. The Navajo code remains the only code in military history to remain unbroken (that we know of). Of the following, which was NOT a listed reason that the code was impossible to break?

(A) It had no alphabet.
(B) It was only spoken on Navajo lands.
(C) It was only written in pictorial representations.
(D) Its tonal qualities were unintelligible to the untrained.

400. The passage describes the complex code as using the first letters of the Navajo words to be translated into an English word. However, some Navajo words were used as direct coded words such as besh- lo (iron fish) being the code for submarine. Another code word was the Navajo word for turtle. Of the following, which is the most likely meaning for this code word during World War II?

   (A) Tank
   (B) Artillery
   (C) Slow
   (D) Take cover

401. Of all the Marine actions in the Pacific Theater in World War II, which of the following was NOT listed in the passage as one in which code talkers played an essential role?

   (A) Tarawa
   (B) Philippines
   (C) Peleliu
   (D) Iwo Jima

Six-Month-Old Word Learners

Suppose a baby's first word is "mommy" or "daddy"—words an infant usually says around his or her first birthday. Of course, the little cherub puts a gleam in her parents' eyes; she's finally talking and is well on her way to becoming the next big opera star or a world famous author.

But new research says infants may begin understanding language much sooner than previously thought. Infants understand the meaning of some words far earlier than parents or even social scientists theorized. In fact, before they talk, walk, or point, infants know the meaning of some words merely from everyday exposure to them.

"By 6 months, infants understand the meaning of words related to foods and body parts," said Elika Bergelson, a doctoral candidate in the department of psychology at the University of Pennsylvania, who recently conducted a study that challenges current views of the developmental sequence of human language learning.

"Unlike previous research, which has shown that young infants know their own name or the words 'mommy' or 'daddy,' or can be trained to learn words for novel objects in the lab, here we show that infants have knowledge about word categories that are a part of their daily life."

Bergelson and her coauthor, associate professor Daniel Swingley, also with the department of psychology and the Institute for Research in Cognitive Science at the University of Pennsylvania, conducted the study. The *Proceedings of the National Academy of Sciences* published the study in its February 13 issue.

"The work by Swingley and colleagues continues a long tradition of research demonstrating that even very young infants engage in complex perceptions and inferences about the world around them," said Peter Vishton, a developmental psychologist in the National Science Foundation's Division of Behavioral and Cognitive Sciences, which partially funded the study. "Babies can't tell us about what they know, but their looking patterns demonstrate that they make sense of the people, objects, and events in their surroundings," said Vishton, "to some extent from the moment they are born."

Using a research method called "language-guided looking" or "looking-while-listening," researchers presented 6- to 9-month-old infants with visual displays, usually sets of two pictures. Then a parent named a picture in each set using a sentence like, "Look at the apple." Researchers then gauged the infant's visual fixations on named pictures as a measure of the infant's word understanding.

Most of the 33 infants in the study recognized most of the 20 items tested, which were food-related or body parts. Researchers compared the tests of the 6- to 9-month-olds with 50 babies 10- to 20-months old.

"We were most surprised that we found evidence of word-meaning knowledge this early," said Swingley. "We knew that infants around this age were very good at discriminating and categorizing speech sounds, but it seemed unlikely that they would be able to show word-meaning knowledge, without training, in the laboratory setting."

Prior research generally classifies infants younger than about 10 to 12 months as prelinguistic, and conventional thinking suggests word learning doesn't start until around a child's first birthday. Because of this, the researchers in this study expected to find that maybe around 9 months there might be some word recognition, but certainly not at 6-7 months.

"In the context of this tradition," said Vishton, "the current finding that 6-month-olds possess knowledge about the meanings of nouns associated with body parts is quite striking."

"The babies surprised us," said Swingley.

"The bulk of current evidence on the language abilities of 6 to 12-month-olds document their savvy abilities to pull out various properties about the sounds of language: Which sounds their language has as separate categories, where words begin and end, what kind of patterns or consistencies there are in the speech stream, etc.," said Bergelson, arguing that this leads to language acquisition theories that suggest infants younger than 10 to 12 months old are not yet "word learners."

"Our findings may lead to changes in the way that we understand language acquisition and its development," she said.

"In terms of the message to parents and caretakers," added Swingley, "our work suggests that young infants understand a little of what is said to them, so it makes sense to talk to them. When we talk to infants as real conversational partners, and talk about what they are interested in, we create the ideal conditions for learning."

"There's more and more work showing strong correlations between how much parents talk to their young children and those children's vocabulary size," he said.

"Overheard language doesn't do it, television doesn't do it. What young children learn from best is when we treat them as real conversational partners."

402. One of the first major developmental milestones for a baby is saying their first word, usually "daddy" or "mommy." Based on what you read in the passage, which would the author most agree is the reason for these being the first words?

(A) Babies spend a lot of time with their mother and father.
(B) They recognize their mother and father.
(C) Parents say those words associated with themselves regularly.
(D) Mommy and daddy are simple phonetic words.

403. The author introduces scientific evidence that suggests babies can understand the sounds associated with words at much earlier ages than one year. These infants are said to be prelinguistic in that they have not spoken their first words yet. Of the following, which would be the best additional evidence to support that infants understand words and meanings long before they can vocalize?

(A) Babies use simple and correct sign language in response to spoken questions.
(B) Babies recognize objects when asked.
(C) Babies laugh when presented a funny picture.
(D) Babies interact with television programs.

404. In the current study discussed in the passage, the author states that the looking patterns of babies can be telling in their understanding and recognition. Of the following, which was NOT listed as one of those things recognized and correlated to the looking pattern of infants younger than six months of age?

(A) Events in their environment
(B) Letters
(C) People
(D) Objects

405. In the study, babies were presented with two pictures and a parent verbally cued the baby to a specific item, such as an apple. These items were food related or body parts. Considering the study, which of the following would most strengthen the assertion that babies recognize sounds and understand what is being verbally communicated?

(A) Chimps and other primates can't perform the same tasks so it isn't likely to be random chance.

(B) Objects other than food and body parts were also recognized by the infants.

(C) Babies still recognized and looked at the objects when presented with three or more options.

(D) Recognition still occurred when a non-parental adult gave the cues.

406. Rather than recognizing words, the author states that babies recognize the sounds of language. Of the following, which was not an example of what the sound of language means?

(A) Hard consonants, which are recognized best

(B) Beginning of words

(C) Consistencies in language

(D) The ending of words

407. Based on the findings of the study, which of the following would the author most likely agree would be a recommendation for parents to follow in the early months of raising a child?

(A) Present them with as many spoken words as possible.

(B) Use letters and word boards to stimulate the association of sounds with language.

(C) Provide variety for the infant to expand their sound vocabulary.

(D) Converse with the baby as most parents already do and continue to do so since they are learning even when we are not aware they can.

CHAPTER **19**

Political Science

Islam and Democracy

The relationship between Islam and democracy in the contemporary world is complex. The Muslim world is not ideologically monolithic. It presents a broad spectrum of perspectives ranging from the extremes of those who deny a connection between Islam and democracy to those who argue that Islam requires a democratic system. In between the extremes, in a number of countries where Muslims are a majority, many Muslims believe that Islam is a support for democracy even though their particular political system is not explicitly defined as Islamic.

Throughout the Muslim world in the twentieth century, many groups that identify themselves explicitly as Islamic attempted to participate directly in the democratic processes as regimes were overthrown in Eastern Europe, Africa, and elsewhere. In Iran such groups controlled and defined the system as a whole; in other areas, the explicitly Islamic groups were participating in systems that were more secular in structure. The participation of self-identified Islamically oriented groups in elections, and in democratic processes in general, aroused considerable controversy. People who believe that secular approaches and a separation of religion and politics are an essential part of democracy argue that Islamist groups only advocate democracy as a tactic to gain political power. They say Islamist groups support "one man, one vote, one time." In Algeria and Turkey, following electoral successes by parties thought to be religiously threatening to the existing political regimes, the Islamic political parties were restricted legally or suppressed.

The relationship between Islam and democracy is strongly debated among the people who identify with the Islamic resurgence in the late twentieth century and the beginning of the twenty-first. Some of these Islamists believe that "democracy" is a foreign concept that has been imposed by Westernizers and secular reformers upon Muslim societies. They often argue that the concept of popular sovereignty denies the fundamental Islamic affirmation of the sovereignty of God and is, therefore, a form of idolatry. People holding these views are less likely to be the ones participating in elections. Many limit themselves to participating in intellectual debates in the media, and others hold themselves aloof from the political dynamics of their societies, hoping that their own isolated community will in some way be an inspiration to the broader Muslim community. Many prominent Islamic intellectuals and groups, however, argue that Islam and democracy are compatible. Some extend the argument to affirm that under the conditions of the contemporary world, democracy can be considered a requirement of Islam. In these discussions, Muslim scholars bring historically important concepts from within the Islamic tradition together with the basic concepts of democracy as understood in the modern world.

The process in the Muslim world is similar to that which has taken place within other major religious traditions. All of the great world faith traditions represent major bodies of ideas, visions, and concepts fundamental to understanding human life and destiny.

Many of these significant concepts have been used in different ways in different periods of history. The Christian tradition, for example, in premodern times provided a conceptual foundation for divine right monarchy; in contemporary times, it fosters the concept that Christianity and democracy are truly compatible. In all traditions, there are intellectual and ideological resources that can provide the justification for absolute monarchy or for democracy. The controversies arise regarding how basic concepts are to be understood and implemented.

408. In the passage, the author makes the statement that the Muslim world is not ideologically "monolithic." Of the following, which most closely represents the meaning of the author in her reference here?

   (A) One set of governing guidelines
   (B) One supreme being in control
   (C) One political party within which to press for change
   (D) One leader in charge of Islam and their politics

409. For Islam and democracy to exist in the same country, such as the U.S., which of the following foundational ideals must be met?

   (A) Individual freedoms must be respected.
   (B) Muslim political parties must be prohibited.
   (C) The constitution must compromise with Muslim law.
   (D) The government must be a blending of several political parties to ensure none has too much power.

410. A conflict arises for some in the Muslim society between what the author calls the sovereignty of God and popular sovereignty. Of the following, which best reflects the concept of popular sovereignty as stated by the author?

   (A) Deity accepted by the majority of the community
   (B) Governing constitution setting one set of standards for all
   (C) Highest religious leader of the society
   (D) An elected government official in charge of the country

411. Based on the passage, which of the following would best represent the sentiment of the author for this topic of popular sovereignty?

(A) Opposed
(B) Supportive
(C) Neutral
(D) Informative

412. In the passage, the author uses the existence of Christianity as an example of how a religious practice can coexist within a democracy. Of the following, which would most weaken this argument?

(A) Christian athletes are derided for expressing their faith in God.
(B) Christian beliefs are being suppressed by the liberal society as being oppressive.
(C) Any and all things Christian are being eliminated from our government.
(D) Christianity is on the decline in America.

413. In the passage, the author states that for Muslims to exist in a democracy, the important concepts from within the Islamic tradition must be paired with the basic concepts of democracy. Of the following, which would make this statement flawed in the United States?

(A) More non-Muslims live in the U.S.
(B) In the statement, Islam is primary and democracy is subordinate. Separation of church and state would make this impossible.
(C) The constitution is a complex and living document, not a basic concept.
(D) Liberals will never allow such a shift in power toward a singular religious group.

Opposition Response to the State of the Union Address

Each January, the U.S. observes a national ritual, the presentation of the annual State of the Union address. The Constitution requires that the president "from time to time give to the Congress Information on the State of the Union," and all but two presidents have fulfilled that responsibility, either in person or in writing. The two who did not—William Henry Harrison and James Garfield—died before they got the chance. It was known simply as the president's annual message until the 1930s, when Franklin Roosevelt referred to it as the State of the Union Address. Harry Truman formalized that title in 1947.

The event has evolved a great deal over the years, and perhaps nothing changed it quite as much as television! Truman was the first to use the new medium, and Presidents Eisenhower and Kennedy followed suit, but it was Lyndon Johnson who recognized the power of television. Whereas his predecessors typically delivered their speeches at midday, when television audiences were small, in 1965 LBJ took the speech to prime time.

"By scheduling his speech in prime television time," commented the *New York Times*, President Johnson "automatically doubled or tripled the size of his audience." Perhaps even more important, the *Times* noted, "since his remarks were a nighttime event, the speech automatically enjoyed much more advance promotion by the networks." The overall effect was to emphasize that the State of the Union had become more than "a report to Congress." Now, it was a report "to the people."

The importance of Johnson's pioneering effort was not lost on members of Congress and particularly Senate Minority Leader Everett Dirksen. The Republican leader was an old hand with the press and understood the impact of media exposure on public opinion. His weekly press conferences with the House minority leaders—dubbed the "Ev and Charlie Show" and later the "Ev and Jerry Show"—became something of a sensation. Consequently, when LBJ went prime time in 1965, Dirksen vowed to get equal time.

Of course, members of the opposition party had been responding to the president's message for years, but such remarks came in the relatively ignored environment of the Senate or House Chamber or at local political events. To gain national attention, Dirksen needed a national forum, and that meant television. And so, after LBJ's next State of the Union address in 1966, Republican leaders Everett Dirksen and Gerald Ford recorded a 30-minute televised rebuttal of the president's speech. For an appropriate venue, the leaders chose the Old Senate Chamber, the setting for some of our nation's most monumental debates. Dirksen covered foreign policy, discussing what he termed the "grim, bloody, and costly business" of Vietnam, while Ford tackled domestic issues, targeting inflation, civil rights, and campaign finance.

It was "a short time for a gigantic task," Dirksen quipped, and the TV networks were not very accommodating—the program aired five days after Johnson's speech and in some areas it competed with the late, late show—but public reaction was positive. The Dirksen-Ford event may not mean that the minority voice will be "more widely heeded in Congress," commented the *Washington Post*, "but it is being more widely heard in the country." Dirksen and Ford made a return engagement in 1967, and this time their response came on the same evening as the president's address and in prime time. Today, thanks to the efforts of Dirksen and Ford, the Opposition Response is anticipated and discussed almost as much as the president's speech.

414. In the history of our country, every president but two have given a State of the Union address, either formalized as such or as an update to Congress. Of the following list, which is the only president to NOT give an address?

(A) Grover Cleveland
(B) James Garfield
(C) Franklin Pierce
(D) Chester Arthur

415. Over the years, the State of the Union address has grown from a simple speech in the chambers of Congress to a major event in our country. Of the following, which does the author attribute most to the rise in its popularity?

(A) The Internet
(B) Radio
(C) Television
(D) Newspapers

416. Our country has existed in its entirety with functional (and dysfunctional) political parties. While the minority party has always offered differing perspectives on the statements of the president, the Opposition Response became popular in the 60s. Of the following, which would the author most agree is the purpose of this speech in modern times?

(A) Much the same as a political debate, to attract voters to their party
(B) To clarify statements of the president and offer support for important programs
(C) For the minority speaker to gain popularity
(D) To offer counter arguments against everything the president says to undermine his authority

417. The Opposition Response grew in popularity in the 60s in response to the State of the Union address of Lyndon B. Johnson. Of the men representing the minority party for the address, which one later was to become President of the United States himself?

(A) Ronald Reagan
(B) Gerald Ford
(C) Richard Nixon
(D) Jimmy Carter

418. The president is a highly visible professional in the U.S. His State of the Union address always stimulates much conversation. However, the author states that the Opposition Response may be discussed as much as that of the president. Of the following, which would the author most agree is the likely explanation for this popularity?

(A) In recent years the country is practically split in half politically, so half of the U.S. population would favor one discourse over the other.
(B) Today, people in general enjoy debate, argument, and drama far more than compromise and peace.
(C) People are familiar with the president's platforms and less so with the minority party, so they are interested in learning what they have to say.
(D) Opposition Responses are typically more direct, lively, and filled with criticism, which appeals to the populous.

419. The president's annual message has been an institution of the Constitution since its ratification. However, it has not always been called the State of the Union Address. Who was the first president to name his speech the State of the Union?

(A) Harry Truman
(B) Franklin Roosevelt
(C) Dwight Eisenhower
(D) John Kennedy

Adam Smith and the Development of Political Economy

Adam Smith, political economist and moral philosopher, was born in Kirkcaldy, Scotland, June 5, 1723. His father, a lawyer and customs official, died before the birth of his son, who was brought up through a delicate childhood by his mother. At fourteen he was sent to the University of Glasgow, where he came under the influence of Francis Hutcheson, and in 1740 he went up to Oxford as Snell exhibitioner at Balliol College, remaining there till 1746. After leaving Oxford, he gave lectures upon English Literature and Economics, and in 1751 became professor of logic, and in 1752 professor of moral philosophy, at Glasgow. The reputation won by his lectures was increased by the publication, in 1759, of his "Theory of the Moral Sentiments," one result of which was his appointment as travelling tutor to the third Duke of Buccleuch. In this capacity he spent nearly three years in France, and made the acquaintance of many of the intellectual leaders of that country. Returning to Britain in the end of 1766, he lived chiefly in Kirkcaldy and London, working upon his *Wealth of Nations*, which was finally published in 1776. It met with immediate success, and in a few years had taken an authoritative place with both philosophers and men of affairs. In the following year Smith was appointed a Commissioner of Customs, and took a house in Edinburgh, where he lived quietly and at ease till his death on July 17, 1790.

Political economy had been studied long before Adam Smith, but the *Wealth of Nations* may be said to constitute it for the first time as a separate science. The work was based upon a vast historical knowledge, and its principles were worked out with remarkable sanity as well as ingenuity, and skillfully illuminated by apt illustrations. In spite of more than a century of speculation, criticism, and the amassing of new facts and fresh experience, the work still stands as the best all-round statement and defense of some of the fundamental principles of the science of economics.

The most notable feature of the teaching of the *Wealth of Nations*, from the point of view of its divergence from previous economic thought as well as of its subsequent influence, is the statement of the doctrine of natural liberty. Smith believed that "man's self-interest is God's providence," and held that if government abstained from interfering with free competition, industrial problems would work themselves out and the practical maximum of efficiency would be reached. This same doctrine was applied to international relations, and Smith's working out of it here is the classical statement of the argument for free trade.

In its original form the book contained a considerable number of digressions and illustrations which the progress of knowledge and of industrial civilization have shown to be inaccurate or useless, and of these the present edition has been unburdened. This process, while greatly increasing the interest and readableness of the book, has left intact Smith's main argument, which is here offered to the reader as admittedly the best foundation for the study of political economy.

420. The author uses the term "political economy" in the title and throughout the passage. While most understand the terms separately as politics and economics, which of the following best summarizes the meaning of the author in linking these two terms?

(A) The financial condition of a country
(B) Risk versus reward of running for political office
(C) Reflections on how individuals in power may affect the economy of their country
(D) The study of how different political systems impact economics

421. Adam Smith, in his work *Wealth of Nations*, introduces the concept of what the author calls natural liberty. Of the following, which best defines what is meant by this doctrine?

(A) Man should only be subordinate to nature.
(B) The freedoms of men must not be artificially inflexible.
(C) Governments only have the power provided them by the people.
(D) The rights of free people are provided by God.

422. Smith's book, *Wealth of Nations*, was said to have met with immediate success and quickly became the seminal piece for philosophers and what the author terms "men of affairs." Based on the passage, which of the following could substitute for that term in the passage?

(A) Economists
(B) Politicians
(C) Businessmen
(D) Bankers

423. The author seems to be making contradictory statements when mentioning that political economy had been studied before Smith; yet Smith is credited for making it a separate science. In what way would the author most align these apparently divergent statements?

(A) Either politics or economics had been the focus before and never linked together.

(B) The role of government and the health of the economy had never before been formally linked into a comprehensive work.

(C) Only select systems of government had been examined to see the impact they had on the fiscal health of their country.

(D) It had only been a peripheral field of study under the umbrella of economics prior to Smith's work.

424. During Smith's life, he had the best of education and training as well as diverse life experiences. Had he lived a portion of his life in communist Russia, which of the following statements would the author most agree would shape his view of political economy?

(A) Socialism is the most effective political system within which an economy can be sustained and thrive.

(B) Socialism is a short-term solution to civil unrest and dissatisfaction for a stable but slow growing economy.

(C) Capitalism will always present itself as the highest reward, greatest risk system.

(D) Capitalism will work only as long as the government does not interfere.

425. There was much political unrest during Smith's life, including the American Revolution. However, the financial disaster of the Stock Market Crash and the Great Depression came well after Smith's life. If he had experienced those financial disasters, how might his doctrine of natural liberty changed?

(A) It would have remained the same.

(B) He would have abandoned it in light of the financial destruction by man.

(C) He would have seen the need to alter his doctrine and include governmental regulation.

(D) He would have seen the flaw in his doctrine which only works if honest individuals are involved in the business of the country.

CHAPTER 20

Population Health

Scientists Predict Massive Urban Growth, Creation of 'Megalopolis' in Southeast in Next 45 Years

Raleigh, N.C.—Urban areas in the Southeastern United States will double in size by 2060 unless there are significant changes to land development, according to a new study by the Department of Interior's Southeast Climate Science Center and North Carolina State University.

The predicted growth would come at the expense of agricultural and forest lands, creating an urban "megalopolis" stretching from Raleigh to Atlanta, which also raises a number of ecological concerns.

"If we continue to develop urban areas in the Southeast the way we have for the past 60 years, we can expect natural areas will become increasingly fragmented," said Adam Terando, a research ecologist with the U.S. Geological Survey, adjunct assistant professor at NC State, and lead author of the study. "We could be looking at a seamless corridor of urban development running from Raleigh to Atlanta, and possibly as far as Birmingham, within the next 50 years."

To understand how urban and natural environments could change, the researchers used NC State's High Performance Computing services to simulate urban development between now and 2060 across the Southeastern United States.

Among the expected impacts of such expansive urban growth, the fragmentation of natural areas would significantly limit the mobility of wildlife, making it more difficult for them to find mates, raise young, find food, and respond to environmental changes.

"This, in turn, increases the likelihood that we'll see more conflicts between people and wildlife, such as the increasing interactions with bears we're seeing in our suburban areas," Terando said.

An increase in urbanization would also make urban heat islands—the warming of cities due to human activities and development—more common, favoring species that can take advantage of the hotter conditions in cities. For example, previous studies have found that insect pests—such as scale insects—thrive in urban environments.

"Unless we change course, over the next 50 years urbanization will have a more pronounced ecological impact in many non-coastal areas of the Southeast than climate change," said Jennifer Costanza, a research associate at NC State and

a co-author of the study. "It's impossible to predict precisely what the specific ecological outcomes would be, but so far, the projections are not good in terms of
biodiversity and ecosystem health."

"This research emphasizes how decision makers involved in community planning will need a well-thought out strategy for future development," Costanza said.

"Given that urbanization poses significant challenges to this region, decision
makers will need to begin serious, long-term discussions about economic development, ecological impacts, and the value of non-urban spaces," she added.

426. Which of the following is NOT an expected impact of excessive urbanization as would occur in the creation of a megalopolis that is stated in the
passage?

(A) Increase in insect pests
(B) Greater species diversity
(C) Limited mobility of wildlife
(D) Increased conflicts between humans and wildlife

427. Which of the following would the author most likely agree with as a factor
in creating the excessive urbanization of the southeastern U.S.?

(A) Healthy economy in the southeastern U.S. compared to other regions
of the country.
(B) Urban sprawl where workers want to be close to their place of
employment yet escape the congestion and problems of city living.
(C) Favorable climate drawing an increasing number of baby boomer
retirees to the southeast.
(D) Increased generational stability causing families to remain regionally
close.

428. Which of the following might the author most agree is the best way to
accommodate increased human presence while maintaining the health of
the ecosystem?

(A) Enforce wildlife zones where human interference is minimized.
(B) Limit the size and population of urban settings.
(C) Create transportation routes via tunnels or raise trains while leaving
the land for wildlife.
(D) Surround the megalopolis with wildlife sanctuaries free of human
influence.

429. Which of the following would the author most agree has been the focus of city planners in the southeastern region of the country?

(A) Ecology
(B) Environment
(C) Economy
(D) Efficiency

430. Which of the following does the author use to support the impact of increased human/wildlife encounters in urban areas?

(A) Alligators representing a threat in Florida suburbs
(B) Large snakes and reptiles increasingly being seen in suburban yards
(C) Wolves and mountain lions being more common in suburbs
(D) Bears becoming more common in the suburbs

On the Frontlines of the Ebola Response: an Inside Look at a Program to Help the Grieving

The West African Ebola outbreak is the worst outbreak in history, affecting four countries. The U.N. World Health Organization declared it an international health emergency.

In Liberia, a country gripped by Ebola, the outbreak has not only taken its toll on health care workers but also on the professionals who comfort the grieving.

"The outbreak of Ebola was very shocking and overwhelming to our country," said Jestina Hoff, a counselor with the Liberian Red Cross. "It brought a lot of fear."

The outbreak has also hampered Hoff's ability to do her job. "As a counselor, I talk to parents who lost a child or to someone who has gotten sick with the virus," said Hoff. "They are feeling so discouraged, and I have to help them accept the situation and comfort them, but without touching them."

Francesca Crabu, a clinical psychologist with the International Committee of the Red Cross, explained that having close contact with those who are grieving is key to providing psychosocial support. But in Liberia and other parts of Western Africa, preventative measures require people to stay at arm's length from each other.

"Here in Liberia, it is very painful that you cannot shake hands. If somebody is dying, I cannot hug you," said Crabu.

To make matters worse, once Ebola claims a life, the body is taken immediately, before families have time to mourn their loss, according to Eliza Yee-lai Cheung, a clinical psychologist with the Hong Kong Red Cross.

"They cannot hold a memorial service or burial according to their culture," said Cheung. "That's why it's very hard for them."

To give psychosocial counselors the tools to help grieving communities, the USAID Ebola Disaster Assistance Response Team (DART) is partnering with IFRC in Monrovia, Liberia's capital city. Among other things, the DART and the

International Federation of Red Cross and Red Crescent Societies are working to raise public awareness of Ebola's mode of transmission, teach disease prevention practices to communities, and train health workers and volunteers.

In a classroom, 19 people—counselors with the Liberian Red Cross, staff with NGOs and social workers with the Liberian Ministry of Health & Social Welfare—are learning from Crabu and Cheung how to organize culturally appropriate activities to help families cope with their loss. They are also taught ways to keep themselves safe from the virus and how to provide support to each other. This group will then go on to train others in affected communities with the hopes that such efforts will help the country come to grips with Ebola.

"It's overwhelming," said Hoff. "But we have a goal. I have a goal. We have to serve our country. We need somebody to take a step to help others move forward. It's scary, but there's hope."

431. According to the passage, what is one of the largest obstacles preventing counselors from adequately comforting grieving family members of Ebola victims?

(A) Unsanitary conditions in Liberia
(B) Sparsely populated areas that make it difficult to reach people
(C) Lack of human physical contact to comfort for fear of contracting the disease
(D) Vastly more people in need than grief counselors in that country

432. Several health assistance organizations are contributing aid and manpower to Liberia during this time of Ebola outbreak and suffering. Of the following, which is NOT a practice provided by these groups to the people of Liberia?

(A) Educating the public about Ebola
(B) Disease avoidance training
(C) Transporting the infected to the U.S. for care
(D) Health training for aid workers

433. The author details the steps taken to help the people of Liberia during the tragedy of an Ebola outbreak. From medical care to emotional support, groups are working to help the affected people. From the passage, which of the following do you believe the author would most support in other countries that may be similarly affected?

(A) Use all resources for disease prevention to negate the need for grief counseling.
(B) Communities should be educated in grief management prior to a tragedy.
(C) Individual countries should have emergency plans such that outside assistance would be unnecessary.
(D) Further support aid groups should assist people around the world dealing with tragedies of all types either biological, natural, or of human causes.

434. The horror of an invisible enemy such as Ebola must be nightmare enough; however, further dealing with the loss of a child, spouse, or parent simply increases an already emotionally terrible ordeal. In Liberia, which of the following would the author most agree was a roadblock to emotional healing for those who lost loved ones to Ebola?

(A) Bodies were burned thus making funerals impossible.
(B) The loss makes the possibility of their personal danger from Ebola even more real.
(C) Fear of others in the family contracting the disease prevents close personal contact.
(D) Lack of grief counselors leaves these survivors to deal with their grief alone.

435. Of all the health and emergency aid organizations worldwide, which of the following was NOT mentioned in the passage as contributing to the people in Liberia?

(A) World Health Organization
(B) Liberian Ministry of Health and Social Welfare
(C) International Federation of Red Cross
(D) Red Crescent

The Changing Face of Health in the South Pacific

Nations around the world both developing and developed alike are waking up and realizing the impact that non-communicable diseases (NCD) such as diabetes, cancer, violence, and drug addiction are having and will have on their population and economic growth. The reality is shocking. According to the World Health Organization, non-communicable diseases, notably cardiovascular disease and diabetes, account for over 75% of the deaths in Pacific Islander populations.

In the United States and in many nations, we observed Breast Cancer Awareness month in October and in November we observe Diabetes Awareness Month and the 16 Days of Activism against Gender Violence. These diseases and phenomena are plaguing and ravishing the lives of our loved ones, our societies, and our economies. Nations around the world are dedicating days, weeks, or months of health promotions to NCDs to bring attention to the problem as they search for an affordable solution for this costly epidemic. In nations such as Papua New Guinea, Vanuatu, Fiji, and Solomon Islands, diseases such as heart disease and cancer have begun taking the lives of more men and women each year. Cancer is now the leading cause of death worldwide.

Diseases that once were only thought of as diseases of the West or the most developed countries are now affecting every nation regardless of its geographic location, social, or economic status. For example, diabetes and heart disease have surpassed infectious diseases such as malaria, diarrhea, and pneumonia as the leading causes of death in countless places including the South Pacific. Each year, hundreds of Pacific Islanders suffer strokes, amputations of limbs, blindness, or even kidney failure due to diabetes and high blood pressure. In many cases where lives are spared, the quality of life is transformed forever.

The shocking truth is that the majority of health systems in the developing world are designed to address health challenges of an infectious nature and are not prepared to deal with chronic, long-term debilitating ones. With the development of new vaccines and drugs, many of these infectious diseases can be eliminated or effectively treated. In order for nations to address NCDs and do it effectively, health systems must be transformed to meet the immediate and emerging health issues of today, all while continuing to meet basic public health needs. Without the proper planning, this transformation can drastically increase the cost of a nation's health system. We must first address the full spectrum of disease management from prevention to treatment, and when possible, to cure. Even for nations that boast amazing access to care, the great challenge is providing the proper services, at the appropriate level, and at a cost that the nation can afford and sustain.

These changes won't happen overnight and will require innovation, creative financing, and changes in the skills of current health workers, infrastructure, modern technology, and resources. By working together, we can ensure we will be ready when the time comes. Through partnerships, regional training programs, centers of excellence, and infrastructural support, we can begin to address the changing face of health issues in the region. There is no time to waste.

436. Based upon the passage, which of the following adjectives would best reflect the author's feelings about countries managing noncommunicable as well as infectious diseases?

(A) Concerned
(B) Demanding
(C) Pessimistic
(D) Passionate

437. Many political agendas and programs have been offered up for debate on how to manage the growing problems of NCD around the world; yet, none has proved to be an effective means that would work in all countries around the world. Of these basic suggested approaches, which would likely be the most successful based on benefit versus cost?

(A) Investments to increase primary healthcare workers
(B) More money spent on education and prevention
(C) Enact laws that restrict the sale and usage of foods and other consumables that lead to NCD
(D) More resources spent on research and development toward more effective management and treatment regimens for NCDs

438. Non-communicable diseases are an every growing problem in developing nations and now many are among the leading causes of death worldwide. Of the following, which is NOT an NCD that was listed in the passage?

(A) COPD
(B) Heart disease
(C) Diabetes
(D) Cancer

439. The author illustrates the spread of NCDs throughout the world as atypical for places other than the "West." Of the following, which would the author most agree is the underlying cause of these NCDs spreading throughout the world?

(A) Affluence leads to less natural diet and more sedentary lifestyle.
(B) Western culture is much more fast paced and leads to hypertension.
(C) More developed countries can import more materials from around the world.
(D) The society shifts from an agricultural base to an industrial one with more pollution.

440. Death rates worldwide for infectious diseases are on the decline while NCDs are rapidly increasing. Which of the following statements best explains this picture of healthcare?

(A) More money is spent on infectious disease control than on NCDs.
(B) Current healthcare systems are designed to eliminate the cause of a disease such as a virus or bacteria. NCDs have causes that are more subtle and complex.
(C) Companies make more profit producing vaccines and medications to treat infectious diseases than can be made for NCD treatment.
(D) NCDs are more a cultural and societal issue and not a healthcare problem.

441. Many diseases are mentioned throughout the passage. Of the following, which is the leading cause of death worldwide?

(A) Stroke
(B) Cardiovascular disease
(C) Cancer
(D) Diabetes

Improved Cookstoves in Peru: A Peace Corps Volunteer's Story

For the more than 3 billion people around the world, who still cook and heat with open fires inside the home, the improved cookstove is a development technology that reduces the health hazards associated with breathing smoke. In rural Peru, I used funding from the USAID/Peace Corps Small Project Assistance Agreement to introduce my community to this brilliant technology by building 15 stoves and training other Peace Corps Volunteers (PCVs), NGOs, and local masons in the stove construction, use, and maintenance techniques.

A successful and sustainable project requires good cooperation between the PCV and the community partners. My first challenge was finding a household that was willing to test a stove, with only my explanation and a diagram. Felicia, who became a tireless advocate and "salesperson" in the community, took that leap of faith and patiently worked with me as we sorted out the details on the construction and use together.

One of the truly unique and powerful aspects of the Peace Corps service is that we volunteers live for two years in close proximity to those we serve. This gives us the advantage of trust, familiarity and, most of all, time. This gave me the opportunity to revisit all of the families, multiple times. The feedback from my community was instrumental in showing me that the improved cookstoves required the user to make many behavioral changes. I also observed many benefits and challenges with the clean cookstoves.

The improved cookstoves not only required more work to start a fire, but they needed smaller sized wood. The stoves only allowed for a limited amount of pots, of a specific size, to fit the stove, and even then, some stoves only allowed 2-3 pots to cook at a time. And in small homes, the larger, improved cookstoves required more floor space, which was a challenge.

However, the health and safety benefits were profound. The open flame and smoke that traditional cookstoves produced was no longer causing issues like damage to lungs or eyes, or causing burns. Cooking fuel was reduced by 50% and the stove resulted in faster cooking times.

Since completion of my project, over one hundred stoves have been installed—a very gratifying and sustainable result. Moreover, it was a real joy to see mothers no longer having to wipe tears from their eyes due to smoke irritation, toddlers no longer getting close to an open flame, and walls and ceilings no longer covered with nasty soot. Folks spent less time or money acquiring firewood, and to my benefit, I was invited to stay for many meals. This face-to-face contact with those we serve is one of the many rewards of Peace Corps service.

442. The people in rural Peru chiefly were preparing their food over open flames. Of the following, which were the principle problems of using open fires for cooking inside the home?

    (A) Breathing smoke
    (B) Causing burns
    (C) Soot covering everything
    (D) All of the above

443. With the assistance of USAID and the Peace Corps, funds were made available to supply cookstoves to the rural people in Peru. However, there were other obstacles that had to be overcome. Of the following, which was the most challenging of these for the volunteers to overcome?

(A) Changing the social norms of how the rural people cooked their food
(B) Providing funds for reconstruction and supplies for the people using the stoves
(C) Finding people willing to try the stoves
(D) Obtaining fuel that would fit the new cook stoves

444. While there are many benefits to using a cook stove versus an open flame in the home, there are some drawbacks. Of the following, which was not listed as a negative to transitioning from an open fire to a cook stove as presented in the passage?

(A) Harder to start the fire
(B) Cooking time was slower
(C) Had to use fewer and smaller pots
(D) Requires more floor space

445. Peace Corp volunteers are required to spend two years in a specific location. If these individuals were only present for a few weeks or months, which of the following would likely have been the result of the cookstove program?

(A) There would have been no effect because the stoves would be welcome by all the people for their benefits.
(B) The rural people would have rejected the stoves completely because they would not trust the strangers.
(C) It would likely have taken longer to find those first families willing to test the stoves, then the program would take off.
(D) It would have increased the rate at which stoves were placed in homes because the new people would be more enthusiastic about helping the natives.

446. The new stoves did present some difficulties and new challenges for the rural people during the transition period. Of the following, which would the author most agree would be a change that likely would have resulted in more stoves being placed more quickly?

(A) Cheaper stoves
(B) Smaller stoves
(C) Stoves that would use the same size wood
(D) Stoves that allowed the use of existing pots

447. In the passage, many of the benefits of cookstoves are listed and detailed. Of the following, which is NOT a benefit as described in the passage?

    (A) Using alternative fuel
    (B) Less time spent cooking
    (C) Lower fuel usage
    (D) Less pollution

"Clean Stoves" Would Save Lives, Cut Pollution

This Mother's Day weekend, most of us will enjoy a home-cooked meal—maybe even breakfast in bed. We'll probably take it for granted that the meal was prepared in a clean kitchen, where the air is safe to breathe. But for nearly half of the world's population, cooking at home is a deeply dangerous act. In fact, it poses one of the most serious health risks in the developing world, and it's a major threat to the environment.

The reason? Smoke from dirty stoves or open flames. Some 3 billion people live in homes where food is cooked on stoves or over fires burning fuels like wood, dung, charcoal, or agricultural waste. These fuels produce toxic fumes, and in poorly ventilated homes, the mix of chemicals can reach 200 times the level that the EPA considers safe to breathe. It can cause lung cancer, pneumonia, cataracts, low birth weight, even death. According to the World Health Organization, smoke from dirty stoves and fires kills almost 2 million people each year, most of them women and children. It kills more than twice as many people as malaria.

Impact on Climate

The impact goes beyond people's health. Burning these fuels produces carbon dioxide, methane, and black carbon, which contribute to climate change. And cutting down trees for fuel causes natural habitats to dry up, forests to disappear, and soil to erode.

On average, women and girls in developing countries spend up to 20 hours a week searching for fuel—time they could spend going to school, running a business, or raising their families. And if they live in areas of conflict, leaving home to search for fuel puts them at great risk of assault or rape.

All of this presents a major challenge—but it can be solved. If we can get cleaner, more efficient cookstoves in wider use throughout the developing world, we can save lives, cut back on carbon emissions, and create new economic opportunities for millions of women.

Fortunately, the technology for clean cookstoves already exists. Several companies are already producing them, and countries like India, China, and Mexico have begun to introduce them in national programs. But the uptake has been slow, because there hasn't been a widescale effort to coordinate these efforts, or to make the stoves affordable in the developing world.

Multiple Supporters

That's why we are excited about the Global Alliance for Clean Cookstoves, a partnership led by the United Nations Foundation that brings together governments, multilateral, private sector, and nonprofit organizations. The Alliance will drive research and development efforts to make new stoves that are more durable, affordable, and tailored to the cooking needs of specific cultures. It will help bring down costs, trade barriers, and other obstacles that have prevented cookstoves from being used widely. And it will promote the benefits of clean stoves, to encourage more families to start using them. A major goal for the Alliance is for 100 million households to take up clean cookstoves by 2020.

Reaching this goal will save lives and reduce pollution. It will also give people, especially women and girls, a new tool to create new economic opportunities for themselves. With the right training and a small upfront investment, women can start new businesses selling, repairing, and distributing clean stoves.

448. Three billion people around the world prepare their food on open fires within the confines of their own homes. Of the following, which was not one of the fuels used by people for their open fires?

(A) Industrial refuse
(B) Dung
(C) Charcoal
(D) Agricultural waste

449. By using the cookstoves, the time for preparing food and obtaining fuel will be drastically reduced. In addition to improving health and reducing pollution, which of the following would be another likely outcome for these rural people?

(A) More men would open businesses.
(B) People would have more time for their education.
(C) Women would obtain better education and/or move into the business world.
(D) Children would have more time for school and play.

450. While the cook stoves will reduce the amount of fuel used and decrease the time spent cooking, there will still be pollution from the natural fuels used in these areas. Which of the following would be the best explanation why alternative fuels such as natural gas or electricity, which are primarily used for cookstoves in the U.S., would not be used in these areas?

(A) Cost prohibitive
(B) Not available in rural underdeveloped countries
(C) Cookstoves which use those fuels are not produced in those countries
(D) Would lead to an even greater societal change and would not be welcome

451. Programs designed to improve health and the environment by offering cookstoves are not a new concept and are already underway in several countries around the world. Of the following, which is NOT a country with such a program?

(A) Brazil
(B) India
(C) China
(D) Mexico

452. Cookstoves, according to the article, will have great benefit on the society, the health of the people, and the protection of the environment. However, the delay is in getting the stoves to the people in an efficient and cost effective manner. Of the following, which would the author most support as a means to supply a greater number of stoves to rural people?

(A) Lobby governments to lower trade costs for shipping cookstoves.
(B) Ask for more donations from companies who manufacture cookstoves.
(C) Help establish local business to manufacture the stoves.
(D) Allow the UN to administer the program to avoid excessive international problems.

453. In addition to a better quality of life for individuals using cookstoves, the transition will also benefit the environment. Of the following, which is NOT an environmental benefit listed in the passage that would occur if cookstoves were used?

(A) Forests would stop disappearing.
(B) More soil would remain and not erode.
(C) Habitats would stop drying up.
(D) More indigenous animals would return.

CHAPTER 21

Psychology

Preventing Suicide

The World Health Organization (WHO)'s report, "Preventing Suicide: A Global Imperative," provides the first global view of how often suicide attempts and deaths occur, and how suicide-related behaviors affect all ages, nationalities, economic levels, and cultures. Every year around the world more than 800,000 people die by suicide. Globally, suicide is the second leading cause of death in 15- to 20-year-olds. WHO reports that for every person who dies as a result of suicide, there may be more than 20 who survive an attempt.

The WHO report offers some important insights by comparing suicide statistics across countries. Policies vary, with suicide considered a crime in some countries and a public health issue in others. In countries where suicide is illegal, decriminalization appears to lower suicide rates. Risk factors differ among countries as well. Research suggests, for example, that mental disorders play less of a role in China and India than in the West. The report also recommends several approaches to reducing suicide, including the importance of surveillance, raising awareness, and educating the media to reduce sensational coverage that can trigger suicides in the wake of news stories.

Throughout, the report emphasizes the importance of reducing access to lethal means. The means used in suicide deaths vary country to country. Worldwide, an estimated 30 percent of suicides are the result of pesticide self-poisoning. Reducing access to lethal means works because suicide is often an impulsive act that is situation specific. Research in Australia provides a provocative example. A 2012 study reported a marked decline in suicide deaths in the late 1990's. One factor in this decline was a sharp decrease in deaths as a result of motor vehicle exhaust poisoning. The attempt rate did not change, but lethality did, likely the result of changes in automobile engineering that lowered carbon monoxide emissions.

Some of the recommendations in this WHO report reinforce points made in the Prioritized Research Agenda for Suicide Prevention, a U.S. report issued earlier this year by the Research Prioritization Task Force of the National Action Alliance for Suicide Prevention. This earlier report identified three strategies that, if fully implemented, could save many thousands of lives in the United States. As 51 percent of suicides are carried out using firearms in this country, reduction in access to firearms was a key strategy. Other recommendations were installing devices to prevent deaths from motor vehicle exhaust and providing evidence-based psychotherapy to individuals who have made suicide attempts. Careful data collection and modeling of the impact of these strategies provides a way forward for accomplishing what has been frustratingly difficult to date: achieving a significant reduction in suicide rates in the United States.

Despite the increased availability of mental health care and medications for depression, the U.S. suicide rate has remained largely unchanged. There are measures we can and must take right away to help prevent suicide—encouraging responsible media reporting, promoting suicide prevention help lines, reducing access to lethal means, raising awareness, and getting at-risk individuals to appropriate care. There are also many unanswered questions about suicide that will require rigorous research. A better understanding of risk, prevention, and treatment along with scientifically based policies will make the difference in reducing the numbers of suicide deaths. As this new WHO report demonstrates, the need is global.

454. As stated in the passage, decriminalization of suicide coincides with a decrease in suicide rates. Which of the following would the author most support as a rational for this decline?

   (A) Decriminalization would also lead to lower sensationalized media coverage.
   (B) The taboo, and thus the attraction, would be removed from the practice.
   (C) Most suicides are planned like other crimes and would become more spontaneous and the rate would decrease.
   (D) The decrease would only occur in countries with greater regulation of firearms.

455. Of the following, which was NOT a stated approach to reduce the suicide rate worldwide?

   (A) Reduction in access to firearms
   (B) Carbon monoxide monitors in vehicles
   (C) Tighter regulation of pesticides
   (D) Psychotherapy for individuals who are a suicide risk

456. Although healthcare in the U.S. has improved its role in the treatment and counseling of those individuals at risk for suicide, the rate in the U.S. has "remained largely unchanged." Of the following hypotheses, which would the author most agree accounts for this apparent illogical statistic?

(A) The treatments and medications are ineffective.

(B) Physicians and psychiatrists are incorrectly treating these suicide risk patients.

(C) The treatments are effective and without them the rate would have been much greater.

(D) While the rate is unchanged, attempts have likely increased.

457. The author discusses making lethal means more difficult to obtain as a method of reducing suicide rates. Although the author does not suggest these individuals have no access to lethal means, which of the following would the author most agree is the condition that occurs when individuals have reduced access to lethal means and, it is the newly created situation that actually leads to lower suicide rates?

(A) Greater difficulty means it would take more time to obtain the lethal means, which would allow time to change their mind.

(B) Without lethal and deadly ways to injure and kill oneself, logically suicide rates decrease.

(C) Seeking lethal measures would lead individuals to encounter others who may give them the support they need to make a better decision.

(D) An easily obtainable means with which to commit suicide may frighten or scare an individual into changing their minds (i.e., the pain of a gunshot or pain of poisoning).

458. Which of the following is the most common means of suicide in the U.S.?

(A) Poisoning

(B) Firearms

(C) Carbon monoxide

(D) Hemorrhage from cuts (e.g., wrists)

459. Sensationalized media coverage has become the norm for developed countries. No longer just the news, these programs are now entertainment and are looking to attract viewers at almost any cost. Of the following, which would the author most agree could and should be done to hold news agencies responsible for the results of their actions?

    (A) Freedom of the press makes this impossible.
    (B) Fines should be levied for overly sensationalized reports that lead to increases in suicides.
    (C) Such reporting should be restricted to just news of the death without explicit details.
    (D) The news producers should face jail time for such reporting to curtail this practice.

Voices from the Field

Senior officers sometimes come to our mental health clinic on back elevators and wait in hallways for their appointments. There are medical staff who refuse to be seen officially in the clinic. Some people who are being seen in our clinic refer to themselves as "crazy" and separate from normal people. There is still stigma.

Service members say it will ruin their military career if they acknowledge they need help and get an appointment. Doctors say they will not be allowed to practice medicine any more if they get help. People fear it will always be used against them if they acknowledge weakness. This is rarely true, and not nearly as often as most people think it is. Only for those who suffer catastrophic mental illness is this true, and they are usually so ill that they rarely even understand how much their illness has changed their lives. For the overwhelming majority, there is no consequence for seeking help, except feeling and functioning better. But fear and stigma remain. I feel it speaks more to the meaning of mental illness for people than the actual repercussions.

Most people fear being labeled "crazy." To many people, those with mental illness are dehumanized. They are "other"; no longer part of humanity. The stigma they experience about mental illness speaks to the fear of being labeled as other. In the military, other often means weak, putting self before mission or unit, or unable to cut it. One's identity becomes that of someone who does not belong, who is a burden. These self-images are all incompatible with the sense of camaraderie, self-sacrifice, and putting team and mission above self that are part of military service. A broken self-image can leave a service member feeling alienated, alone. Fundamentally, it comes down to connection to others, and the fear of losing connections by acknowledging problems often keeps many service members from getting the help they need.

But I think that stigma is also a manifestation of a much deeper, personal fear. Outside of military settings, there are psychoanalysts who talk about the hope and dread of seeking treatment. In fact, there is a book by a very well-known contemporary psychoanalyst, Stephen Mitchell, by the title *Hope and Dread in Psychoanalysis.*

Basically, people hope for improvement when they seek treatment, but they also fear repetition of their past. They fear that the provider will reinforce a self-image of being broken. They fear they will not find empathy and acceptance, but a relationship in which once again they are a failure, or not good enough. Their fears will then seem true and unchangeable. They also fear that the person they seek help from will not understand them. They fear they will be alone, lost in their failings forever.

A very wise mentor of mine, Dr. George Atwood, once told me that there is nothing more powerful than being understood by another human being. We all seek that. We also all dread not being understood. Many suffering from depression, PTSD, and anxiety disorders have a shattered sense of themselves. They do not feel understood. Others tell them, or maybe they have told themselves, that their reactions to situations are not acceptable, maybe not even human. They feel that they cannot share their perspectives with others and are left feeling overwhelmed and alone. Feeling understood and accepted by another person is the antidote to isolation and stigma.

Patients often do not know it, but they are seeking understanding from us as mental health providers, or other care providers they seek. They arrive via back elevators or worry about their medical licenses out of fear of not being understood, or dread that prior rejections will be repeated. But there is also hope in seeking treatment. Often, once people feel understood, they lose this stigma and fear.

I have had patients change from hiding to sitting in our waiting room. They might say they see it as part of leadership. But they also say with their actions, "I have been understood. I have found someone who is willing to wade into and dwell in the horrors I have experienced. This person does not look away from me. So I will sit in public and wait to speak with this person again." This is often all they want and need to right their lives. They need help overcoming the danger they see in shame, stigma, or weakness so they can accept themselves. Living in one's skin is the one way we can thrive as human beings. If we can give that to each other by not looking away from suffering, then maybe much of my business will disappear.

460. According to the passage, is the stigma of seeking psychiatric care still an issue in our current culture?

(A) No, there are laws that protect individuals who are seeking psychiatric assistance yet can still perform their jobs effectively.

(B) Yes, how society views mental assistance is still prevalent in our culture.

(C) Yes, the stigma is self-inflicted since society views seeking mental care as worthwhile.

(D) No, psychiatric care is well accepted in society as a normal healthy practice by the majority of people.

461. The author makes it very clear that while there are many factors that influence the decision of an individual to seek psychiatric care, there is one major underlying factor that can prevent a person from seeking that care, which would be:

(A) Fear of the psychiatric problem (being in denial)
(B) Fear of what other people may think
(C) Fear of repercussions at work
(D) Fear of weakness, having failed to control their own emotions

462. Considering the stigma of seeking psychiatric help, the author goes to lengths to explain the underlying relationships and the rational for seeking professional help. However, he makes it abundantly clear that the individual who is most responsible for the creation and the elimination of the stigma is who?

(A) The support group of the patient, be it family, co-workers, or friends
(B) A spouse or significant other of the patient
(C) The psychiatrist
(D) The patient

463. In the final paragraph, the author states that one way to thrive as human beings is to "live in one's skin." Which of the following best represents the author's meaning?

(A) Be proud of who and what you are.
(B) Understand and accept yourself regardless of others.
(C) Be as mentally healthy as possible and understand it's normal to seek help when needed.
(D) Seek out like-minded people with whom to form connections.

464. The author describes many situations that can destroy self-image both among military personnel and civilians. Of the list below, which was NOT one described in the passage?

(A) Bipolar disorder
(B) Anxiety disorder
(C) Depression
(D) Post-traumatic stress disorder

465. Of the following statements, which best reflects the main theme of this passage?

(A) The stigma of seeking psychiatric help is slowly being overcome to help more and more people.
(B) Psychiatric assistance is needed by many former military members.
(C) The stigma of psychiatry still prevents people from seeking help today.
(D) More resources and financial assistance need to be directed toward the psychiatric care of military veterans.

Why People Live in Wildfire Zones

The California wildfires in 2007 led some people to wonder why anyone would live in terrain as vulnerable to natural disasters as parts of California. Now, with the 2008 fire season in the headlines, people will no doubt ask similar questions as homes and communities are threatened once again.

Do people have no choice but to live on land that regularly suffers fires, landslides, and earthquakes? Do they love the beauty and weather so much that they are willing to live with exceptional risks? Is it possible that they do not really understand the risks they face?

"Understanding risk and taking acceptable action is complex," says Paul Slovic.

For decades, scientists like Slovic, a psychology professor at the University of Oregon in Eugene, Ore., and president of Decision Research there, have studied aspects of these difficult questions.

For example, researchers have identified why some people tend to overestimate or underestimate the risks of certain hazards. Hazards that are familiar, visible, and well understood draw less concern than new, invisible, or less understood hazards.

Wildfire is a good illustration. In general, people are familiar with fire and understand a good deal about its mechanics, so fire risks are often underestimated or discounted. In contrast, the unfamiliar, invisible hazards posed by electromagnetic radiation tend to appear riskier and draw more concern and demands for government control.

"Understanding risks in a democratic society means understanding that there are multiple perspectives that should be considered when making risk decisions," says Slovic. "Risk decisions do not purely belong to scientists or government officials. The public has important contributions to make."

Slovic's perspective comes from his early days as a decision and risk behavior researcher in the late 1960s. It was then that he met one of the early pioneers of decision, risk, and management sciences, Dr. Gilbert White, who put Slovic on the path to one of his most significant research findings.

White was studying risk decisions related to natural hazards—fire, hurricanes, and the like—and was aware of Slovic's work with risk and gambling experiments. White asked Slovic why people rebuild on the same spot after a natural hazard, a question Slovic could not answer. But it spurred him to further research.

That research resulted in the development of the psychometric paradigm of risk perception, a theory influential in convincing policymakers that experts are not necessarily better at estimating risks than lay people. By introducing a quantitative, survey-based method for studying risk perception, Slovic showed risk could be studied scientifically.

"The public is not ignorant or irrational when they disagree with the experts," says Slovic. "They may know things scientists do not know. It's important for us to bring public values into risk management decisions."

Taking cues from Slovic's research methodologies as well as from others' work, a number of scientists are examining the psychology of risk in order to help people make better decisions about risks. Much of this work is supported by the National Science Foundation (NSF). For example, scientists are exploring questions about which risks people are or are not willing to take. An individual and his neighbor both may think the probability that a wildfire will damage their homes is exactly the same, yet one of them might move to a rainy climate to escape while the other would not dream of moving.

"We can't underestimate the importance of place, weather, and beauty to people," says Slovic. "It's important that policymakers, government officials, and insurance companies take these risk elements into account.

"It may be that government officials want to restrict new development in a risky area, or that insurance companies want to ask people to share the cost burden," he adds.

466. Many of us are often confused when natural disasters destroy homes and property yet the owners continue to rebuild on the same spot each time. Of the following, which was NOT a possible consideration that would lead people to stay in such unsafe locations?

(A) The cost
(B) The place
(C) The weather
(D) The beauty

467. Based on information in the passage, to which audience is the author directing this work?

(A) Real estate agents
(B) Meteorologists
(C) Psychologists
(D) Actuaries

468. The author states that hazards that are familiar, visible, and understood draw less concern than new invisible hazards. However, the author also illustrates how neighbors react differently to the same situation. Of the following, which would the author agree most likely influences those individual decisions?

(A) Financial status
(B) Security for a spouse and children
(C) Prior experience with loss and recovery
(D) Precautions made possible for protection or property and life

469. People live and build homes in some of the most inhospitable and dangerous environments on the planet. Of the hazards listed in the passage, which of the following is NOT described?

(A) Earthquakes
(B) Tornadoes
(C) Fires
(D) Landslides

470. Tornadoes are certainly natural forces that can cause great amounts of damage and great risk to the lives of people who are in their path. Of the following, which would the author most agree is a plausible explanation for why people would live in areas where tornadoes occur?

(A) They are not as widespread as earthquakes.
(B) Less damage is caused by tornadoes than by other natural disasters.
(C) Tornadoes are fairly well known and predictable so people are less concerned with them.
(D) Tornadoes may occur anywhere so any location will present some risk of them.

471. Toward the end of the passage, Slovic says that "they may know things the scientists do not know." This was his reason for bringing public values into risk management decisions. Which of the following best reflects what Slovic meant in the statement?

(A) In certain situations, the people are more aware of the real risks than are the scientists.
(B) Historical memory may in fact reflect patterns in these occurrences unfamiliar to scientists but known by the locals who have generations worth of oral history.
(C) Financial health and insurance may play a role in the decision to stay, and, if the worst happens, recovery is not financially devastating.
(D) Scientists and lay persons may be looking at entirely different data trying to predict the disasters and the choices of people.

Stressed Out: Teens and Adults Respond Differently

Stress can be compared with the pressure that a sculptor places on a piece of marble: the right pressure and it becomes a masterpiece, but too much pressure and the marble breaks into pieces.

The right amount of stress helps us to meet our goals and do good work. Too much stress can produce serious damage to the heart, the vascular system, and the immune system, and it also causes changes in some areas of the brain.

With support from the National Science Foundation (NSF), Adriana Galván, a neuroscientist at the University of California, Los Angeles (UCLA), is studying the effect of stress on brain function in adolescents and adults.

"Studies on stress and cognition across development have mostly focused on chronic, severe, and, often, traumatic stress, such as child abuse or neglect," Galván said.

"In our new research, we will determine what normative, daily stress, and associated stress hormones, do to decision making during adolescence."

When we are exposed to stress, the brain interprets the event as a threatening situation. The hypothalamus secrets adrenocorticotrophic releasing hormone (ARH), which stimulates the pituitary gland to produce adrenocorticotrophic hormone (ACTH). ACTH stimulates the adrenal gland, located on top of the kidneys, to produce adrenaline and cortisol, increasing blood pressure and heart rate. When the stressful situation is over, the hippocampus (in the brain) stops the production of these hormones so the body can return to its normal state.

Studies in animals show that chronic stress produces a decrease in the size of the neurons in some parts of the brain, such as the hippocampus and the prefrontal cortex, which are involved in memory and attention.

Chronic stress also produces an increase in the size of the neurons in the amygdala, the part of the brain involved in aggression, fear, and anxiety. These changes in the brain can influence one's ability to make decisions.

Other studies have shown that the decision-making process, in situations that involve choosing between a risky versus a safe response, produces high activation of the insula (in the brain) and that chronic stress can decrease the activity of the hippocampus and prefrontal cortex, weakening memory and attention.

The way an individual responds to stress can be very different based on previous experiences. Normally, a stressor factor, such as a project for school, turns on the stress circuit, and it is turned off again when the stressor factor disappears. This can change for different reasons such as repeated stressors, failure of an individual to adapt to the stressor factor, or defects that prevent the circuit from turning off.

Galván monitors the level of stress in her study participants four times per day. When an individual records high or low levels of stress, he or she immediately comes to the lab for evaluation.

Data suggest that the greatest sources of stress for teens are parents, while for adults stress tends to come from work or schoolwork.

There are also differences based on the time of day. While adults are most stressed in the morning, teens are most stressed in the early evening. Data also suggest that teens show greater cognitive impairment when stressed than adults.

Once the individuals come to the lab, their levels of cortisol are evaluated. Galván explained, "We expect diurnal patterns of cortisol release to differ between adults and adolescents and that this distinction will correlate with levels of stress. Previous work has shown that, under identical stress conditions, teens show greater cortisol release than adults."

Participants also get a functional magnetic resonance imaging (fMRI) scan that allows the researchers to see which parts of the brain are working during a specific task.

According to Galván, "We anticipate greater ventral striatal and ventral pre-frontal cortex activation during risky choices in the adolescent group, compared to adults. In adults, we expect greater insular cortex activity during non-risky (safe) choices. These effects will be exacerbated during times of high stress. In addition, we expect that adolescents will show greater recruitment of the amgydala during high versus low stress conditions."

The researchers predict that these findings will have a broad social impact. They will provide information to a broad range of specialists, including those in public policy, psychiatry, psychology, human development, and education.

472. According to the author, stress and hypertension can lead to biological stress and damage to various organs and systems in the body. Of the following, which was NOT listed as a system negatively affected by stress?

(A) Brain
(B) Heart
(C) Immune system
(D) Urinary system

473. The passage describes many ways in which stress may affect the brain and thus the functional capacity of the individual. Of the following, which would most likely illustrate the way in which stress may have a negative impact on the brain and performance ability?

(A) Test anxiety
(B) Performance anxiety of an athlete in a big game
(C) An individual awaiting punishment
(D) Financial burden

474. The amygdala is a deep region of the brain associated with control of several behaviors. Of the following, which was not a behavior listed in the passage that is attributable to the amygdala?

(A) Fear
(B) Aggression
(C) Pleasure
(D) Anxiety

475. As part of the sympathetic nervous system, the release of epinephrine (adrenaline) is rapid and systemic. Within the passage the author describes the sequence of hormones that result in the release of adrenaline throughout the body. Of the following, which is NOT involved in the adrenaline release pathway?

(A) Amygdala
(B) Adrenal gland
(C) Hypothalamus
(D) Pituitary gland

476. For soldiers, combat and the threat of death are among the most high stress situations to which a human can be subjected. In light of the passage, which would the author most agree is the best means by which the military can assist officers in high stress situations make the best decisions?

(A) Include high stress situations in their training.
(B) Repetitive training leads to actions and decisions being instinctual rather than intellectual and thus not easily effected by stress.
(C) Only have officers in combat who have demonstrated good decision making in prior combat situations.
(D) Choose officers who score the highest on psychological predictors for stress and decision making.

477. As the study illustrates, teens and adults respond to different stimuli with different levels of stress. Of the following, which is the most significant source of stress for teens?

(A) Parents
(B) School
(C) Significant other
(D) Friends

CHAPTER 22

Sociology

Making a Decision? Check the Data

Working in a data-driven business culture is a jargon-y way of saying, "We use science to decide what to do to reach our desired outcomes at work." Science is, at core, a method of logical inquiry and testing. The scientific method starts with a hypothesis—a hunch or a guess at what makes something happen. The rest of science is testing and analysis: Is the hunch the cause of the outcome? Is it the only cause? Is something else happening? If you have a hunch in science, you test it to see if it's true.

Data-driven business culture applies the scientific method to business decision making. It's an alternative to gut-instinct and "Highest Paid Person's Opinion" decision making, bereft of hunches, feelings, instincts, and personal preferences. Management must support this methodology, decision makers must have the knowledge required to use the data as input and feedback on their projects, and the data must provide reliable insights on which to stake business decisions.

Management Support

In a data-driven business, executives believe that their organization's success is based on doing the right things to achieve a measurable outcome.

We have leadership support already from some parts of the Broadcasting Board of Governors for web analytics—some editors set targets for their traffic and are evaluated on how well they meet those targets. At a strategic level, the BBG has emphasized establishing a set of key performance indicators (KPIs) that illustrate the impact the BBG has in target markets. Having these clear targets in mind lets everyone determine the most effective method toward achieving their goals, including identifying products that do not yield adequate results.

Education

In a data-driven culture, decision makers base their choices on evidence rather than hunches. They work towards targets, using metrics that tell them whether or not their project (or article or affiliation) is successful.

Here's an example of turning a gut-based decision into a data-driven one:

> Not data-driven: "I'm going to start a podcast about environmental issues because my boss told me to make a podcast about something, and I think I have enough to say about environmental issues."

> Data-driven (note the evidence, hypotheses, and goals): "I've noticed that we get lots of comments and questions about environmental issues when we include them in our general interest programs. Environmental articles get 100,000+ page views over several weeks after I post them, 30% of which are from one target country, so I infer that environmental issues are evergreen and have broad appeal AND specific reach in a target area. Any podcast we promote gets at least 45,000 downloads per episode, 40% of which are from that target country. I think that there's an audience for an evergreen podcast just focusing on environmental issues, and I expect that if I promote it in regular programming and on related articles, it could get at least 30,000 downloads per episode after 2 months of publishing them weekly."

Reliable Data

Trustworthy and readily available data fuels the data-driven decision-making process; data must be reliable, and stakeholders must review and analyze results regularly. In order to ensure BBG's web analytic data are reliable, we're undergoing an initial audit of our setup and will have maintenance audits to make sure data continues to measure activity in our target regions precisely and correctly.

Strong, relevant data on its own will not yield results. In a data-driven business culture, everyone is attuned to their data on a regular and systematic basis so they can identify outliers and trends over time. The most effective decision makers make a habit of monitoring their data, making changes to their projects in accordance with what they think will improve performance, and then observing if these changes caused the outcome they hoped for. Decision makers who do not look at the data throughout their project's lifespan forgo the opportunity to improve based on the feedback they could be getting.

478. Of the following, which would be the least important criterion for data when making business decisions?

    (A) Trustworthy
    (B) Systematic
    (C) Relevant
    (D) Available

479. In which context does the author use the phrase "highest paid person's opinion" in decision making?

(A) The boss makes the decisions.
(B) The best trained person makes the decisions.
(C) The financial officer makes the final decisions.
(D) Stockholders influence business decisions most.

480. A data-driven business is most closely comparable to which of the following?

(A) Teacher
(B) Accountant
(C) Scientist
(D) Doctor

481. Which of the following would be the main theme of the passage?

(A) Business as a science cannot be successful.
(B) Science can be a business.
(C) Applying the scientific method to decisions can improve businesses.
(D) Data management is a growing business opportunity.

482. Which of the following would most weaken the author's assertion about the success of data-driven decision making?

(A) Entrepreneurs recognizing a niche and profitably meeting that need
(B) Pharmaceutical company that creates a new beneficial drug
(C) Inventors working for years to develop a device that becomes popular and profitable
(D) Authors whose books in a new genre become overwhelmingly popular

483. In the final paragraph, the author states that the most effective decision makers utilize a definite sequence of activities to help them be successful. Of the following, which most closely resembles that plan of action for these decision makers?

(A) Risk versus reward assessment
(B) Scientific method
(C) Business model of supply and demand
(D) Mathematical algorithm for cost versus profit

Ending Child Labor

Global social movements have proven we can end child labor. An ambitious social movement to eradicate child labor globally came together two decades ago—and has enjoyed unprecedented success. Civil-society organizations in over 100 countries on every continent launched a Global March Against Child Labour in 1998. The march crossed 103 countries and culminated in a conference at the International Labour Organization (ILO) in Geneva in June 1998 where activists called on governments, international organizations, companies, and civil society to come together to end child labor.

The ILO launched the World Day Against Child Labour in 2002. Each year on June 12, the day brings together governments, employers' and workers' organizations, civil society and millions of people from around the world to highlight the plight of child laborers and what can be done to help them.

The movement is succeeding in its ambitious goals. In the late 1990s, the estimated number of children in various forms of child labor was nearly 250 million. Today, that figure has dropped to 168 million. The decline has particularly benefitted girls; total child labor among girls has fallen by 40 percent since 2000, compared to a drop of 25 percent for boys.

Child labor is defined as work that is hazardous to a child's health, education, or physical or mental development. Too often, it traps children in a cycle of poverty. Too many children in the world still work instead of going to school. For example, an estimated 98 million children worldwide work in agriculture. Children harvest tobacco, cocoa, rubber, and other global commodities. Children also work in dangerous industries like shipbreaking in Pakistan and Bangladesh, and in services such as construction and restaurant work. However, the U.S. Government has made a substantial contribution to ending this vicious cycle for tens of millions of children.

What Have We Learned About What Works?

Social mobilization and awareness-raising: Like so many of the world's 'wicked' problems, addressing child labor requires a concerted effort by multiple stakeholders acting together. Work to promote awareness of child labor among citizens and consumers in developed countries, and among families and communities in developing countries where children are at risk, has proven to be an important part of the solution . . .

Another very important part of the solution is mobilizing communities and empowering them to work at a grassroots level on practical solutions to address root causes of child labor . . .

Businesses are also an important part of the solution to the child labor problem. Awareness-raising campaigns have succeeded in flagging this as a business issue for many companies worldwide in many industries, and those companies and industries are working on innovative new approaches to ensuring their supply chains do not exploit workers . . .

Finally, governments also have a very critical role to play in addressing child labor, through their role in establishing laws and policies to protect children, and equally important, their role in ensuring that all children have access to basic education.

484. According to the passage, "tens of millions of children" are subjected to child labor every year. However, the author describes this as a "vicious cycle" for children. What statement best exemplifies the meaning of the author and the choice of wording?

(A) Every year children are forced to work.
(B) Children forced to work are more likely to force their own children into the workforce.
(C) Year after year, the same children are forced to work.
(D) Child labor occurs in the same country every year.

485. The author is clear that when children work there are detrimental consequences for the child. Of the dangers child labor presents that were listed in the passage, which was NOT mentioned?

(A) They have less access to healthcare.
(B) Children remain economically disadvantaged.
(C) They lack a proper education.
(D) Emotional development may be impaired or delayed.

486. Within the passage, the author details the global movement toward eradicating child labor worldwide. While progress has been made, which would the author most agree has been the reasoning for child labor to still involve over 160 million children annually?

(A) Children working is necessary for the survival of the community.
(B) Social and cultural acceptance for child labor is the norm.
(C) There is a lack of education of the negative consequences of child labor.
(D) Poor countries lack the resources to combat the epidemic of child labor.

487. Which of the following adjectives would best describe the attitude of the author as it relates to child labor as described in this passage?

(A) Informative
(B) Supportive
(C) Appalled
(D) Neutral

488. Communities and governments are working diligently to educate people about the dangers of child labor. However, the author also includes businesses in the list of entities that must be made aware and educated about child labor. Which would the author least agree is a motivating factor in businesses using children for their labor force?

(A) There are more children than adults available for a workforce.
(B) Businesses pay children less than adults.
(C) Businesses operate at lower cost in countries that allow child labor.
(D) Adults are more demanding about work place quality than children.

489. Based on the passage, which of the following statements would the author most agree represents the main theme of this passage?

(A) Child labor is a worldwide epidemic.
(B) For the future of all countries, worldwide child labor must be eliminated.
(C) Child labor must be eliminated through education and societal change.
(D) International laws must be passed and enforced to immediately halt child labor.

Respect for Sacred Values Is Key to Conflict Resolution

A team of researchers funded by the National Science Foundation is investigating the role of ethical and religious beliefs, or "sacred values," in motivating human behavior. The team's most significant finding is that individuals who hold sacred values are rarely willing to barter them for economic gain.

"It's easy to assume that all players approach the world with similar sets of rational choices, but ignoring or disregarding the sacred value frameworks across cultures may exacerbate conflict, with grievous loss of national treasure and lives," said Scott Atran, visiting professor of psychology and public policy at the University of Michigan Ann Arbor.

Atran is also a presidential scholar at John Jay University and holds a tenured position as director of research in anthropology for the National Center of Scientific Research in Paris. The Michigan-led research team included members from Northwestern University, the New School, Harvard University, and the John Jay College of Criminal Justice.

The team's research results suggest the "rational actor" theory that has dominated strategic thinking since the end of World War II is often of limited value in today's increasingly global world. The theory assumes adversaries model the world on the basis of rational choices that are similar across cultures. Most transnational organizations, such as the World Bank, NGOs and U.S. military and diplomatic services, still set policy based on the assumption of rational actors.

"The Michigan research on sacred values demonstrates some limitations of the 'rational actor' framework and could transform the way the U.S. handles some geopolitical issues because it provides scientific evidence for the role sacred values often play in decision making and in resolving conflict," said NSF Program Officer Robert O'Connor.

The researchers combined experiments, surveys, and interviews of students, refugees, settlers, and leaders involved in the Israeli-Palestinian conflict. They asked participants to respond to a series of proposed solutions involving compromises while measuring their emotional response and their propensity for violence. They found that most of the participants responded negatively if the proposed solution was an economic trade-off of some sort, responded extremely negatively if offered a trade-off along with some substantial material incentive, and responded more positively to a trade-off that also involved a symbolic concession.

"Our research tells us when there is a confrontation involving sacred values, then offers to give up or exchange sacred values for material incentives is taken as a deep insult, which only increases disgust and the moral outrage that inspires violence," Atran said.

The researchers' findings appear to hold true for groups outside of the Middle East. Scientists at Northwestern University and the New School recently replicated the study's findings for a conflict involving Hindus and Muslims in India and also Madrassah students in Indonesia.

The research results also appear relevant for sacred values not necessarily tied to an organized religion. In the U.S., many European-American hunters have sacred values concerning gun control while at least one group of Native American hunters did not. The Native Americans, in turn, had sacred values on issues of eminent domain and sovereignty. In another study, the researchers found that Amish and Evangelicals hold similar sacred values, but only Evangelicals translate them into political action, and only for a subset of issues. A key finding of all the studies is that sacred values do not correspond to a generalized tendency towards extremism or some set of personality traits, Atran noted.

Their work today suggests government leaders should discard the rational actors' theory in favor of the "devoted actors" when negotiating with groups such as suicide terrorists that live within a rigid framework of sacred values because they are willing to make extreme sacrifices with little or no guarantee their actions will result in success, material or otherwise.

"The utilitarian position of the U.S. may play into the hands of terrorists who turn it around to show that America and its allies try to reduce people to material matter rather than moral beings," Atran said. "A more productive strategy may be to allow moral alternatives that provide non-violent pathways of expression, even if they do not match our own moral values."

490. This passage deals with the importance of sacred values to the peoples of the world and how people from different belief systems resolve conflict, especially when their values are not aligned. Of the following, which best demonstrates what can result when sacred values are not aligned and resolutions aren't achieved?

(A) ISIS and other groups around the world
(B) Christians and Muslims during the crusades
(C) Native Americans and Colonists in the new America
(D) All of the above

491. The findings of research performed by a team is reported in this passage. Which of the following institutions WAS involved in this research?

(A) Yale
(B) Stanford
(C) Harvard
(D) Oxford

492. Based on the findings of the passage, which of the following would the author most agree would be the most likely means with which to resolve the conflict between non-Muslims and ISIS?

(A) Give them a country of their own.
(B) There can be no resolution for this form of extremism.
(C) Provide monetary ransoms for the hostages.
(D) Allow them a position of authority within a governmental system in which their voices can be heard.

493. The research groups surveyed a number of groups to learn about their motivations and feelings surrounding sacred values and conflict. Of the following, which might the author agree is a group, not surveyed, but that could yield interesting data?

(A) Soldiers
(B) Businessmen
(C) Religious leaders
(D) Local residents

494. The research results have led to a shift in the existing paradigm from "rational actor," which assumes that adversaries model the world on similar rational choices. The passage states that several businesses utilize this theory as a basis for their business operations and decisions. Of the following, which is NOT an organization listed in the passage?

(A) World Bank
(B) United Nations
(C) U.S. military
(D) NGO

495. The outcome of the research has been to shift from an older dogma and move to one that reflects the events and people of the global community. When dealing with the extremists of today, which of the following does the author believe governments should be using?

(A) Devoted actor
(B) Rational actor
(C) Utilitarian actor
(D) Terrorist actor

Why Contribute to the Good of the Group?

Would you refuse to house-sit for a vacationing neighbor if you knew that she never participates in the local PTA or neighborhood watch program? If so, according to a study funded by the National Science Foundation, you may be partly responsible for maintaining social order in your community.

The question addressed in the study is as follows: why do people engage in collective actions—behaviors for which an individual pays a cost to provide a benefit to the whole group—rather than simply freeload on the actions of others? Examples of collective actions range from villagers draining a swamp to limit disease to U.S. citizens paying income taxes to provide for the national defense.

"If the help and support of a community significantly affects the well-being of its members, then the threat of withdrawing that support can keep people in line and maintain social order," said Karthik Panchanathan, a UCLA graduate student and first author of the report. "Our study offers an explanation of why people tend to contribute to the public good. Those who do will be supported by other community members and thus outcompete freeloaders."

...Panchanathan and anthropologist Robert Boyd modeled four strategies that people might use in large-scale societal cooperation. The model has two stages: collective action and mutual aid. In collective action, individuals work for the good of the group, for example, helping to drain a swamp. In mutual aid, individuals help others in order to be included in future cooperation, for example, in helping neighbors with home repairs. Those who contribute to collective action gain good standing, and this good standing may influence others to help them in the mutual aid phase.

A "Cooperator," who will help the community drain a swamp AND help anybody with repairs, is using a strategy that will be eliminated by any of the other strategies. Nice guys finish last in this game.

A "Defector" won't help the community drain a swamp AND refuses to help anyone with repairs.

A "Reciprocator" won't help drain the swamp AND helps only those who have helped others with repairs—that is, he does not base his decision to help others on whether they helped drain the swamp.

A "Shunner" will help drain the swamp AND help others with repairs only if the others also helped drain the swamp. The Shunner is the guy whose strategy links action for the public good to whether or not a person gets aid.

Over time, a society tends to become made up of Defectors, Reciprocators, or Shunners. While Shunners can invade Defectors if the conditions are right, the opposite is not true. While Reciprocators and Shunners cannot invade the other, a number of selection processes can account for a transition from pure reciprocity (Reciprocators) to linked indirect reciprocity and collective action (Shunners).

496. As you read the passage and consider the different types of individuals based on their willingness and desire to help the society and help individuals, stereotypes will undoubtedly enter into your mind. Based on those descriptions, into which of the following would most people place politicians?

(A) Cooperator
(B) Defector
(C) Reciprocator
(D) Shunner

497. In the example from the passage of refusing to house-sit for the neighbor who never helps the PTA, which of the following explanations would the author most agree is how that refusal helps maintain the social order?

(A) The person will be punished for not contributing to the community.
(B) The defector will be forced to become either a shunner or cooperator.
(C) The defector will be forced to become either a reciprocator or shunner.
(D) The person will be ostracized from the community.

498. Which of the following would the author most agree is the main theme of the passage?

(A) The give and take of social order in the modern world
(B) Members of society all contributing to the whole in one way or another
(C) Individuals choosing what programs and individuals they will assist
(D) Society dictating how people contribute to a group

499. In the U.S., a record number of individuals are on the welfare and assistance roles in the country. In light of the passage, how are these individuals contributing to the greater good or the society and into which group would they be placed (generally speaking).

(A) Cooperator
(B) Defector
(C) Reciprocator
(D) Shunner

500. In several states, laws are being proposed and enacted that will require people on the welfare rolls to volunteer in the community, and/or obtain training/education in order to raise themselves off the welfare rolls. In light of this passage, these programs are attempting to shift these groups into which role of society?

(A) Shunner to reciprocator
(B) Reciprocator to defector
(C) Defector to shunner
(D) Defector to cooperator

ANSWER KEY

This answer key will provide you with explanations for the correct answer as well as indicate which of the three skills tested by the Critical Analysis and Reasoning Skills section is being considered by the question:

- Foundations of Comprehension
- Reasoning within the Text
- Reasoning beyond the Text

PART 1: HUMANITIES

Chapter 1: Architecture

1. (C) Foundation of Comprehension. This question asks you to recall from the passages those benefits the author confers to the presence of the post office within the community. While the post office is in fact a government office, the author states that it is more a symbolic presence (paragraph four). Additionally, the author states that the post office is one of the several government buildings that form the civic core for the community.

2. (C) Foundation of Comprehension. The designers of post offices incorporated their tastes and their status in society into the architecture. Certainly, city fathers expected a nice, updated, if not lavish, governmental office when these were built, a practice which did in fact cater to the egos of the government officials of the community. Of course quality materials would be used in the building of the post office. However, class in this case refers to societal station rather than the materials and furnishings being used. While people from lower economic status may have been unable to afford a mailbox or would frequent the post office less than middle or upper class individuals, this classism was in no way meant to exclude any social group. As with distractor B, government officials and designers, while typically from higher classes in society and thus the post office was a reflection of their tastes and community pride, in no way designed them to be exclusively used by a select few individuals.

3. (D) Reasoning beyond the Text. While the passage mentions the architectural design of post offices, their role in communities is at the heart of this passage. Several positive impacts on communities are listed in several of the paragraphs; thus, in addition to delivering the mail, much more is contributed to the community by the postal service. Choice C is a true statement and discussed in the body of the passage. However, as with choice A, it does not encompass the breadth of benefits mentioned in the passage. Thus, when compared to choice D, this selection is not the BEST response.

4. (B) Reasoning beyond the Text. As the author discusses in the passage, the post office is a gathering place for many individuals, especially those of smaller communities and rural areas. While the electronic age has minimized the use of paper mail, the post office remains necessary and continues to provide a central location within their communities for people to meet, interact, and find a commonality, even if just in a zip code. Regarding choice D, when considering the modern electronic messaging age, foot traffic at post offices will be much less than in past decades. Thus, the influence of the post office on economic development would be less today than in previous years.

5. (A) Reasoning beyond the Text. This is a somewhat tricky question. However, based on the nostalgia with which the author writes as well as the fact that the post office does far more than just send and receive mail, the author would likely agree that the modern post office still serves many vital roles for its community and still does so better than any of the other choices could for the same community.

6. (C) Reasoning within the Text. This passage is clearly about the architectural history of the post offices in the United States. It does in fact lend itself to being a purely informative article. However, throughout the passage, the historical connotations, the reference to fine materials, and art, paint a more glowing picture of the buildings of the past rather than the functional ones of today. Thus, the author is found to be rather nostalgic (as well as informative) throughout and results in this being the best selection for this question.

7. (A) Foundations of Comprehension. While in all likelihood, affluent countries will be better able to build ever larger structures, this was not among those listed as being representative of Big Buildings in paragraph four. Of the remaining list, stability and longevity were specifically mentioned in the passage. Although power was not spelled out in the passage, it is an appropriate synonym for strength that was listed. When reading through the passage, make mental notes of lists not only for the specific wording used but also the meaning the words convey.

8. (C) Foundations of Comprehension. This passage introduces the concept behind the new TV program "Building Big." However, it does more than simply provide the background and the concept for the show. It continues to also introduce the topic of an episode on the Brooklyn Bridge. Take care not to speed through the passages and choices without considering the FULL passage and not simply excerpts, especially when considering questions on theme, objective, and main point of the passage. Each of the distractors can be found within the passage and some (such as the introduction to the "Building Big" TV show) are actually a major portion of the passage. However, when the choices are compared, the reader will realize that only selection C captures the full extent of the passage while each of the other choices are only selected portions that together could make up the entirety of the reading.

9. (A) Foundation of Comprehension. Many of these FOC questions are straightforward for those who carefully read the passage or, at most, require a quick look back at the passage to confirm your selection. This question, however, may have tripped up many of you. Each of the selections was discussed in the passage, yet only three were on the list in question. The correct choice (in this case a negative selection) was also a BIG building project and one which the author devotes much of the passage to describing. This may have easily led you to believe it was important and part of these Great wonders. Based on the list in the passage and the specific question posed, you must take care to critically understand the QUESTION just as much as you should carefully select the BEST choice.

10. (C) Reasoning beyond the Text. Each project, vehicle, and building listed could certainly be a target for awe and wonder in the modern age. However, the question is about which particular one would most likely be added to the list by the author. In our passage, the author mentioned BIG buildings, and we think immediately of skyscrapers. However, there is much discussion in the passage about the Brooklyn Bridge. Additionally, the five listed wonders are not all tall buildings but include a tunnel and a dam. Thus, we are left to reason that BIG can mean difficult, ingenious, almost impossible feats being made possible by the creativity and persistence of the human mind and collective. With the Mars Rover, the great accomplishments are in the distance that was spanned to bring us information on our nearest planetary neighbor. The rover itself isn't a massive machine nor is it technically unique in what it can accomplish. When considering the deep ocean, massive oil platforms that can house hundreds of workers or submersibles that can take humans to unthinkable depths are great achievements for mankind. Yet, each of these seems almost routine in this day and age when compared to the living facilities of the international space station. The time to completion of the livable facility, the number of countries involved in its construction, and the simple fact of the inhospitable vacuum of space as the surrounding environment would make it the most amazing of those listed and likely the choice of this author.

11. (A) Reasoning beyond the Text. This is another deeply thought provoking question that in a quick glance may have at least three selections that could NOT be easily eliminated. The passage goes into detail in paragraphs 10 and 11 about the inventions that made this project come to life. Certainly their ingenuity and creativity played a tremendous role in its success. However, after several personal and professional setbacks, John Roebling continued with the project. In paragraphs seven and eight, the author mentions the "ambition" of the architects, and the "fearlessness" of the workers, which clearly speaks to their internal drive and motivation. Finally in paragraph 13, a quote from the project director that says it was built upon "layers of effort" is the last bit of data needed to make the correct selection for this question. In the building of the Brooklyn Bridge, the needs of commuters and the economic benefit to the city certainly factored into the genesis of the project and the risk both financially and personally to the designers and workers of the project. However, these external motivators were not the best rationale for the completion of the project. Many great ideas and start-up projects sit uncompleted because of difficulties in financial backing as well as technical or physical obstacles that cannot be overcome.

12. (A) Reasoning beyond the Text. The Titanic has become iconic and representative of arrogance as well as of disasters in our modern society. However, that tragedy did not prevent other ocean liners from being built and transporting passengers across the oceans of the world. In contrast, the destruction of the Hindenburg brought air transport by dirigible to a complete halt that largely continues even today. When we see blimps in the sky, they are usually crewed by only a few people and do not function as a safe and effective means of rapid transport of passengers around the world. The other two selections, the Bent Pyramid and the Leaning Tower, are designs that could have been planned better; yet, they still exist today and thus were made well enough to stand (albeit leaning) the test of time.

13. (B) Reasoning within the Text. Faith is a term often associated with religion and religious practices. However, one can also have faith in an airplane when they board for a flight. In this case, Hughes was stating that the Supreme Court Building was an investment in the future of the new country. This was accomplished because enough people believed (had faith in) the new government to sustain itself that funds could be raised and appropriated to build a structure to house the third branch of our government.

14. (C) Reasoning beyond the Text. In this day and age of big government, it is a rarity for projects to come in under budget. Almost daily, the media sheds light on government excesses and how money is spent without thought about the expense and the final product. Thus, all features and size of the building likely would increase; however, a modern project for the federal government will be unlikely to come in under budget.

15. (B) Foundations of Comprehension. William Howard Taft was the 27th president of the United States and the only person in American history to serve as both president and chief justice of the United States.

16. (D) Reasoning beyond the Text. The Supreme Court of the United States has always been and will always be an equally important branch of our tripartite government. However, for seemingly practical reasons, the justices and the Court did not obtain their own separate building for over 146 years. While the author makes no direct hypothesis for such a delay, the knowledge that the court is made up of nine justices may assist in answering this question. It is reasonable to speculate that little room was needed for the Court, as compared to Congress or the presidential residence. With only nine justices, it may have seemed unreasonable and impractical to spend the amount of money, as required for Congress, on such a building.

17. (B) Reasoning within the Text. With politics, there may not always be a logical or practical reason for programs, projects, and decisions. Often, these are decided based on the influence, popularity, and promised future support of individuals. This certainly was the case for the Supreme Court Building. In paragraph four, the author mentions that, "Finally... Chief Justice William Howard Taft.... persuaded Congress . . ." Thus, his power, influence, and reputation as a former president of the United States was clearly the momentum behind initiation and completion of this important building.

18. (D) Foundations of Comprehension. In paragraph six, the author states that the Corinthian style was chosen to be similar to the architecture of the surrounding buildings, which would also include the Capitol. This was to denote the Supreme Court as an equal, albeit separate, branch of the federal government.

Chapter 2: Art

19. (A) Foundation of Comprehension. Ambiguity is a great strength to the artist when a smirk is used. Since this expression can mean so many things to so many people, it allowed for the personal interpretation by the viewer (which can also change depending on the emotional state of the individual when the painting is observed). Consistency of a smirk would only be applicable in the case where all portraits were of people smirking. Otherwise, this is one of the most openly interpreted expressions of all human facial expressions possible.

20. (A) Reasoning beyond the Text. Presidential portraits are historical works of art that will be displayed for generations to come in the White House and in museums. Thus, many display the same expressions of presidents of the past, which is the serious facial expression and accurately represents the seriousness of the position and the title of President of the United States. Models often do not show the full open smile, but smirks are in many photos of models. When compared, this would not be a better choice than A.

21. (D) Foundation of Comprehension. All of the included selections can be found in paragraph three except for calculating, which is the correct choice for this question.

22. (C) Reasoning within the Text. Sfumato as defined in the text as blurry or smoky is in reference to the inability to consistently interpret the expression of the *Mona Lisa* either from moment to moment or person to person. This ability of Leonardo was one of many ways in which he was a master artist of all time. Leonardo's mastery of color, light, etc., truly is unmatched in historical and contemporary art. However, this reference is about perceived emotion more than simply his technique to convey such feelings.

23. (D) Reasoning within the Text. While the focus of the passage is on the smirk as a means to equivocate emotion, it is in fact that emotion which the observer is unable to consistently capture in the expression of the *Mona Lisa*; so, the author can't determine if she is happy, bored, flirting, etc. As stated in the passage, with every glance her expression appears to change. However, it is not the smirk itself that is the focus but the emotion conveyed beyond the expression that is of frustration to the author.

24. (C) Reasoning within the Text. Enigmatic as used by the author in this passage may not be a term which you have encountered routinely. However, in the context of the passage, especially the discussion of *Mona Lisa*, among the choices, mysterious is the best selection. In that same paragraph, the author mentions the long line of authors who have written millions of words about her smirk. This would lead the reader to understand that the smile is not something easily defined and described.

25. (D) Reasoning beyond the Text. The fact that there is an article on the smirk versus the toothy smile demonstrates how important facial expressions are to convey emotion. In the case of the *Mona Lisa*, her smirk is frozen in time to be that mysterious expression left open to the interpretation of all who view her. In light of the magnitude of photos that flood social media today, the facial expression can speak volumes to the viewing audience and in all likelihood would be the theme of another passage from this same author on the importance of the smile/smirk in selfies.

26. (C) Reasoning within the Text. Jim Crow refers to the law that separated blacks and whites in almost every aspect of society. The paragraph goes on to exemplify this by the description of separate water fountains for the different races.

27. (B) Foundations of Comprehension. This label is clearly explained in paragraph three when it describes the sale of their art from the trunks of their cars along the busy highways of Florida.

28. (D) Foundation of Comprehension. These early African American artists, while not seen as noteworthy during their lifetime, have carved an important place for themselves in the history of America and of the African American people. A and B are certainly true of the human spirit in general and of that spirit which thrived in the Florida Highwaymen. However, the passage is about that and more. It is clearly about the specifics of this group of talented and brave men and women of the arts.

29. (B) Reasoning beyond the Text. In the same way that the Florida Highwaymen went to great lengths and distances to have their art displayed and appreciated, many minorities and inner city young artists will use any blank wall within their reach to display their art or to send an artistic message of their passion or cultural or political beliefs. This is not unlike the protests of the Highwaymen by selling their art in places that were largely off limits to African Americans of the day.

30. (C) Reasoning beyond the Text. Much like any commodity available today, when the demand outpaces supply, the price goes up. Likewise, when an interest in a particular work or works of a certain artist goes up, so do the prices of their works of art. This would be the case of the Highwaymen who had stopped painting while the demand for their works increased. Although articles in *The New York Times* in fact did introduce much of American to the Highwaymen, that exposure alone would not have been sufficient to cause the increase in value of the paintings. However, it did increase the demand for the limited supply of the paintings.

31. (C) Reasoning beyond the Text. Throughout the passage, the author talks about the hardships of the Highwaymen, the quality of their art, and their movement throughout the south. While the art does elicit an emotional response, the passage speaks to the content of the art as landscapes. Thus, while one may be inclined to select all of the above from a personal visceral reaction, if you consider the question in light of the passage the best choice would be C. This selection encompasses both the quality of selection A but also enhances their amazing contribution by the fact that they didn't always have an abundance of supplies and materials.

32. (D) Foundation of Comprehension. All of the benefits present in the list can be found in paragraph two of the passage, with the exception of selection D. In paragraph five, there is a reference to the "busy-ness" of life; however, that is how a natural free flowing dialogue can be established in a museum as opposed to amid the busy-ness of life that interferes with conversation normally. Thus, D is the best selection for this question.

33. (B) Reasoning beyond the Text. Students can learn and be exposed to a wide variety of experiences through programs, online-interactive programs, traveling exhibits, and guest speakers and demonstrations. However, to approximate the similar experience of a museum visit, along with parents and adults, the trip to a local, albeit small, zoo is one of the closest experiences for children from small rural communities. This would provide experiences with unique animals as well as the interaction with adults as mentioned in the passage. Likely, all of the other selections mentioned would provide the students with some experience but without the presence of many (if any) parents along with the students.

34. (A) Foundation of Comprehension. Certainly levels of interest may be similar for adults and children while they are exploring a museum; however, it most likely will be on a very different level. In a similar way, communication will not always be the same for adults and children as the kids usually are busy exploring and not always paying attention to adults (especially parents and teachers). This leaves the final two selections to logically deduce the best response for this question. However, if you were reading carefully, you would have realized that selection A was specifically addressed in paragraph three of the passage.

35. (C) Foundations of comprehension. In paragraph four, the author states that intergenerational learning is where adults and children grow together through the learning experience. It's more of a communal learning and sharing than simply adults asking students what they like. In this way, both the adults and children are learning, sharing, and experiencing at the same time, yet, in their own unique way.

36. (D) Foundation of Comprehension. The author interviews curators from "Blue Star" Museums (as mentioned in the first paragraph) for her article here. However, it isn't until the fifth paragraph that she defines what Blue Star actually means, which is an organization to provide experiences for families of soldiers about to deploy. Thus, of the selections, only D was not mentioned nor does it fit the definition of Blue Star from the passage.

37. (B) Reasoning within the Text. This may have seemed like an easy and/or a trick question, and in a way it is. Certainly the main theme of the passage is the benefit of taking kids to the museum. However, from the passage, we see that it's not the museum itself that is the important facet of the learning and interaction that occurs. What is actually important, as the author states in paragraph four, is sparking an interest in history, art, and science. While this can happen at a museum, it can also happen in many other settings. Thus, B is a better choice than the simple and almost too obvious selection of A.

38. (A) Reasoning within the Text. *The Apotheosis of Washington*, in the case of George Washington, elevates him to the highest level, almost to the point of deification. Sitting in the midst of parted clouds and surrounded by patriots of history, one can see how this high level would be appropriate to the first and possibly the greatest President of the United States.

39. (D) Reasoning within the Text. Each of the selections for this passage are impressive in their own right. However, while the size, the speed, and the location of the painting are remarkable, the fact that Brumidi did the work at 60 years of age make this all the more impressive. This fact was pointed out by the author in paragraph two when he mentions that he was 49 years old when he accepted his first Capitol assignment. Additionally, throughout the passage, the author comments on the 25 years Brumidi dedicated to the effort. Thus, time, tireless work lead the reader to believe this was what most impressed the author about Brumidi and his work.

40. (B) Reasoning within the Text. While there is no clear explanation for Brumidi's immigration to the U.S. from Italy (paragraph two), based on the information in the passage, we know that he immigrated to the U.S. in 1852 at 47 years of age. Likely, he was an established artist in his own right in Italy; however, the freedoms and opportunities in the U.S. in the 1850s were unique for the world and likely were the key attraction to the U.S. even before he was offered the painting of the Capitol Building (two years later).

41. (D) Reasoning within the Text. Over the 25 years of painting in the Capitol, there were many politicians who were elected and also left office. All of this change resulted in different artistic tastes and differing ideas on how the Capitol should look. Thus, the artist in charge of this project would need to possess the skills to not only paint, but to be able to work with people in such a way as to continue the project as originally assigned and not yield to every changing whim. Additionally, this would need to be done in a diplomatic fashion so that everyone could work together.

42. (C) Foundation of Comprehension. In the first and final paragraphs of the passage, the "august hallways" are mentioned as the location of the Brumidi Corridors.

43. (A) Foundation of Comprehension. The author clearly states in paragraph five that artists were hired to repair his art and that it was in an era before modern conservation. This implies that the artists were simply painting over damaged areas in the way they felt like the painting would have or should have been rather than trying to restore and reveal the work of Brumidi (which has been done since).

44. (B) Foundation of Comprehension. Working in Washington D.C. in the 1850s-1879 would have spanned the period of the Civil War (mentioned also in paragraph four).

45. (D) Foundation of Comprehension. Near the end of paragraph six, the author explains that it was the innovation of his projects that attracted the attention of the people at JPL and resulted in him obtaining the job, albeit with a six-month probationary period.

46. (B) Foundation of Comprehension. In paragraph three, the author highlights Good's piece "Beneath the Surface," in which he designed an interactive and immersive experience of walking into a room that resembled the clouds of Jupiter as the Juno spacecraft descended through the atmosphere.

47. (C) Reasoning within the Text. Throughout the passage, the author is clear that Dan Good's position is more than simply an animator and an artist. His knowledge of science as well as his creativity and artistic ability has allowed him to create illustrations and exhibits that truly immerse and educate the public about critical JPL and NASA missions in space.

48. (A) Reasoning beyond the Text. Through creative and unique vehicles, Dan Goods has the ability to connect with the layperson in a way to help them better understand and more easily appreciate the complex missions carried out at JPL. Given the highly technical training of those who design and implement the missions, the average person on the street would be entirely unable to understand those technical details. However, in the context of the natural world, everyone can visualize those parts of the mission illustrated and demonstrated by Dan Goods.

49. (B) Foundation of Comprehension. The lightning in the room was purposefully made by using light invisible to the naked eye. This could have been either infrared or UV, both of which are invisible. However, infrared light is detectable by most digital cell phone cameras and would appear when these were used by the visitors. Additionally, infrared in the amounts used in the room are far less hazardous than UV light exposure.

50. (D) Foundation of Comprehension. Even without the author's statement in paragraph one that "... he wanted them to feel it," the reader should clearly have arrived at the conclusion that through all of Goods' described projects, he wants viewers to experience and be in awe of the natural world. Thus, while he will use every technology available to him, the goal is the real and visceral response of the viewer much more than mastery of the art and the technology. Case in point, the soda-bottle pipe organ didn't require great expense or advanced technology; however, people who experienced that exhibit were likely left with a long-lasting memory and a clear understanding of the organ's operation.

51. (A) Reasoning within the Text. Regardless of the field of science, Goods was an expert at taking the "big ideas of science" and making them something "meaningful" for the average person. This was his statement at the end of paragraph five, and whether it was gene expression throughout mouse embryonic development or the appearance of the clouds of Jupiter (which resulted from mountains of data returned to Earth from the Juno spacecraft), Goods was able to simplify and convey meaning to the casual observer.

Chapter 3: Dance

52. (C) Foundations of Comprehension. As stated in the passage, the East side of Austin is a low-income area which would typically make exposure to modern art a difficult proposition at best for the people living in that area.

53. (A) Foundation of Comprehension. The final paragraph begins with the single word "exposure." This was the key aspect of what Ballet East set out to accomplish—the exposure of dance to as many students as possible.

54. (A) Foundation of Comprehension. As stated at the end of paragraph three, "Seeing dance live keeps their attention better than viewing a tape."

55. (C) Foundation of Comprehension. Since the focus of the passage is the functioning project of Ballet East, this should have been the first selection that caught your attention. It goes further to state what this particular exposure to the arts facilitates. Thus, this is the best selection for the passage. Exposure to the arts does not guarantee that an interest will develop; however, without exposure at some point, an interest simply can't develop. As with many areas and topics, including an interest in science and math, exposure at an early age greatly increases the likelihood of success. However, many of the students went to their first live performance when in the 11th and 12th grade and thus early exposure is not a focus of the passage.

56. (C) Reasoning within the Text. While most of the distractors would be valuable goals for Ballet East, the primary goal as stated in the passage was "… creating a new generation of dance audiences." Thus providing a means with which to promote an interest in the arts was the focus of this project.

57. (B) Reasoning beyond the Text. While many students were exposed to modern dance through the program, it was specifically directed at the students who might pursue a career in dance. While the directors would hope more students would develop an interest in the arts, they are more focused on the performers. If none of their students ever worked in dance, that would indicate failure of the program.

58. (B) Reasoning within the Text. Although the passage specifically deals with people using dance as a psychotherapy, it would not be restricted to only those who were having a dire psychological experience. Certainly individuals who have been abused may close off from other people and be unable or unwilling to communicate their feelings and dance may be a safe vehicle with which to do so. However, throughout the passage, psychotherapy is used as a means in which to help anyone and everyone who has difficulty within their own skin to be able to express themselves. Thus, selection B and its broader range of individuals who could benefit is the better answer than selection C.

59. (D) Reasoning beyond the Text. This question challenges the reader to apply what was learned in the passage to their own knowledge of physical therapy. In this case, much of what is described as benefits from dance therapy can be used to compare and contrast with what you know from physical therapy. Choice A may have distracted you (as intended). Physical therapy does in fact deal with increasing range of motion and strength; however, dance therapy was stated to NOT be about dance technique. Rather, dance therapy was about the connection to others and the emotional safety and freedom to express oneself.

60. (C) Foundation of Comprehension. While strength and better cardiovascular health are collateral results of dance therapy over time, that is not a major goal as stated in the passage and would be the best NEGATIVE selection for this question. Care must be taken not to confuse words with meaning. Strengthening positive feelings is a stated benefit of dance and may have been a distractor in this instance if you were moving too quickly through the section.

61. (A) Reasoning within the Text. In this modern electronic age, there are a number of ways in which people connect. While those virtual venues for interconnectedness exist, the author in the passage is describing the connection between groups of people in the same physical environment. Thus, selection A is the only choice that would allow for that physical as well as emotional "with-ness" that the author describes.

62. (C) Reasoning within the Text. The key to this question, as found in the passage, is the connection that dance therapy enables for an individual to fit into a larger group of people. That safety in numbers as well as the feeling that everyone is doing their own thing while the group is collectively expressing themselves is where the real value of dance exists. The actions of individuals who feel they are the best dancers and who are dancing to show the world their moves and to attract attention are diametrically opposed to the tenets expressed in this passage.

63. (B) Reasoning beyond the Text. As with learning, maturing, or building a business, change is that part of the process that must occur for successful growth to be complete. However, much like dance, change will be a part of our lives, throughout our lives as we grow internally and intellectually.

64. (D) Reasoning within the Text. To understand the meaning of the author in this sentence, when a word is not known, try reading the sentence without the word and let your mind fill in the blank. In this case "there could not have been a more...for the creating of a new center...," could have been "could not have been a better opportunity or a more fortunate series of events that lead to the creation of a new center."

65. (B) Foundation of Comprehension. While this is a comprehension question, it borders on being a reasoning question since Hill was the main topic of the passage and thus the reader may have assumed she was one of the greats of modern dance. However, while crucial to the establishment of the dance summer program, she is not listed among those other "Giants" who trained the dancers that carried the movement out into the world.

66. (C) Reasoning within the Text. The job opportunity at Bennington college came in 1932 "... in the midst of the Depression" as the author states in paragraph three. While the other factors listed may have contributed somewhat to her decisions, likely the chance to obtain additional money in the most difficult times was more of a motivating factor.

67. (D) Reasoning beyond the Text. Fall and spring terms for universities have been in existence for almost as long as there have been institutes of higher education. Thus, the most likely rationale for summer offerings was the availability of students who were not taking classes at their schools. This is supported by the fact that while 60 students would have been a successful enrollment, Hill ended up with 103 in the class before she closed it.

68. (C) Reasoning within the Text. Many people protect themselves from disappointment by always expecting the worst. However, those individuals are usually very negative and not enjoyable to be around. Most people do often expect the worst, yet they are hopeful for positive outcomes. This was the case for Horst. He didn't believe the program would last but he worked tirelessly to make it the best it could be and HOPED it would be successful.

69. (A) Foundations of Comprehension. The list of curriculum components can be found in the final paragraph of the passage. Of the selections, only A is missing from the listed topics taught in the summer program.

70. (B) Reasoning beyond the Text. While the Great Depression was a difficult time for everyone and men were working tirelessly to find and keep as many jobs as possible, in the 1930s, the vast majority of men did not view professional dance as a socially acceptable or profitable means by which men could live and support a family. This is clearly exemplified in the fact that two-thirds of the attendees to the summer program were female teachers, who in all likelihood would return to their institutions and teach dance. Had men been more involved, more of these teachers would have been men.

Chapter 4: Ethics

71. (D) Foundation of Comprehension. Through the avenue of interpersonal communication and education, the people of Yemen have begun to affect change in their society that will benefit their people and communities for years to come. Although A is certainly an important point that the author of this passage would support, it was never expressly mentioned in this passage. However, the details and theme of this passage are certainly a means with which that end may ultimately occur.

72. (D) Reasoning within the Text. The solution to this question is not overtly stated. However, in light of the fact that the statement of poverty in paragraph five follows that of marriages with no dowry in paragraph four, it is logical to link the two together. Although the remaining selections may be in fact reasons for a couple with a child bride to remain impoverished, these were never stated or implied in the passage.

73. (C) Reasoning within the Text. This passage was clearly about the problem (child marriage) and the solution (interpersonal, face to face education) leading to the positive outcomes. While this author may not limit any suggested approach to solving the problem, certainly he or she would support this approach given its success, which will likely be perpetuated in the culture through the coming generations.

74. (A) Reasoning beyond the Text. In the model community, the passage states that most are illiterate and implies that they are uneducated. With the delay in marriage age as well as the increased time for education, more females will gain greater education, increasing the likelihood of females playing a larger role in the decisions made for the community and society. Choice D may have been a selection made by many readers. Clearly this model of education and impact on a community will be used in other areas to influence the society and benefit women in a larger geographical area. However, the underlying impact and theme will be on educating the people leading to greater benefit and opportunities for women to become more educated and have a more influential voice.

75. (A) Foundation of Comprehension. This is a more difficult reasoning and comprehension question. Although poor health of infants born to child brides is mentioned in this passage, when compared to the other selections, which were clearly stated in paragraph five, this appears to be the least favorable choice. Additionally, the poor health of these infants is due to the young age of the female whether she is married or not. Thus, this statistic and factor relates more to the age of the mother than to the age at which she is married and represents the best choice for this negative selection.

76. (A) Reasoning beyond the Text. From the passage, it is clear that the author opposes child marriages. These pilot programs are showing progress as exemplified in the increased age from 14 to 18. However, in the U.S., this is only the first time where females can independently marry. This age likely reflects the first period in which the girls may have some say in who they marry, but in all likelihood, the parents will pressure the child until they reach the minimum age and then force them to marry. Until the process is eliminated and all females have a free choice in who they marry, the author will likely not feel it has been fully successful.

77. (A) Reasoning within the Text. In the context of the passage, "longest" means anti-Semitism has occurred continually for the longest period of time while "oldest" refers to its early beginnings in human history before any other prejudice.

78. (C) Foundations of Comprehension. India was the only country in the list not to have been discussed as jointly speaking out against anti-Semitism in the passage. All other countries were mentioned in paragraph six of the passage.

79. (C) Reasoning beyond the Text. "Ancient" and "ugly" are direct terms that give vision to the problem of prejudice in general and anti-Semitism specifically for this passage. They also convey the deep-seated negative feelings that exist and how difficult these problems will be to unlearn and remove from society. These negative sentiments about people different from ourselves and the distrust and dislike that follows have been the foundation of many (if not every) war in human history. While the distractors are all true to various extents, the adjectives used in the passage refer to a historical context and one of shame as it relates to historical human nature and behaviors of the past based on prejudices. None of these fulfill those components better than selection C.

80. (A) Reasoning within the Text. Germany was not included in the section of paragraph two about violent anti-Semitism examples. An incident in Paris (France) was described, Sydney (Australia) was the site of an attack on Jewish children, and Casablanca (Morocco) was the location of a beating of a Jewish Rabbi.

81. (B) Foundation of comprehension. John Kerry, Secretary of State, and the tragedy that befell his grandparents was described in paragraph four of the passage.

82. (C) Reasoning beyond the Text. Hate and terror groups that are thriving in the world today do so as they prey on fear and on peaceful people who demonstrate little resistance or retaliation. However, the main thrust of their motivation is that their frustration with their lives that they see as miserable and downtrodden must have an outlet and a target for their external demonstration of vengeance.

83. (B) Reasoning beyond the Text. Staying informed and knowledgeable about the current state of our country's foreign and domestic issues is an essential task for every American citizen. However, the populous by in large have conceded the reigns of governing over to the politicians. Thus, even when informed, the majority of Americans do NOT accept an active role in any form of the governmental process.

84. (C) Reasoning beyond the Text. Today, the news is simply another entertainment program that is seeking higher ratings. Thus, there are many flavors of news and you can pick how you want your information delivered.

85. (A) Foundation of Comprehension. This was the only selection not mentioned in paragraph three as an important provision that the information from the media supply and assist the general public in decision-making processes.

86. (C) Reasoning within the Text. According to the author in the sections on reporting in Kenya, he attests to the motivated yet untrained volunteers that provide news. With the harassment discussed in the previous passages, it is most likely that these laypersons are unfamiliar with exactly what actions and consequences the government has the authority to enforce when it comes to the news and free media in Kenya.

87. (B) Reasoning beyond the Text. While the news (free press) has been rich with reports of all such activity by the federal government over the years, the most common, likely, and legal means to restrict the media is by determining who sits in on a press conference and news briefing and which reporters get to ask questions.

88. (B) Foundation of Comprehension. In paragraph six of the passage, visa assistance is the only service listed that was not described.

89. (A) Reasoning within the Text. Being sensitive in the reporting is a two-way street. Being sensitive to the will of the government as well as to that of the people is important. This will be successful if it is a balanced article that does not choose sides nor place blame on any particular group. Remember, it takes two people to have a fight. Thus, knowledge of how to get the information to the public without placing any personal bias or feelings in an article is very much a skill that takes training and practice.

90. (C) Reasoning within the Text. The Great Depression lasted from 1929 until 1939 and was broken only by the industrial demand of World War II. However, in his address of 1933, President Roosevelt was instilling confidence in the American people that in this darkest hour, there was hope and that there was a plan. The financial resources of the United States of America had not vanished, they had simply been mismanaged by the banking industry and could be recovered through the work and industry of the American people. Thus, the financial rescue for the American people was close, and it was up to them to make it happen.

91. (A) Foundation of Comprehension. In paragraph three, he states that happiness does not lie only in the possession of money but in (B) joy of achievement, (C) creative effort, and (D) moral stimulation of work. The quest for employment was actually a task on which far too many Americans were expending great effort, and they would have found little joy or happiness in that venture.

92. (B) Reasoning within the Text. Welfare states are unlikely to survive. When a government provides everything a populous requires, then that government is in a position to take everything away. Roosevelt was encouraging the people to persevere. He knew that through the determination, work ethic, and dedication of the American people, they would overcome the disastrous economic episode in our history and be the better for it. Furthermore, he knew that if the people were self-sufficient, such a tragedy would be far less likely to occur in the future.

93. (A) Foundation of Comprehension. Roosevelt was speaking to the American people as an equal citizen in the Republic. His message was not what the government could or would do, but it was more what the American people HAD to do to return to a place where individuals and thus a nation as a whole would be financially secure again.

94. (D) Foundation of Comprehension. Roosevelt suggested that the populations of the nation should be shifted to remove the employment burden of the cities and shift people into rural communities where there was an increasing need for agricultural resources. These would supply the growing nation as well as provide opportunities for more people and help stimulate the stagnant economy and inject revenue into the pockets of the American people.

95. (B) Reasoning beyond the Text. Bad loans that resulted in many foreclosures and bankruptcies for individuals eventually led to banks on the whole failing and filing for bankruptcy. The U.S. economy was teetering on the brink of collapse when the federal government began to infuse money into the failing banks in order to keep the economy from tanking and causing another depression. While the other events were detrimental or led to difficult economic times in the U.S. and in foreign countries, the banking failures were as close as the U.S. has come to another great depression (they called it a recession).

96. (A) Foundations of Comprehension. All of the following were proposed by Roosevelt in the final paragraph of his address with the exception of unemployment benefits. While these were certainly short-term measures to assist the American people (and never meant to be a means with which to exist for perpetuity), this would have gone against his measures to get people back to work.

Chapter 5: Literature

97. (B) Foundation of Comprehension. As stated in the passage, the best translations do not appear to be translations at all. The sound, tone, and wording of the translation can appear to be an original work. When this occurs, readers forget that it is in fact a translation in a completely different language from the original. This makes the work an art that is often unnoticed, thus invisible.

98. (D) Foundation of Comprehension. The importance of the work and the challenge of the task may both factor into the decision to accept a translation assignment for a literary work. However, the passage clearly states that all translations will be inherently flawed due to the subtle differences in languages. Thus, translators do the best they can in the translation to achieve as much as possible of the original author's sentiment.

99. (A) Reasoning within the Text. In paragraph six, the author goes into detail about "sound maps" and their use in trying to find similar sounding patterns as would have been created in the original language. Thus, languages that sound alike would make this a much easier task. All distractors used draw on the understanding of the reader in light of the difficulties of translating from language to language. However, only choice A was specifically singled out in the passage as presenting a unique challenge to the translation of poetry and thus is the best selection.

100. (B) Foundation of Comprehension. In this basic comprehension question, grammar is the only choice which would fulfill this NEGATIVE response. Some may confuse syntax with grammar; however, syntax also being a choice, grammar is clearly the correct option. All other choices ARE given in the text and thus leave choice B as the only negative response.

101. (D) Reasoning within the Text. Given that the work of translators is painstaking, time-intensive, and thankless, there is no wonder so few people translate literary works. The difficulty of the task in addition to the fact that the resulting work will never be exactly as the original author intended lend to the lack of literary translators in this country.

102. (C) Foundation of Comprehension. Yevtushenko was a Russian poet from whom she took the quote used in the final sentence of the passage. All other names were of those who had written materials that she translated.

103. (B) Reasoning within the Text. In the same paragraph (one) in which the statement occurred, the author goes on to describe Alexie's work and his preference for writing about the realities of contemporary Native American life and obstacles they face in society and on reservations. If you are moving too quickly and not fully and critically considering all selections, you may have selected A. It does in fact state many of the concepts of the passage; yet, it is a more generalized statement when compared to the most specific selection of choice B. As to choices C and D, while there may be truth to these statements, there is nothing to indicate so in the passage.

104. (A) Foundations of Comprehension. In the context of inspiration, Alexie distinguishes between individual occurrences (which a moment would be considered) and the inspiration that sets his mind to writing. All other selections were detailed in paragraph two as what inspiration really is to him. Inspiration could also be two of those smaller instances happening at the same time (i.e., phrase or line of dialogue).

105. (D) Foundations of Comprehension. While the distractors are true when considered individually, in the context of this passage about Sherman Alexie and his thoughts on inspiration, selection D is clearly the best choice.

106. (B) Reasoning within the Text. In the final paragraph, when describing the old abandoned mattress, Alexie goes on to say when you are at the bottom, you see everything above you. Thus this description of bottom to top lends itself to the comparison made in selection B. While each distractor is true in reference to the passage, B is the best selection comparatively speaking to the passage and the specific statement.

107. (D) Foundation of Comprehension. In the final paragraph, each selection was listed as inspiration for one of his stories except for the new house. In fact, he used that comparison with the old mattress to say that the new modern house was of no interest (no inspiration) to him at all.

108. (B) Reasoning beyond the Text. Alexie mentions in paragraph two that he writes down every observation, idea, and thought that comes to mind. This isn't unlike a scientist making observations or reading from the literature. However, he says that when two thoughts come to mind, that's when inspiration hits. Thus, two or more observations that lead to the formulation of a hypothesis would most closely resemble that idea in scientific terms.

109. (B) Foundation of Comprehension. Dodgson was Carroll's own pen name as also stated in paragraph one.

110. (C) Reasoning within the Text. The author does mention in paragraph one that Carroll's more serious writings were "inferior" in many ways to his more humorous works. However, he goes on to specify that these works were overly "sentimental." This suggests that his writings had a personal touch that while important to Carroll had less appeal to the general audience.

111. (D) Foundations of Comprehension. According to the author, "Hunting the Snark" is a very unique piece of literary work. While it may not have accounted for a new literary vehicle or genre, the uniqueness for Carroll was that the last stanza was written first in a moment of inspiration. Thus, as mentioned in paragraph two, the piece was written backward from the last stanza forward.

112. (A) Reasoning beyond the Text. In the modern digital age, the art and pleasure of reading is fast becoming a lost art. With online videos from professionals and amateurs alike, visual entertainment is by far more effective than textual communications of the day (we even have emoji rather than letters in text messages). Thus, *Alice* being presented in a visually rich means in the movies and on television likely accounts for its popularity and would likely gain the author's agreement.

113. (A) Reasoning beyond the Text. While people have searched for meaning in both the *Snark* and *Alice*, Carroll insists that both are total nonsense. The statement in response to his question in *Alice* is as nonsensical as the question itself and reflects his playful and humorous nature.

114. (C) Foundation of Comprehension. As stated in paragraph four, "Hunting the Snark" was released on April 1, 1876. The author suggests this was intentional by Carroll.

115. (A) Foundation of Comprehension. Gertrude Chataway was the friend to which Carroll dedicated this book. In doing so his acrostic poem included all of the above list with the exception of "stay" (he used away in the book).

116. (B) Reasoning beyond the Text. According to the passage, White spent much time alone, near the stable of his farm, and preferred the company of animals to people. Thus, it appears his own life was the inspiration for his fictional character Fern in Charlotte's web.

117. (D) Foundation of Comprehension. At first you may feel this is an impossible question (or unfair at the least). Possibly you haven't read *Charlotte's Web* and thus would not be able to answer the question. However, there is a solution simply based on the passage. Of the list, there is only one animal NOT mentioned in the passage and thus could be the only possible answer to this question. In fact, the RAT (Templeton) in *Charlotte's Web* is the only animal not mentioned in the passage from the list.

118. (C) Reasoning beyond the Text. In the original *Charlotte's Web*, everyone could see the writing in the web at the corner of the doorway in the front of the stable. Here it would be obvious and seen by everyone. Thus, the storefront on the busy street of New York would likely have been the setting into which White would have placed the character of Charlotte the spider.

119. (A) Reasoning within the Text. A gimlet is a tool used to make holes in wood without splitting it. Thus, along with the term exacting, the reader should be able to deduce that "cautious" is the statement of writing style that White preferred and did not perform well under the tight schedule of a newspaper deadline.

120. (D) Reasoning beyond the Text. As a child, the author states that E.B. White was always the "first" child on the block with a certain toy and always had the "best that money could buy." Thus, in this modern electronic age, he would always have the latest smart phone technology on the market.

121. (B) Reasoning within the Text. Just at the time White was looking for a forum for this writing, the New Yorker was looking for just such a writer. While this was in fact lucky, fortunate, and became profitable, it was at just the right time. Thus, the providential turn was most opportune for White.

122. (A) Reasoning beyond the Text. There is no indication that White was a prophet by any stretch of the imagination. Thus, the meaning of this passage must be found illustrated by facts other than the 911 tragedy. White found no attachment to the city, especially the people. In light of war, or nuclear attacks, city life may in fact be dangerous and lead to people living in rural areas for their own safety thus ending city life as we currently understand.

123. (C) Reasoning beyond the Text. Too often, readers equate "books" with reading. However, this could not be further from the truth. While society has a large appetite for the latest sound bites and memes online, the sale of digital literary works is a booming business. Thus, while the paper versions of books seem to not be in vogue, digital reading remains a valued pastime for millions of readers worldwide.

124. (A) Reasoning within the Text. This term is used in reference to the new digital age in which we exist, thrive, work, and play. However, the context is more than the medium used. She paints a vivid picture of the virtual world technology and how this has led to people being dispersed and rarely communicating face to face.

125. (B) Reasoning within the Text. Whether on paper or digitized, the words, feelings, and meanings of a book are identical. Thus, with this statement, Elizabeth Taylor is pointing out the different means in which people acquire those words.

126. (D) Foundations of Comprehension. Bette Cerf Hill says in paragraph four that her job was to get people to come to this part of town. Thus, as a leader of the planning board and an integral part of the festival planning, she played a role in using the festival to increase personal traffic in that area of Chicago.

127. (A) Reasoning beyond the Text. The human species from early ancestors have exhibited artistic ability. However, not all people are inherently artistic. There are in fact many who are completely unskilled in any artistic form. Yet, of that population, most if not all will find some form of art within which they identify and have an appreciation.

128. (A) Foundations of Comprehension. Hill mentions that the driving force that will bring the community together is not the act of reading (which is solitary) but is the enthusiasm for the written word. The ideas, feelings, and thoughts to be stirred in the reader are those things that can be freely shared, exchanged, and will unite a people with a common thread of artistic enjoyment.

Chapter 6: Music

129. (D) Foundations of Comprehension. John Adams is mentioned in paragraph one as one of the artists that a student had the honor of working with. He was not one of the artists mentioned associated with Internet2. Augusta Tomas may have been your selection if you failed to read carefully and critically. While not included in the list of artists on Internet2, she is mentioned specifically as having met with a student on Internet2 at the end of paragraph two. Choices B and C were listed as participants on Internet 2 in paragraph two.

130. (A) Foundations of Comprehension. During the time in the fellows program with the New World Symphony, all of the skills listed as selections were discussed except for composing. This is likely something that the fellows will do, but it is not a listed focus of the project and thus is the best selection for this negative response.

131. (D) Reasoning beyond the Text. Whether 10, 20, 50, or 100 years ago, live performances for an audience remain the same, fraught with the same perils and reaping similar rewards. Although decades prior, the fund raising, media interactions, and camera appearances were important, today these are essential, required, and emphasized to a greater degree.

132. (B) Reasoning beyond the Text. Teaching will always be a means through which music and musical talent and ability is perpetuated through the generations. This is as valuable a skill and as important an aspect of a musical community as developing the individual skills of the artists themselves.

133. (D) Foundations of Comprehension. This was the only professional artistic group mentioned in paragraph one in which fellowship graduates had become a part.

134. (C) Reasoning beyond the Text. By the time adults have completed college, much of their talent and skill has already been developed and programs like this one are able to further hone those talents into the higher quality expected in symphonic settings. Many children will display musical talent at early ages; however, to predict which will continue to improve and develop would be difficult at best.

135. (A) Foundations of Comprehension. In paragraph four, the Kuba people are stated to be from the Democratic Republic of Congo. Certainly this is a country in Africa and that may have confused you and gave you pause in thinking of Africa as a selection here. Remember, Africa is the continent, not a country. The other countries listed are simply random African countries used as distractors.

136. (D) Reasoning within the Text. The author mentions that some instruments were essentially works of art, impossible to be played. However, this was not a generalization, so selection C is incorrect. Also, while many were used in religious ceremonies and practices, not all were used in that way and thus selections A and B can be eliminated. This leaves D as the remaining choice, since the author stresses the importance of the music they produced.

137. (A) Foundations of Comprehension. While it is likely that many of these instruments found their way into South African culture, the lute is the one specifically mentioned in paragraph six as being the type found in South Africa. The other instruments mentioned were those present throughout other sections of the passage as indicative of other African regions.

138. (C) Reasoning beyond the Text. All of these expensive and exquisite items listed are likely to be used much less because of their value than similar items that are less expensive and/or ornately designed. However, in attempting to select one from this list of four, the vase and the piano are the two that are likely to be used much more than the other two items in the list. Additionally, while the passage describes musical instruments, it is also more importantly talking about items that have artistic value and the musical aspect is secondary. The piano would not be as likely to be distinguished in its look as much as in the quality of its sound. This may likely be the case of the violin. Possibly more recognizable as a rare and exquisite instrument, to the layman, it may appear as simply another violin. However, there would be no mistaking a Ferrari in any showroom or on the road. Thus, the sports car because of its value and its appearance is likely to be driven much less than other cars and also more likely to be displayed for others to see more than to give them a ride to work!

139. (B) Foundation of Comprehension. In paragraphs 9 and 10, the author states that slaves did not bring the musical instruments or any other personal items with them to America. Thus, their ideas, their songs, and their talents were what infused African musical culture into the fabric of America. While it is possible that Europeans or other travelers may have obtained these instruments and brought them to America, not just anyone can make music when given an instrument.

140. (C) Foundation of Comprehension. While much of the early portion of the passage deals with African musical instruments, it does so as a prelude to how African musical culture was infused into American society and music. Much more than simply the tone of the instruments, the musical style has become as much a part of American music culture as any other genre or social group.

Chapter 7: Philosophy

141. (A) Foundation of Comprehension. While the first portion of the passage sets the stage and provides the reader background on the author, more than half of the article describes Jean-Paul Sartre's perspective and virtual disdain for what he views as American culture as exemplified by the areas he visited. Although an existentialist himself, the article was not about existentialism in America.

142. (C) Reasoning within the text. Sartre's use of "footloose" referred to the mobile nature of American families and stood in stark contrast to the French and European culture in which families lived in the same location for generation after generation. All distractors for this question are plausible definitions of footloose in various contexts. However, in regard to the passage, footloose referring to the temporary and mobile American families he encountered is the best selection.

143. (D) Reasoning beyond the text. Given the view of Americans as footloose and inherently detached and mobile, to have visited areas in the country such as a town in the south with stable, nuclear families who have also lived on their land for generations would have been a more familiar and welcome sight for Sartre. Additionally, Sartre's view was not that of comparing rural to urban; rather, it was temporary versus grounded and stable. While Sartre was visiting the industrial wonder of the TVA, industrial cities may have done little to distract his attention away from the temporary towns he visited.

144. (A) Foundations of Comprehension. While much of the TVA focus was on power and industry, it is likely that the harnessing of water would additionally provide resources for water consumption. However, in this passage, drinking water was not listed as a value of the TVA. All other distractors were mentioned in the above passage.

145. (D) Reasoning within the Text. Sartre experienced the lack of connection of the workers for their town at Fontana as well as with the people in the four cities he visited. This detachment from the location and people allows for ties to quickly be severed if jobs and the economy provide better opportunities elsewhere in the country. Cities will surely have more of an identity the longer they exist; however, if the people do not provide the foundation for legacy and heritage, the connection will never be realized. Also, Americans are inherently adventurous, but moreover they are practical, hard workers who will do whatever it takes to provide for their families even if that means being extremely mobile. While true, this is not within the context of the statement made by Sartre.

146. (B) Foundation of Comprehension. A great philosopher of his day in Europe, Sartre was present at the TVA project as a journalist for a French magazine as stated in paragraph six.

147. (A) Foundation of Comprehension. Much of the text is invested in the description of the tour that took Sartre and his colleagues throughout much of the U.S. It was in their viewing of these great engineering marvels that Sartre made his assessment of culture and American life.

148. (B) Foundation of Comprehension. As stated in paragraph seven, the U.S. war department organized the visits from foreign politicians, writers, etc., in an effort to "show off" the great war effort of the mighty U.S.A.

149. (C) Reasoning within the Text. The Church had a tremendous influence over the governing and the society of the day. Thus, when the religious leaders feared the contrast between Averroës' ideals and their teachings, they quickly moved the public to condemn his teaching and ideas as controversial or even heretical (paragraph three). The distractors used here may have had varying levels of effect on his standing in the culture; however, they were not as clearly spelled out as was the struggle between philosophy and religion.

150. (C) Reasoning within the Text. All of the above choices likely had an influence on the development of Averroës' intellect and his world view as described in the passage. However, from the passage it is stated in the first paragraph that his father and grandfather were prominent scholars as well as religious figures. This educational and spiritual heritage was highly valued in these early cultures and likely allowed for all of the other choices to be correct and true as well. However, without this legacy, none of the others might have occurred at all and the world would have lost out on a great mind.

151. (A) Foundation of Comprehension. From the passage, it would be clear that had Averroës made the statement in choice B there would have been more than a banishment for such a heretical statement. The other statements, as described in the passage were opposed to the religious teachings of the day.

152. (C) Reasoning within the Text. Throughout the passage, we hear of the struggle between philosophy and religion. However, what is really occurring is the resistance of one group of people to allow themselves the possibility of other perspectives from what they believe. It was not a struggle between the institutions of religion and philosophy, and the author states as much in the final paragraph when he quotes Averroës: to ban philosophy would be "a wrong to the best sort of people and to the best sort of existing things." From the passage, it appears that the people are the scholars and the religious leaders and the things are philosophy and religion.

153. (D) Reasoning within the Text. Averroës as a philosopher would not have been an exclusionary. From his writings it is clear he was expanding on the religious ideals using philosophy to be more expository and inclusive. Thus, of the selections given for this question, the one that is most inclusive, open to the broadest group of people, would be selection D. The qualifiers of faithful, educated, scholars, etc., are the distractors in this case where the focus should be on the numbers: who would be the largest "best" group of people from the list.

154. (D) Reasoning beyond the Text. Regardless of the religion of the late twelfth century, his philosophical ideals would have been met with the same resistance and even hostility. Much of the foundational theology of Islam and Christianity are similar if not identical. Thus, the outcome for his life would have been very similar.

Chapter 8: Popular Culture

155. (B) Reasoning beyond the Text. Many players such as Alex Rodriquez are heroes and role models for adults and children alike and have an obligation to represent those things best in Americans. Alex chose to use PEDs and to lie about their use and has been punished for that indiscretion. In this passage about the oversight of baseball by the federal government, the author could easily have used this example. Although a scandal in baseball at the time, the Pete Rose incident wouldn't have garnered the attention of the author. In fact, at the time of the writing, this scandal was very well known. While another PED scandal, little else remains connected between the American pastime of baseball and the French spectacle of the Tour de France. Barry Bonds was an easy target for accusations of PED use for his capturing of the home run record. Little evidence has been produced other than these accusations to support their validity.

156. (C) Reasoning within the Text. Baseball and the federal government have co-existed with various levels of interaction for the lifetime of baseball. However, as "baseball grew into an American institution," the government had also grown into a powerful enough body to insure the influence was the will of the people who elected them.

157. (C) Foundations of Comprehension. In paragraph three, the author explicitly states that only a few players have ever been convicted of lying to congress. All distractors, while illegal in baseball and other sports, have resulted in the conviction of many players and coaches over the decades. These may have been convictions but none of which were acted upon by Congress and the federal government as a whole.

158. (D) Foundations of Comprehension. Paragraph four is about the court hearing of Roger Clemens on charges of lying to congress. Both Mark McGwire and Rafael Palmeiro were mentioned in paragraph two as giving testimony before Congress, but they were not charged with perjury. Barry Bonds was not mentioned in the article.

159. (D) Foundations of Comprehension. Baseball was becoming an ever increasing part of the "national identity." This would have an impact on the younger generation as well as reflect the integrity and ethics of the nation as a whole through the example of the players. All selections are plausible reasons one may have for investigating and maintaining the levels of ethics and integrity of the huge industry of professional baseball. However, only choice D was expressed in the passage.

160. (B) Foundations of Comprehension. In the final paragraph of the passage, the author makes the interesting statement that the archives which contain these legal documents can be "profitably researched" in the records of Congress.

161. (A) Foundation of Comprehension. As listed in paragraph four of the passage, credibility, authority, and likeability may all be lost when conversational journalism is attempted unsuccessfully.

162. (B) Reasoning within the Text. This statement relates directly to the choice of which informational items are newsworthy and should be broadcast and which are not. Editors in the newsroom used to make these decisions. Today, each individual with a computer and a Twitter, Facebook, or Instagram account can be a purveyor of news items of their choosing.

163. (C) Reasoning within the Text. Although crowdsourcing may be an unfamiliar term to you, you likely have been a participant in this activity on social media. Adding your comments, descriptions, video, or photos about or to a news item is this new means of conveying information through the vehicle of social media and/or the Internet.

164. (B) Foundations of Comprehension. This is in fact the opposite of one of the suggestions made by Marchionni in the list at the end of the passage. Putting reporters on video engages the audience, humanizes and personalizes the reporter which is a positive in conversational journalism. All other selections are present in the list of recommendations listed.

165. (A) Reasoning beyond the Text. TV anchors of the 70s, such as Walter Cronkite, were held in high regard as being a part of the fabric of America, trustworthy, looking out for the best of what this country was founded upon, and the news stories were those which were needed to keep the American people apprised of events in the nation and world. On any of the three networks, you could expect to see stories that were 99% the same and presented practically from the same apolitical perspective. This yielded a feeling of simply conveying the information without political interjection, opinion, or skewing toward a preference or agenda. That fostered a trust and dependence on those individuals that is largely missing today.

166. (A) Reasoning within the Text. The author states in paragraph five that the "gatekeeper" no longer sits in the newsroom. She is speaking of a news editor or producer who directs the stories and the timing in which they are delivered. Today's Internet news is customized by the reader into what news to view and when to view the stories.

167. (A) Reasoning within the Text. From the passage, we see the author describes the "Mastermind" as that entity that forms when two or more minds come together in the creative process and result in a combined, yet separate result and can be stated as two minds are better than one. In the paraphrased statement in selection A, the product is greater than simply the sum of its parts is a direct correlation to the statement made by the author. The author introduces the reader to the concept in paragraph one; yet, he defines the term and concept better in the next paragraph.

168. (C) Reasoning beyond the Text. For the creative process, there is always a goal or objective that the collective is working toward. In the case of our selections, all choices are groups or organizations that are works in progress. Whether it is decision makers debating a budget, a boss obtaining data and input before making a major decision or stock brokers carefully weighing the risk versus gain options, they are all part of this creative process. However, C, the ineffective committee, would be an illustration of how this group creativity process would have failed. In all likelihood, the process is not flawed in this case, the failure would be the result of the individuals not working together (as is often the case when groups fail to achieve a goal).

169. (C) Foundation of Comprehension. The entire passage is about creativity and innovation; thus, it would be natural to make this connection between choice C and the validity of the question. However, after careful reading, recognizing the list of networks in paragraph seven, you should have immediately recognized all of the networks as being discussed and listed there with the exception of the innovation network.

170. (D) Foundation of Comprehension. Much of this passage it spent detailing the medium of the Internet as the modern creativity pool into which analysts dive in order to glean relevant information from the resources of the world. However, the real underlying message that becomes clear toward the end of the passage is not the means (the Internet) to the end (creativity); rather, the message is how human creativity and innovation is the driving force behind the advancements we see in society and culture. The Internet has only allowed for the growth of these resources to be more readily available.

171. (D) Reasoning within the Text. As the information analysts data mine the vast expanses of the global Internet and social media, they encounter a mountain of information, much of which is not relevant to their particular interest. Thus, while each of us has experienced first-hand all of the adjectives from this list in our social media news feeds and public posts, the real meaning here for the "noise" would be meaningless information for the analysts and is data that is ignored in order to more quickly find the useful information.

172. (D) Foundation of Comprehension. In paragraph six, Jack Matson is quoted as saying, "… cultures are innovation driven." Even if you missed this quote in the passage, this was taken from his book entitled *Innovate or Die*. Thus either would have helped with this selection.

173. (B) Foundation of Comprehension. While some may view graffiti as criminal and unpleasant, the author states that tourists thought that the art on the subway trains was "quite charming," rather than the plain grey color typically seen on the railcars.

174. (B) Reasoning within the Text. In the passage, a description of street artists who sought only to destroy the work of others is given. For these individuals, it was not about the art, but about the deed. In fact, the author states in paragraph four that "if they destroyed something nice, everyone was talking about them…" Thus, street art is for the notoriety and fame and not simply for the art.

175. (A) Foundation of Comprehension. Jennifer Kreizman was the only person not mentioned in the list of first street artists in paragraph seven. In fact, Jennifer Kreizman is the author of this passage. Familiarity with a name should not lead you to a false sense of confidence in making a selection. Rather, as you read the passage and map out lists and details, make sure to note the author's name and gender.

176. (D) Reasoning within the Text. While there is discussion in the text of artistic display as well as the fame obtained by elite artists who perform "epic deeds," paragraph three is very clear that the thrill of street art is "knowing that you were naughty and you got away with it." This is not unlike the feeling of most criminals in the events leading to their crime. The difference here is that the art remains.

177. (B) Reasoning beyond the Text. Lady Pink attempts to justify street art as a rebellion that is essential for society to grow. Her statement speaks to change for the sake of change as essential for the beneficial evolution of society and makes the argument that the American Revolution lead to our country. However, the American Revolution was about lack of representation in the governance of the colonies and its people. It was not merely for the sake of "something different." Thus, her hypothesis falls apart in light of the motives of each group.

178. (D) Reasoning beyond the Text. For all its beauty and beautification of plain areas, street art is still a criminal activity (unless permitted by the city) that has consequences for the artists. If their efforts were directed into more socially accepted venues, their work might very well lead to the fame and notoriety they seek. However, that path requires dedication, sacrifice, and time. In modern society, these past few generations have grown more and more accustomed to immediate gratification.

179. (A) Foundations of Comprehension. Lights are the only selection of the list not described in the next-to-last paragraph of the passage as materials used by street artists today. This may be due to the fact that lights would hinder their ability to conceal their illegal activity at night as they create their works.

180. (C) Foundation of Comprehension. You may have selected supportive for this question. While the author clearly is in support of allowing limited tweeting during a live performance, she goes much further in that she is excited about the possibility of doing so to enhance her own experiences as well as share with people unable to attend the live performance. Thus, C is the BEST selection for this question.

181. (B) Reasoning beyond the Text. Traditionally, the university classroom includes students taking notes while a professor lectures. Decades of this practice led to established and accepted etiquette within which the classroom culture functions. However, technology has introduced digital projectors (rather than chalk) and computers/tablets have replaced notes and textbooks. When used appropriately and for the specified tasks, these can enhance the learning experience just as tweeting can for watching a live performance.

182. (A) Reasoning within the Text. The author is very clear in her enthusiastic support of live tweeting in the theater. She is also equally clear that as long as it enhances your experience and does not distract others, it should meet specific but limited constraints. In the passage, the author directly or indirectly supports all with the exception of the time limit on tweets. The desire to tweet will clearly be related to significant events during the play which will be different for each individual.

183. (B) Foundation of Comprehension. In the opening paragraph, the author states that technology allows artists to "utilize Twitter to engage a broader audience." Additionally, the last sentence of the first section refers to "sharing the performance by hashtag for a whole other audience over the Internet." Clearly these are directed at those not in attendance.

184. (A) Foundation of Comprehension. In paragraph four of the passage, the author notes that while tweeting is a way to share the experiences with those unable to attend events, care must be taken to not do so in such a way as to be distracting and disrespectful to the performers or the live audience members.

185. (C) Reasoning beyond the Text. While most of the list is in practice in the theater and classroom, the most important on the list would be selection C. This is a rather inclusive listing that when considered as an umbrella guideline will influence many specific activities while in the theater or classroom setting. If more people would consider this as an important rule, the theater and classroom would always be an enjoyable and effective setting.

186. (C) Foundation of Comprehension. Regardless of the specific details of the event, even the repetition of the act, if there is no intent of the accused to do harm, then there is no bullying. Often jokes among friends do not end well and the victim does not find the humor in the act. While this may be seen by others as bullying, without the intent to do harm, it is simply an accident or an ill-timed and poorly planned joke.

187. (C) Foundation of Comprehension. Of the list given in paragraph three, video messaging was not listed. However, YouTube, Vines, etc., are clearly vehicles through which cyberbullying can occur.

188. (B) Reasoning within the Text. While a physical bully would not always demonstrate a greater intelligence over the victim (in fact it's usually reversed), in cyberbullying the author states that often a "greater technological expertise" is a means through which to gain an imbalance of power over another and enable cyberbullying.

189. (A) Reasoning beyond the Text. As we have seen in many videos taken in recent months of the riots in various cities, the vast majority of those acting out and looting businesses wear masks. In all likelihood, if masks were not available, knowing their identity would be discovered, most would NOT act in that manner and break the law. The anonymity emboldens the perpetrator and provides somewhat of a shield against the negative consequences they understand should be levied upon them.

190. (B) Reasoning beyond the Text. The author describes the lack of social cues that prevents virtual communication from being most effective. These can be a smile or a wink that may not be seen through an email or texting. Thus, in light of those comments, video chatting so the individuals can see those facial cues may help reduce or eliminate misunderstandings that arise through routine virtual communication.

191. (A) Foundation of Comprehension. While a sense of anonymity may in fact be present and lead to cyberbullying, it is not a requisite factor for cyberbullying and is impossible for real world and face-to-face bullying.

Chapter 9: Religion

192. (B) Foundations of Comprehension. In paragraph one as the categories of Buddhists are defined, Zen Buddhism is defined through meditation and mindfulness. When lists are encountered in passages, summarize in your mind and take keys with you into the question/ solution section which will minimize your need to return to the passage to review. Accuracy is critical in the CARS section; however, speed is also crucial for the completion of this section. You MUST balance speed and accuracy without sacrificing either too much.

193. (B) Reasoning within the Text. Based on the passage and the teachings of Buddhism, Americans view this religion as peaceful and all inclusive in that all living things are important and all living things may have both a positive or negative impact on all others.

194. (C) Reasoning within the Text. This statement about indirect Buddhism is in paragraph two and is followed by a discussion of the use of meditation in dealing with stress and improving health of individuals. This is the best selection for this question. Selection A may have been your choice if you were moving too quickly through the answer selections. Choices B and D can be easily eliminated, leaving A and C. The difference between the two is the reference to religion. While certainly an indirect practice with Buddhism would not preclude someone from practicing a different religion, this passage is specifically talking about using the teachings and practices of Buddhism in a nonreligious manner.

195. (C) Reasoning within the Text. In paragraphs 11 and 12, the author is clear that the multitasking society in America presents a clear and very real obstacle to those who wish to practice meditation as described in Buddhism. In every aspect of American life and culture, multitasking is the norm, and it is rare to find Americans simply being much less meditating (Americans call that sleeping). The author does mention the overwhelming popularity of Christianity when compared to other religions; however, in America we have Freedom of Religion and may practice in any way (or no way) that we believe it best without fear of retribution. For Americans, the greater flexibility of scheduling, meaning not going to church, would appeal to vastly more than would having to set aside communal time as is the norm in other religions. Thus, this statement would likely increase interest in Buddhism in America. With the Internet and instant access to information about any topic imaginable, lack of knowledge about a topic of interest simply is not plausible.

196. (A) Foundations of Comprehension. Paragraph four describes engaged Buddhism as more of an evangelical and externally influential practice than the others. From promoting peace to environmental advocacy, engaged Buddhism reaches out, whereas other Buddhist practices are more focused on the individual spiritually interconnecting in a peaceful and positive way to the living world.

197. (A) Foundation of Comprehension. This passage discusses the presence, the historical foundation, and the practices of Buddhism in America.

198. (B) Reasoning beyond the Text. Even without an understanding of the word, philia, meaning loving or favoring, the reader will be aware that the Zen (practice of meditation) is one that can elicit peace, harmony, and joy for the person.

199. (A) Reasoning within the Text. This may have been an easy selection given the press of ISIS over the past few years and their destruction of anything that is not Islamic. The existence of extreme religious fanatics is horrific in its own right, but the spread of this movement, largely allowed by many countries throughout the world, is beyond appalling. Selections C and D would actually greatly support the movement and acceptance of religious freedom in the world. Peoples of different religious practices peacefully coexisting would be the pinnacle of human achievement around the world. Choice B may have caused some to pause and consider if this is truly an example of religious freedom or in fact a move toward religious restrictions. In the media these laws to protect the freedoms of religious individuals (Christian, Muslim, etc.) is viewed as a license to discriminate. However, compared to the beheadings that are done in the name of religion by ISIS, this is clearly not the best NEGATIVE choice for the question.

200. (C) Reasoning within the Text. The writer of the passage clearly spells out the evidence for the role of the U.S. as leading the world toward religious freedom. However, this is not simply a news article; it clearly voices the positive aspect of all that the U.S. has done in the name of religious freedom around the world. While the tone is clearly not negative, the choice between positive and enthusiastic may have been more of a challenge for you. There are words used in the passage that illustrate the "commitment" to religious freedom and the "efforts" made by the U.S. government, but the words that would signify an enthusiasm for what the U.S. has done simply are not present.

201. (D) Foundation of Comprehension. This is another question in which, if you are moving too quickly, you may have erroneously selected the first choice that sounded reasonable: selection C. The main difference between C and D is in the description of the U.S. effort. In C the U.S. is said to "LEAD" whereas in D the descriptor is as a "vital role" in religious freedom. Nowhere in the passage does it say the U.S. is the leader and all other countries are following. Thus, C assumes that the U.S. is doing the BEST of all countries. Selection D, however, paints the role of the U.S. as vital to the more global effort from many countries to facilitate religious freedom and is therefore the best answer to this question. Although A and B may in fact be true, they are not listed in the passage. Additionally, the U.S. demanding these things from our allies likely would not be the best political approach to solving this global problem.

202. (B) Foundation of Comprehension. This selection is the only one mentioned in paragraph four about the role of embassies in the march toward religious freedom. The "support of victims of religion-based persecution" would be synonymous with providing aid to those persecuted individuals. The other choices to these questions, while possibly mediated through embassies, were discussed throughout the chapter as being services that come through the State Department.

203. (D) Reasoning within the Text. Much of the effort as described in the passage deals with education and training of people and communities to recognize and prevent religious persecution while promoting acceptance of all peoples regardless of their religious practices (or lack thereof). The other efforts listed in the passage and that are seen in this list of choices are additional means to minimize existing persecution and to penalize countries and people who fail to recognize the need for this level of acceptance throughout the world. However, if the penalties and negative consequences were the only means with which the world would attack the problem, little would change. The hearts and minds of the people, once changed, will take care of the rest.

204. (B) Reasoning beyond the Text. With global terrorism on the rise, particularly those of extreme Islam, there are countries that tolerate and in fact harbor those criminals in their country. However, while the Office of International Religious Freedom has the authority to demand economic sanctions against those countries, the U.S. has failed to do so.

205. (B) Foundation of Comprehension. When making your selection, you may have considered either Shiva or Nataraja for your answer. While Shiva is the god represented, Shiva may do so in one of three incarnations. Thus, the Lord of the Dance incarnation of Shiva as Nataraja is the best choice for this question.

206. (C) Foundation of Comprehension. Paragraph three makes it clear that Shiva only made appearances in an enshrined sanctum into which only "privileged" individuals could enter and commune with the god.

207. (D) Foundation of Comprehension. Worshipers in the sanctum who had seen and been seen by the god (experienced darshan) received grace from Shiva. This is detailed in paragraph three of the passage.

208. (B) Foundation of Comprehension. The only way for a worshiper to experience darshan (seeing and being seen by Shiva) was to actually be in the presence of the god. The passage describes the move to bring statues of Shiva to public events and in that way the god was able to be seen by many more worshipers.

209. (B) Reasoning within the Text. There is no definition of who belongs to the group called the Brahmin. The assumption immediately is that this is a very select group of people. From the list, we can eliminate the monarchs and the priests because in paragraph three, they are listed as two of the three groups that includes the Brahmin, so they can't be of that group. This leaves high ranking officials and the elders. While elders may in fact obtain a high social rank, the honor of entering the sanctum is likely reserved for individuals of even higher social status.

210. (D) Foundation of Comprehension. The passage describes the need for "smaller and lighter" images to be used for the public appearances of the gods. This statement immediately precedes the discussion of the use of bronze for the statues. Thus, it is logical that bronze made possible such small and lightweight images to be used.

211. (A) Foundation of Comprehension. While the passage focuses on Taoism, it begins with an explanation of the creation of the universe by the Tao. From this the roots of Taoism are explained in detail as this became an accepted cultural and eventually a religious practice.

212. (B) Reasoning within the Text. From the words and phrases used in the passage, the author maintains a rather informative tone throughout. This does not lend the reader any evidence in any way whatsoever that he is either in support or resistant to the teaching of Taoism; thus, the conclusion is that the author is merely informing the readers and allowing them to shape their own perception of this practice.

213. (C) Foundation of Comprehension. Laozi (Lao-Tsu) was described in the first paragraph as the sage who first revealed the way. You may have mistakenly chosen the final selection (*Tao Te Ching*), since the name includes Tao. However, that is the name of the book written by Laozi describing the way.

214. (A) Reasoning within the Text. In the final paragraph, the author is clear that Taoism has no need for one or multiple gods. In fact, the ultimate goal of Taoism is to lift humans above gods and heavens by unifying all humans together with the Tao.

215. (D) Foundation of Comprehension. Following the use of the term transubstantiation, the author states that Laozi's mother died because mother and son were one and the same person. This indicates that transubstantiation would be the transfer of a "life force" for one entity from one body to another.

216. (B) Reasoning beyond the Text. Even in the American vernacular and with little knowledge of Taoism, most people are at least acquainted with the image and the idea of yin and yang. Those opposing forces unite to form one whole.

217. (D) Foundation of Comprehension. In paragraph one, the author lists the five relationships described in the Confucian idea of filial piety. However, only friend does not have a counterpart listed because the counterpart of friend is also friend.

218. (A) Reasoning beyond the Text. Today's Americans are mostly egocentric, which is diametrically opposed to the close-knit family unit of ancient China in which the family unit had become so important as to evolve into ancestor worship.

219. (B) Reasoning beyond the Text. A Biblical teaching that has made its way into our culture and is often considered as folk wisdom would be "do unto others as you would have them do unto you." Basically, "treat others as you wish to be treated" is a common lesson throughout history that has been taught to many.

220. (C) Foundation of Comprehension. The third feature of Confucian doctrine states that the chief moral force in society is the example of superior men. He states that "virtue in superiors will call out virtue in common folks." This ideology is flawed and only works when there are virtuous men in leadership positions within the society to be exemplified.

221. (D) Reasoning beyond the Text. In our society, we wish to give everyone the benefit of the doubt and rise above the level of barbarians and evil. Many feel that justice and punishment only lowers us to the level of evil individuals. However, Confucius realized the social benefit of consequences and personal responsibility, which is greatly lacking in our country today.

222. (D) Foundation of Comprehension. In paragraph four, the author is clear that while Confucius practiced a faith in a supreme being and a heaven, he simply did not dwell on such things as it was impossible in our world to truly understand them. He simply spent his energy focused on the present world, people, and how those interactions could make this time on Earth the best it could be.

Chapter 10: Theater

223. (A) Foundation of Comprehension. Being from the "Bay Area" is a descriptor of the San Francisco area. Additionally, that she was a part of the San Francisco Mime Troupe is a big enough clue that this selection should have been an easy one. While Los Angeles and San Diego are also in California, these are not mentioned in the passage. New York, while an area filled with theater and art, it is not the location specific in this passage.

224. (A) Foundation of Comprehension. While this may be true for the initial part of an acting career, it was not expressly mentioned in this passage along with the other negatives. All three distractors were mentioned in her third and fourth answers to questions.

225. (A) Reasoning beyond the Text. To Cohen, the importance of theater is bringing the community together for an in-person experience. Being at a baseball game, live and surrounded by others, would most closely provide a similar experience. Watching a movie with the family does provide additional interaction with others, but it fails to provide the same level of community as does the theater or a live sporting event or concert. This would be a selection made in haste and without considering if there are better choices available. The real benefit and experience of a LIVE concert would be the energy and interaction of the audience, which is totally lost when you stream the music and are withdrawn from the actual venue. Virtual communication also withdraws the person from the actual physical interaction and experience with real people. The communication is live, spontaneous and real; however, all of the other facets that are available in an audience situation are lost over electronic devices.

226. (C) Reasoning within the Text. The physical aspect and live nature of theater do not allow for the same special and visual effects that are provided on film and television. This requires the imagination of the audience to fill in those parts of the play that are implied but not visually provided and makes the viewer a larger and more active participant in the event. Plays are often as long or longer than many full-length movies, so length would not have an impact on level of detail or use of imagination. Screen plays are often as detailed or more in the theater when compared to movies. More information has to be given to provide the context and background of the play as opposed to settings and visual effects that can provide that in film and television.

227. (B) Foundation of Comprehension. Cohen states in her final answer that students can understand "who they are…" when exposed to the arts in public schools. All distractors are reasonable and worthwhile justifications for providing exposure and training in the arts in public schools. However, the only one specifically mentioned in her final answer was their self-identity recognition.

228. (A) Foundation of Comprehension. In the first paragraph, all were listed accept for the first choice, Bay Area Theatre.

PART 2: SOCIAL SCIENCES
Chapter 11: Anthropology

229. (C) Reasoning within the Text. Meso (meaning middle) America refers to a region in the middle of Central America where early cultures arose independently from outside influence. While the passage describes early cultures and peoples of America, this term would be too broad and could include populations from any location in the Americas. Additionally, B and D bound the Mesoamerican portion from the south and the north respectively.

230. (D) Foundations of Comprehension. The Olmecs are suggested to be the ancestral group in Mesoamerican culture in paragraph seven. In paragraph six, all other selections were suggested to have arose later than the Olmecs and use a similar system of calendars and writing as do the older ancestral Olmecs.

231. (C) Foundations of Comprehension. Although these cultures likely shared this cultural ritual and ceremonies, it is not mentioned in this passage. All other selections can be found in the passage. Writing similarities, rulership and its representation, and the use and style of calendars were all similarities mentioned between these Mesoamerican people groups in paragraphs eight and nine.

232. (D) Foundation of Comprehension. This is the best choice based on the information in the final paragraph. A combination of factors including environmental changes as well as being overwhelmed by a more powerful group would have led to the abandonment of their settlements as well as elimination from the historical record. Flooding is a natural disaster and was mentioned in the passage. However, it was the change in river pattern due to repeated flooding over time that led the Olmecs to move. Additionally, environmental changes led the people to abandon their settlements, but they should have founded new ones if not for other factors. Thus, D is the better selection.

233. (B) Foundations of Comprehension. Several times throughout the passage, the Olmec 260-day calendar was mentioned.

234. (A) Reasoning beyond the Text. Often the simplest answer is the correct one. While there may have been reasons for the appearance of the Mayan writings in the historical record more so than any others, when only theirs has been found and it dates the oldest known, then logically that will account for it being the oldest known writings from Mesoamerica.

235. (D) Reasoning beyond the Text. As stated many times in the passage, the ultimate goal is walking, not the means with which infants grow and progress toward that goal. For the other selections, the author makes statements and comments on practical issues of babies learning to walk. However, none fully are supported by the passage and its main theme. For example, the delay in walking is just that. It doesn't say that Au babies fail to learn how to walk.

236. (A) Foundation of Comprehension. In paragraph five, the author describes Tracer's original interest in studying the relationship between Au mothers and their children. It was only through attention and observation that he noticed the Au children did not crawl before they walked.

237. (A) Foundation of Comprehension. As stated in paragraph nine, crawling may have developed as recently as two centuries ago as wooden floors replaced dirt floors in human homes.

238. (A) Reasoning beyond the Text. Hardwiring in biological terms most often is used to describe the genes via which an organism is encoded and can function. In contrast, instinct is often used in reference in some innate activity or function of an organism, and while this may be an attractive selection in relationship to the animal kingdom, when compared to selection A, it is clearly not the best of the choices for this question. While D is a true statement from a biological perspective, it would not be the best choice for the author to use as a replacement for the "hardwiring" statement from the passage.

239. (A) Foundation of Comprehension. While the article describes the Au people and their babies, the more global lesson in this passage is that cultures have differing ways in which they nurture infants. This results in different opportunities for these babies to develop the strength and confidence required to walk. However, regardless of the means, the ultimate goal of walking is achieved. Selections B and C represent specific aspects found within the passage. These are individual portions of the more global message of the passage that the vehicle for gaining strength and confidence depends on the culture into which the baby is born. Selection D may have caught your attention and at first glance appears to be a good choice. However when compared to selection A, choice D loses some appeal since the means used by infants is irrelevant to the task of walking but is totally relevant to the culture as described in the passage.

240. (C) Reasoning beyond the Text. The author's claim is that the developmental progression toward walking is unimportant. It is the goal of walking that is essential. The Au babies are delayed in their learning to walk, but it is only a short delay. However, if there was a culture in which the babies were significantly delayed in their learning to walk, that would suggest that crawling is essential for the more rapid progression toward walking, which would greatly weaken the author's thesis. The first selection (A) appears to suggest the same; however, there are no qualifiers to determine the delay in walking. This then makes choice C the best of the selections here.

Chapter 12: Archeology

241. (C) Foundation of Comprehension. The passage contained information about a golden treasure (A) and described how the treasure was found in a Bactrian tomb (B). It went on to describe the many dangers that could have resulted in the dispersal of the items and possibly their loss. However, the selection that most encompasses the content of the passage is C, in which the survival (against the stated armies) as well as the rediscovery (of the golden Bactrian treasure) of the tomb and its contents was described. Thus, C is the best and most complete description of the full passage.

242. (D) Foundations of Comprehension. Although many military forces, including Russian, Taliban, and participants in the Civil War within Afghanistan were threats to the treasure's survival, tomb raiders from Afghanistan were not among those threats detailed in the passage.

243. (A) Foundations of Comprehension. Leaving coins with the dead is an ancient practice to allow the fare to be paid to the ferryman to cross the river Styx and enter the realm of the dead. While some cultures placed these coins over the eyes of the corpse, possibly in order to help keep the eyelids closed, in the Afghan culture, these coins were placed in their mouths, as stated in paragraph seven.

244. (A) Foundations of Comprehension. Although not explicitly stated in the passage, the timing of the most recent incident was related to the arrival of the American forces. It seems unlikely that the author would include this detail for any other reason than to provide an explanation for why the Taliban "ran out of time" as they were trying to obtain the treasure. The implication here is that they ran out of time before the American troops would arrive and they did not want to have an encounter with that force. This can be found in paragraph three of the passage.

245. (B) Reasoning within the Text. This passage reads much like an informative news story whose main objective is to provide information to the reader. There are no specific words or phrases that would lead one to believe that the author is anything but neutral (almost by default without indications otherwise) about this particular topic. One can understand that there would be interest or at least someone would have positive feelings about these ancient treasures being preserved. However, in the absence of any other indicators, neutral is the best adjective to describe the tone of the author for this passage.

246. (C) Reasoning beyond the Text. From what may be known about the Taliban in recent history and in the media, their terrorist activities are widespread in Afghanistan. Thus, to maintain such a large group, financial resources must also be available. Many terrorist groups in fact use the money raided from communities which they invade. In this case, the passage states that the Taliban was about to blow the central bank's vault. This is clear that the Taliban was seeking to obtain money or items of value. The likely connection between these treasures and their activities would lead one to deduce their intended use from the selections.

247. (C) Foundations of Comprehension. In paragraph three, Cancuén is defined to mean the Place of Serpents.

248. (D) Foundations of Comprehension. Although the first paragraph mentions the funding agency, lack of finances was not stated as a reason for the site being undisturbed for hundreds and thousands of years. In fact, excavations, such as the ones in Egypt, were much better funded in the earlier golden years of archeology.

249. (B) Reasoning within the Text. To be Machiavellian is to put power and authority above morality and ethics to achieve the goal of rule and power. Thus, calculated would be the best alternative in this case and is clearly evidenced in the remainder of the paragraph. When considering choices A and D, while both would be factors behind the King's motives and actions and certainly his choices would be calculated based on risk versus reward, the best choice for a substitute deals more with the morality and lack of ethical thought in deciding on a course of action.

250. (B) Foundations of Comprehension. As stated in paragraph eight, Cancuén and its people were never drawn into or initiated a war during the existence of their culture.

251. (D) Foundations of Comprehension. In paragraph five, the dense vegetation was a stated cause for the abrupt end of an investigation and mapping expedition in 1967. This likely had been the drawback to expeditions for much of the 20th century.

252. (D) Reasoning within the Text. Stucco is a layer much like mud that is placed on a support wall and used as a canvas upon which to paint. This was the case at Cancuén. While the vines and foliage of the jungle supported the walls themselves, the thinner stucco layer was able to slide off the wall and land in such a way as to be covered, preserved and relatively easily recovered.

Chapter 13: Cultural Studies

253. (D) Foundations of Comprehension. From the passage, it is immediately obvious that the funding agency does in fact contribute to all of the choices given above. However, in the wording of the selections there are some subtle but important differences. That being the case and in light of the author's detailing of the types of businesses funded, providing needed resources on the reservation by its own people is the best selection for this question. While selection A at first appears a logical benefit of the funds, enhancing economic development of the reservation and increasing the diversity of services offered are different issues.

254. (A) Foundations of Comprehension. The author paints a clear picture of the Four Bands Fund and its assistance to the community through encouraging, recruiting, and training small business owners. The start-up funds are essential for success and for obtaining the additional funding to launch the business. These entrepreneurs weren't looking for funds, the agency sought them.

255. (B) Reasoning beyond the Text. With the focus of the funding agency being to bring needed services onto the reservation (and in doing so benefit individuals from the community as small business owners), this selection would be indicative of a failed program. Half of the businesses, although possibly making money, not providing necessary services to the community, would be outside of the focus of this agency and be used as an example of their failure.

256. (D) Reasoning within the Text. The passage is clear that the Four Bands Fund was created to stimulate economic growth by identifying needed services and by finding and mentoring small business owners to success. Thus, providing the guidance, training, and support to outside individuals would also help them be as successful as the examples given in the passage.

257. (B) Foundations of Comprehension. Although eating and feeding a family is essential to the survival and growth of a community, eating at a restaurant is a luxury and not an essential service for a community. Other selections (some being comparable to the examples given in the passage) would be far more essential, in light of the passage, than would a restaurant.

258. (C) Foundation of Comprehension. Although there is much detail about the specifics of the loan program and business model, the message is about how money and experience can be invested in people and communities to grow their businesses and bring economic security to their reservations and families.

259. (B) Reasoning beyond the Text. Productivity and personal interaction are independent functions, and while creativity may enhance one, it does not always enhance both. Thus, people with different personalities may not enjoy the company of one another; yet, that same pairing may lead to valuable productivity within the business setting. Selection A is similar to selection B; however, it is much less detailed and fails to mention creativity, so while it is a perfectly valid reason for this disconnect, it is not the best selection for this question.

260. (C) Foundations of Comprehension. In the second paragraph where the distinctions and characteristics are described and defined, the biology professor is listed as a Pro-C creative person.

261. (B) Foundations of Comprehension. Being open to new ideas, settings, foods, etc., is one of the behaviors suggested to foster creativity in paragraph five. While being creative in a specific area can help you climb the C ladder into the Pro and then the Big C range, initially focusing in an area will likely inhibit creative thinking.

262. (A) Reasoning beyond the Text. Stephen Hawking is one of the greatest minds (if not THE greatest) of this generation and will likely go down in history along with the names of Newton and Einstein. While the passage suggests it takes hundreds of years for history to judge who makes it into the Big C ranks, it is safe to say that from this list, Dr. Hawking is the only one worthy of that distinction.

263. (C) Reasoning beyond the Text. This is a difficult question and two of the selections are extremely close to being equally suited for an answer. However, the passage talks about coping with stress better. It does not suggest that creative people experience more or less stress. When anxiety is mentioned, that leads you to believe that they do in fact experience more stress which builds and feeds into the anxiety.

264. (A) Foundation of Comprehension. Although the author describes creative people as being able to cope with stress more easily and to heal faster after trauma, he also states, in the first paragraph, that creative people are often more anxious than their non-creative counterparts.

265. (A) Foundations of Comprehension. Although the passage did mention oil, it was in reference to the oil shortages of the 1970s and how that brought travel to a halt almost overnight. Certainly increased usage in millions of cars and trucks on the road will elevate the costs of oil and gas, but those were not mentioned in this passage. Take care to not let your logic lead you to an incorrect selection.

266. (D) Reasoning beyond the Text. Culture is about sharing ideals, feelings, history, and hopes with people. Before the highways, people were more isolated and it was more difficult to interact with people different from your own world. The highways made this much more possible and allowed the blending of peoples and their cultures.

267. (B) Reasoning beyond the Text. Just as the highways allowed for greater interaction of people with different histories, beliefs, and lifestyles, the Internet has brought the world together into a huge melting pot of social consciousness. While this is not the physical blending that highways facilitated, it has nonetheless made an indelible impact on the world, which will never be the same.

268. (C) Reasoning beyond the Text. Paragraph seven begins with stories told by individuals about their experiences as children on family outings. Invariably they illustrate the speed with which travel is accomplished and how the enjoyment of the scenes, sights, and experiences along the way are missed now due to the importance of getting to the destination "on time."

269. (B) Foundation of Comprehension. The description of those who contributed to the documentary "Divided Highways" can be found in paragraph six. From that list, only the car manufacturers were not discussed.

270. (D) Foundation of Comprehension. Paragraph eight describes a conversation with a Native American who says "the speed is a sadness." This statement reflects the need for people to move from place to place and not enjoy all the land and beauty that is between.

271. (D) Reasoning within the Text. While a boiler room is typically where hard and hot work occurs, in this regard, the sales tactics were dishonest at best. This is detailed in the final paragraph of the passage and is followed with several examples of the illegal activities used by the salesmen.

272. (B) Foundation of Comprehension. The author makes it clear in the first paragraph that the attraction to Florida during the post-war times was because so many soldiers from across the country experienced the culture, climate, and the good life in Florida during their training.

273. (A) Foundation of Comprehension. If you have never lived in the south or in Florida during the late summer months, you cannot truly appreciate the oppressive heat along with the humidity of the region. This is illustrated in paragraph five of the text in the discussion about the essential nature of air conditioning for hotels and houses being built.

274. (D) Foundation of Comprehension. "Instant City" is the description used by the author to describe Cape Coral and how it came into existence after 1950 based on the dreams of the developers of the land in Florida. While it is stated to be the largest city in southwest Florida, it is by far one of the youngest.

275. (B) Foundation of Comprehension. As happens today, much of the decision making in purchasing a home or relocating a family all comes down to the price. You must live within your means or else the dream will be short-lived indeed. This certainly was the case for the people in the post war migration to Florida.

276. (B) Foundation of Comprehension. The author states in the final paragraph that the upward mobility of the working class was the force that led many to be able to afford the move and the living expenses in Florida. Thus, the middle class was the group that benefited most in this shift of culture and life in America.

277. (C) Foundation of Comprehension. In paragraph two, the author states that in Yemen poetry is used to negotiate and settle disputes. While it may also be used in the other ways listed, they were not described in the passage as being specifically applicable for Yemen.

278. (A) Reasoning beyond the Text. The contradiction between peaceful sharing of poetry as we may imagine the 70s flower children sitting and listening to all forms of poetry is painted against the backdrop of our daily influx of violent images from the Middle East as political and religious ideologues seek to destroy those who think differently than them.

279. (B) Foundation of Comprehension. The winning poem of the festival, as described in the fifth paragraph, was inscribed in gold and placed on a door of Mecca, the holiest and most heavily trafficked place in the Arab world. This would ensure that all would see the poem and result in fame for the writer.

280. (B) Reasoning beyond the Text. In a manner similar to the social disputes in Yemen, rap artists and the poetic lines of their raps will have rap-offs to determine whose lyrics are the best and thus settle the dispute in question much like is done in the Arab world and has been done there for centuries.

281. (B) Foundation of Comprehension. The description of nomadic tribes and their use of poetry can be found in the final paragraph of the passage. Of the selections listed, the only one not mentioned in the passage is poetry as used in oral business contracts.

282. (B) Reasoning beyond the Text. This is not an easy set of selections to consider for this question. Since poets convey information, certainly they are popular, any or all of these selections may be applicable. However, in the next to last paragraph, the author clearly states that the poet is the "voice of the tribe, its defender and representative… its provocative force." In light of that description, the most provocative voices that are heard today are those of the comedians and many on late night television. They meet the controversies of the day head on, often in extremely provocative and direct ways, all with the use of humor as their protection and shield.

Chapter 14: Economics

283. (C) Foundations of Comprehension. In addition to listing the minerals and mineral materials that are produced and recycled in the U.S., the importance of these commodities to the U.S. economy is the central focus. If you were focused on the title alone, you may have selected A. However, the passage goes into much more detail on the impact of this business sector on the economy of the U.S. While the passage does detail the minerals and materials produced and recycled in the U.S., it also goes much further into the role of these on the economy. Although it was mentioned that these numbers on sales of minerals and their rise and fall on global markets impacts policies, the details of how policies are made is not described.

284. (D) Reasoning within the Text. The fundamental importance of mineral resources to... technology (paragraph two) is clarified later in the passage where the production of metals is stated to be important to the production of electronic devices (paragraph six). Logically, the more funds available for a country, the more financial resources can be shifted into the technology sector. However, with the specific description in the passage, A is not the best choice.

285. (B) Foundations of Comprehension. For a commodity that contributes so much to the U.S. economy, any shift in price, production, and/or export could have a huge impact on the economy of the country and the world. While selection A is a true statement, it fails to stress the more fundamental importance of minerals to the economy of the entire country. Choice C focuses on one area mentioned in the article to distract from the better selection. Although the housing market does play a role in interest rates and the economy, this choice is too focused and restricted to be better than the more global choice B.

286. (D) Reasoning beyond the Text. The basic principle of supply and demand is being addressed in this question. For the price to remain unchanged, the supply of mineral goods must have kept pace with the demand for those same goods. Otherwise, the price would increase (with greater demand) or decrease (with less demand). Increased exports without data on the production and/or use of domestic minerals would be useless information relating to the price. Also, global increase in production may or may not impact the price. The demand for the minerals is the critical missing factor for this calculation given in this statement.

287. (C) Reasoning beyond the Text. Since minerals are used in road construction (paragraph five) and given the thousands of miles of roads in the country, this would have a huge impact on mineral prices and the U.S. and global economy. Relative to this passage and minerals, alternative energy would have little impact on this sector of the economy. While minerals are used in new building construction, the vastly larger area required for road construction and improvement makes choice C a much better choice and would have a larger effect on the economy. Also, technology does rely on metals for production. However, a new infrastructure does not preclude the use of metals or a vastly greater demand for metals that would impact the economy.

288. (C) Foundation of Comprehension. In the final paragraph of the passage, the twelve top producing states are listed. You must have observed that they are listed in descending order with regard to productivity to be able to answer this question.

289. (D) Foundation of Comprehension. In the passage the author refers to New Orleans as the "Crescent City " in the first paragraph. While Bourbon Street and Mardi Gras are certainly associated with New Orleans, they were not mentioned in the passage. Also, the capital of Louisiana is actually Baton Rouge.

290. (B) Foundations of Comprehension. As stated within the passage, healthcare is one of the listed disaster-resilient industries and a hospital would fall into that category. All of the distractors are certainly of value to communities; however, upon careful reading of the passage, the choice of a service associated with healthcare is certainly the best selection for this question.

291. (C) Reasoning within the Text. With the resources made available with the first EDA grant, the Idea Village helped New Orleans become, as stated in paragraph seven, a "self-sustaining entrepreneurial community" and thus generated its own financial and intellectual resources and did not require the same injection of outside money to accomplish the intended goals. While funding agencies often will decrease individual awards to provide some funds to more worthy programs, in this case it is clearly stated that the Idea Village had helped create a self-sustaining community of entrepreneurs, so C would be the best choice for this question. As with most funding sources and renewals of grants, rarely if ever will a program request less funding in the subsequent year. The economy may have a profound impact upon available funding. However, nothing in the passage gives any indication this is the case.

292. (B) Foundations of Comprehension. This may have presented a problem for many readers. In paragraph four, the author discussed the means by which New Orleans developed their critical mass, which was knowledge-intensive industries. The passage mentions the need for disaster-resilient industries as a way to have a long lasting and secure community of businesses. However, when compared with the information in paragraph four it becomes clear that B is the better of the selections when compared to A.

293. (D) Reasoning within the Text. The focus of this passage was about the Idea Village and how it assisted the rebirth of New Orleans business sector with the input of money from the EDA. The main targets of the Idea Village are entrepreneurs and small businesses aided by an intellectual input from college graduates with the knowledge and creative thinking to help identify, develop, and implement a business plan in the areas needed for New Orleans to be successful. The distractors are such that each could be seen as an alternative way to explain the growth of New Orleans on a purely logical basis. However, the entire passage is about the formation, assistance, consulting, and advising of local entrepreneurs and small business owners. Thus, none of the distractors are valid in relation to the passage nor would they be a better selection that choice D.

294. (C) Reasoning within the Text. Capital usually refers to financial resources. In this case, the resources are the people who will bring their talents, skills, understanding, and drive to the city in need of rejuvenation.

295. (A) Foundation of Comprehension. Buying supplies in bulk is typically a cost savings plan. However, it was not one of those listed in the text. What was listed was buying supplies from the government at or below costs.

296. (B) Reasoning beyond the Text. One fee included in the passage was the state incorporation fee. Depending on the state and the location, the municipal fees and tax codes may be decidedly different and it would benefit a new small business owner to locate his or her business in a state and area that is business friendly with lower costs for small business startup.

297. (B) Foundation of Comprehension. The items to be identified as expenses versus assets are described in numbered paragraphs one and two of the passage. From the selections, only equipment (an asset) may not be considered as an expense in the startup.

298. (D) Foundation of Comprehension. The author states that assets incur a "one-time cost" to the new business owner. This implies that once paid, the business professional owns the items and are considered assets after their purchase.

299. (B) Foundation of Comprehension. All of the selections were mentioned in paragraph two with the exception of franchise.

300. (D) Reasoning beyond the Text. In the age of immediate response and access, a business owner will likely be out of touch without the technology of a smart phone as well as the website (expected now). Accounting software would be absolutely essential for the professional to monitor expenses versus income. However, the biggest, best monitor on the market, while enjoyable and nice, would not be an essential expense (although likely highly coveted).

301. (A) Foundation of Comprehension. Certainly an accountant would be someone who could help a new business startup as well as assist with the operation of the business. However, this is an additional expense, it is not essential to the business, and relative to this question, was not listed along with the other selections.

302. (C) Reasoning within the Text. While there is no direct definition of sourcing strategies in the passage, the entirety of the text is about utilizing the strengths of others to enhance the diversity and innovation of your own business. Thus, that partnership (as mentioned in paragraph two) benefits all parties.

303. (B) Foundation of Comprehension. Paragraph two includes three examples of how sourcing may be accomplished with other companies. These include all of the selections with the exception of incorporating.

304. (B) Reasoning within the Text. Organic in the sense of sourcing and business innovation refers to the natural process of utilizing the strengths of others to compliment the areas of your business that could be improved. This could also be considered somewhat of a symbiotic relationship for organisms in which both benefit from the relationship.

305. (A) Foundation of Comprehension. The list from Clayton Christensen can be found in the middle of paragraph three and includes all of the selections with the exception of item A, products. While this is very much an important factor for the success of any business, it was not listed in this section of the passage.

306. (D) Reasoning beyond the Text. For this type of ecosystem to work, it must be mutually beneficial. In the case of our selections only two examples could even possibly meet that criterion. Of those two, the dog and owner match the best. The dog gets shelter and food while the owner gets affection and protection. Both benefit from what the other can do best.

307. (C) Reasoning beyond the Text. The strength of any country is largely based on the health of its economy. As the money flows, so grows the government and the country. Thus, it is critical to the U.S. that all businesses thrive and stay competitive with each other and with the worldwide market.

308. (D) Foundation of Comprehension. The list of characteristics for small businesses can be found in the next-to-last paragraph of the passage and includes all of the selections with the exception of diversity.

309. (D) Foundations of Comprehension. The problem during the dry season was NOT lack of produce but rather lack of refrigeration to store the fruit during the dry season. This was described in paragraphs three and four.

310. (B) Reasoning beyond the Text. Since the passage is all about the obstacles that were met and overcome by Marie Kigoma, it reasons that this would simply be seen as another in a series of difficult moments she and her business faced. It also allowed her never give up attitude to be displayed for her employees. Success can be measured in many ways and not simply by the bottom line. Profit or not, success was providing jobs and a service for the people in her community.

311. (C) Foundations of Comprehension. The grant money did not exclusively go to FRUITO but also to the farmers in the communities. This not only was a benefit to the production of juice but also allowed for the increased productivity of the passion fruit produce that is the first step of the process. In doing so the grant aided the community as well as FRUITO. Choices A and B may have tripped you up. These were in fact aided by the grant money, and if you were not carefully considering all choices, you may have incorrectly selected one of these.

312. (D) Foundation of Comprehension. In paragraph six, the author clearly describes the use of grant money to obtain trucks for the direct transport of their fruit by FRUITO and reap the cost savings rather than paying trucking companies a higher cost to move their produce to the processing plant. You may have chosen C erroneously since the statement is about trucking and cost savings via shipping. However, they did not create their own company nor did the passage mention diversification of shipments of their produce to anyone other than FRUITO.

313. (D) Foundation of Comprehension. This passage was about the character and determination and leadership of one woman who had a need, found a solution, and grew it into a worldwide business with the help of her community. This is key to the passage as are the individual parts that illustrate the obstacles she faced as well as her never say quit attitude. Although the passion fruit business was a means with which she met a need to provide for her family, the passage is more about her than the business. A key motto that illustrates her character, statement B is only a portion of the qualities, character, and the history for Marie Kigoma. Statement C would be the least appealing of all the choices in that working as a part of the community of people was the portion of the passage least discussed.

314. (B) Foundation of Comprehension. In the opening paragraph, the author states that Marie began producing juice to help financially while raising three children and working as a full-time nurse.

Chapter 15: Education

315. (A) Foundations of Comprehension. Although Lincoln University is a historically black college or university in Pennsylvania, it was the only one of the selections that was NOT mentioned in the second paragraph of the passage.

316. (A) Reasoning within the Text. While social pressure, internal anxiety, and the uncertainty of future success and safety all likely played a role in the choice of colleges for black students, it is likely that the greatest internal motivator was to stay with what was familiar. This is not unlike those feelings of the black students in these early days of desegregation.

317. (C) Foundation of Comprehension. It is likely that money spent on black and white universities was meant to be the same, but was not and thus wouldn't have been equal. Furthermore, that was not directly discussed anywhere in the passage.

318. (A) Reasoning beyond the Text. Much like the Separate but Equal doctrine led to inequality for black students and schools, any division in the institution of marriage would also be "different." From the passage, it is clear the author does not, nor would anyone, favor the separate but equal doctrine in light of its failure, thus this is the best choice for this author's likely opinion and preference.

319. (B) Foundation of Comprehension. Accountant was the only career not mentioned in the discussion of career preparation in HBCUs in paragraph two.

320. (B) Reasoning beyond the Text. The author of this passage is clear in his optimism in the opportunity for people, black students, to succeed. This was primarily done through their opportunities at the higher education level. Today, so much of primary education is head counting and exam prep that students are only helped to the exam as the finish line rather than college and a career being the driving focus of their education at the secondary level.

321. (B) Reasoning beyond the Text. In the past, states particularly and the federal government to a lesser degree assisted universities with state and federal money (subsidies) to keep the cost of higher education affordable for all students. These started being reduced as the economy contracted years ago until finally all subsidies have practically ceased to exist. Thus, keeping doors open and programs being offered, universities were forced to pass the cost on to students in the form of tuition and fees.

322. (D) Foundation of Comprehension. These benefits are discussed in paragraph six and all are listed except for choice D. In fact, the passage states just the opposite—that individuals with higher degrees have greater mobility with their jobs.

323. (A) Reasoning within the Text. This statement reflects the choice that is made on a risk versus reward basis. While college is seen as a definite means by which to earn a better living and have a better quality of life (than without), in some cases that is not true. Often, people will miss out on a BETTER employment opportunity immediately out of high school in favor of a college education when, in retrospect, they would have been better off taking the job initially. You may have chosen C if not considering critically the difference between A and C. Here we see the philosophy behind the decision and the basis for the choice. However, the wording of the passage is most relevant when presented with an actual choice between a job and college.

324. (B) Reasoning within the Text. The author discusses this benefit of higher education in women in the section of the passage on social value. Thus, the consideration is more social and developmental rather than financial. The other selections for this question focus on a financial aspect of the career and family time as if it is a contest or tug of war and that a choice has to be made. The importance of time spent developing the future skills and interests in children is seen as essential to highly educated women who will continue to improve their position in their career as well as making the time needed for their children and family.

325. (D) Foundation of Comprehension. The final paragraph lists these benefits to the community of having college educated individuals in the work force. Selection D is similar to the stated benefit elsewhere in the passage as a benefit to the individual. However, this is actually the opposite of the benefit to the community which is increased workplace flexibility and would function to keep the individual within the community and prevent them from moving elsewhere.

326. (A) Foundation of Comprehension. The author of the passage is extremely pro-college and describes all of the areas in which a college education will create "value" financially, socially, and personally. Thus, its worth cannot simply be seen as a bottom line on a spreadsheet.

327. (B) Foundation of Comprehension. Many children find pleasure and joy from attending school, being with their friends, interacting with teachers, and in learning. However, happiness was the only selection of the list not present in paragraph two of the passage.

328. (B) Reasoning beyond the Text. Humans are social animals with highly complex social norms and expectations which require the young adult to achieve a moderate level of understanding of our written and spoken language as well as mathematical skills and socially accepted practices in order to cope (survive) in society. This is not unlike the mother (teacher) training her young how to feed, avoid predators, and find mates. These are all skills required of young animals, while young humans have much more to learn to "survive."

329. (B) Foundation of Comprehension. In paragraph three, the author states that half of all school aged children not attending school were refugee/displaced children.

330. (D) Foundation of Comprehension. Among the countries listed as having a significant problem of educating displaced children, in paragraph seven, three countries are listed as dealing with this problem in light of an Ebola outbreak. Those countries are Guinea, Liberia, and Sierra Leone.

331. (B) Reasoning within the Text. Although groups of children may be attacked and forced into some kind of service, it is much easier and less visible and dramatic for them to be taken solitarily with little resistance. Thus, the immediate positive impact for the children is the security of being together in a class setting, which doesn't have to be a structure as much as it does the collective of individuals. Paragraph 11 is clear that school ".. can help.. shield them from adults who might harm them."

332. (B) Reasoning beyond the Text. While most of these suggestions are possible solutions, the financial constraints of new buildings (which would be left empty when the students leave to go home) or the increased financial burden on the states for additional funding (simply to hire more teachers) won't solve the issue fully. Thus, allowing teachers and students to use the existing facilities and expand their school year will be the most beneficial and least burdensome on the budgets for the states and the schools when compared to the cost of new buildings for a shorter school year. This would also be reflected in those countries who taught their students in double shifts to make sure all children received their education.

Chapter 16: Geography

333. (B) Reasoning beyond the Text. Using words and phrases throughout the passage such as "our corner of the South" and "we don't..." implies a personal perspective of the TVA and the Copper Basin. This would immediately lead to the elimination of the national and foreign selections. Given the two remaining choices, an administrator would likely have done more to describe the actual facilities of the TVA rather than the external impact on the area, as would be the viewpoint of a local individual.

334. (B) Reasoning within the Text. The passage discusses the damage due to the mining of copper and the disregard of the environment over profit, which clearly converted a lush environmental area into a dead zone resembling a desert that could be observed from space. Although deserts can be areas other than arid sandy deserts, there is no analogy in this case to the natural deserts of the world.

335. (A) Foundations of Comprehension. In paragraph four, all listed areas including the moon were stated with the exception of the Sahara desert.

336. (D) Reasoning within the Text. In the final portion of the passage, the author takes care to mention the return of the songbirds "on their own..." to the region. This is the best selection for this question. While all of the distractors are positive benefits to the region, they all resulted from human intervention (even the reduction of acid rain from reduced sulfur burning). Thus the only "natural" restoration was the return of the birds. Birds and fish are typically the best indicators of ecological health in a region.

337. (D) Foundations of Comprehension. The Panama Canal is certainly an engineering marvel and a testament to human persistence and ingenuity, but this man-made structure was not listed in the passage.

338. (C) Reasoning within the Text. This statement occurs in the paragraph about the former desert being reforested. While the sentence about native fish being reintroduced stands between the reforest statement and that of the songbirds, it stands to reason that the reforestation, and a return to natural habitat for the songbirds enabled them to migrate to the area once again to live and raise their young in the branches of the new trees.

339. (B) Reasoning within the Text. Moving across the country. Selling everything they had to make the trip. Working tirelessly without sleep for days on end. These are some of the symptoms people displayed when they contracted "Gold Fever." Actions rare for stable individuals, these were common for those who could not resist the possibility of instant fortune. Thus, the irrational behavior is the basis for the genesis of this term.

340. (B) Foundation of Comprehension. This is a straightforward comprehension question. There are some trends of human nature and the mind that must be overcome here. First, only a single selection does NOT start with the letter E. Our minds tend to seek out those distinctions and may have caused you to make an incorrect selection if you were moving too quickly. Also, when we think of modern California, glaciers are not exactly an everyday occurrence, although we know that erosion is a powerful geological force. Thus, you must have read carefully and comprehensively and realized that while erosion certainly does have an impact, it was not listed in paragraph one.

341. (C) Reasoning beyond the Text. The typical volcano is seen as a pyramid-shaped inverted cone. There is the rim of the volcano and the depression of the interior. Large volcanoes will have lower sides and broader openings revealing a sunken inside, which is the caldera of the volcano and would in many ways resemble much smaller raised areas with central depressions such as impact craters on the moon.

342. (A) Foundation of Comprehension. While all the statements are true and in many ways reflective of the passage, the first selection includes the specifics of the Long Valley Caldera which is the backdrop for the larger explanation on geological activity.

343. (A) Reasoning within the Text. In geological terms distance and time are relative factors that we who live in the moment fail to appreciate. However, even a 2.5 foot increase in elevation suggests that the volcanic activity has increased and that could mean the beginnings of even more activity in the future (either sooner or later). Thus any geological change is worth noting and being cautious about.

344. (B) Reasoning beyond the Text. Normal human physiology will account for changes in blood pressure and temperature as we go from waking hours into sleep. Pain is also not something to be overly concerned about when in low levels. However, just as a slight change in the caldera raised immediate concerns among geologists, a skin change in humans can indicate skin cancer and should be examined immediately by a physician.

345. (D) Reasoning beyond the Text. While fewer data points and inferior equipment may have resulted in less reliable data, the readings will likely show little variability that cannot be accounted for. However, if the measures were in deeper or more shallow water or in different regions of the coastline that may have altered the flow of the ocean, the data may not be solely reflective of the temperature change as much as the location/depth change in where the thermometer was located.

346. (B) Reasoning beyond the Text. If the symbiotic algae are resistant to the warmer temps yet they are not found on the coral, this would suggest that the algae are abandoning the coral for a more hospitable environment. Even if food resources may be less abundant, the lower temps will allow the algae metabolism to also decrease and result in lower raw material requirements away from the coral.

347. (D) Reasoning within the Text. Data from the studies on water temperature as well as statements by the author only demonstrate that higher water temperatures lead to the loss of symbiotic algae. This then results in the starvation of the corals turning them white (bleaching). There is no evidence that the coral is sensitive to the higher temps at all. It is simply the heat sensitive algae that may be the actual cause of coral bleaching thus making D the best selection.

348. (D) Reasoning within the Text. There is far more detail and data presented in this article for it to have been written for the lay public or politicians. Thus, this must have been written for professionals interested in the topic (such as oceanographers).

349. (B) Reasoning beyond the Text. Selection D may have been your choice as it does sound like a valid piece of data to support the direct impact of coral growth from water temps (not algae depletion). However, by demonstrating that the coral cells will decrease their mitotic activity would be an even more direct measure of coral growth and thus the best selection here.

350. (A) Foundation of Comprehension. Although Pensacola is in Florida, it was not one of the three locations listed in the passage.

Chapter 17: History

351. (B) Reasoning beyond the Text. The burning of the U.S. Capitol was in fact retribution for the burning of a Canadian Capitol by the Americans earlier in the War of 1812. However, the fact that private property was spared is likely a lesson learned from the Revolutionary War, where the British burned many towns in an attempt to subjugate the colonists. Rather, this emboldened them against the British and was a principle reason for the American victory. This was a tactical mistake the British did not wish to repeat.

352. (A) Foundations of Comprehension. Stone and masonry, while common in the day and area, were used for their aesthetic value (paragraph two). This proved to be fortuitous since these materials are also resistant to fire. Likely the choice of stone (for its beauty) also contributed to the life expectancy of the building (as a secondary consequence). Yet, this is never mentioned in the text. Selection D is another consequence for the choice of building materials and would be speculation to consider this a deciding factor for its prior choice.

353. (A) Reasoning within the Text. Fire has amazed man since the earliest of our ancestors for its destructive power, its warmth, and its production. Even today, fire being commonplace in our lives, when an inferno, much like that of the capital, is present it will draw our attention and awe to its power and changing colors in much the same way as one may view a work of art. All of the choices that follow are distractors that draw on your understanding of American history, the relationship with the French and their distaste for anything British. However, each one is simple speculation and has no foundation from the text or from any inference from the text.

354. (D) Reasoning beyond the Text. All entities of the U.S. government were to have an equal standing as is the foundation for the separation of powers in the U.S. Constitution. Early on in the history of our country, the facilities, land, and buildings simply weren't available or affordable. Thus, the Library of Congress and Supreme Court were temporarily housed in the Capitol Building.

355. (C) Foundations of Comprehension. As stated in paragraph three, the bonfire in the clerk's office was so hot that the British soldiers setting the fires had to leave for their own safety. None of the distractors are ever stated in the text, unlike choice C which is clearly stated in paragraph three. This is merely an attempt to cause you to waste time logically considering possible rationales for their action rather than focus on the comprehension from the passage.

356. (B) Foundations of Comprehension. As stated in the opening paragraph, the burning of the American Capitol by the British was in retaliation for the American burning of the British Capitol in Canada in 1813.

357. (D) Foundations of Comprehension. As with most leaders, they will accept the brunt of the blame and reap the rewards of success regardless of the true nature of their involvement. This was certainly the case for Abraham Lincoln in having all the blame for the early failures of the Union efforts in the Civil War. Other individuals in the list were players in the story and of the time; yet, as the author states at the end of paragraph two, the public blame was laid at the feet of the president.

358. (A) Reasoning within the Text. If you were not reading carefully, a personal bias and the current political climate may have influenced your choice. Many Democrats identify themselves as admirers and followers of Abraham Lincoln and that may have led to your selection of that political party incorrectly. As stated in the passage in paragraph three, the Republican Party chairman was advising the president on his reelection campaign and what political moves to make to increase his chances. This conversation would likely have only occurred if Abraham Lincoln belonged to that same party. However, Lincoln actually ran as a candidate for the National Union Party in 1864.

359. (B) Reasoning within the Text. When confronted with the lack of military progress and an impending loss in the election, Lincoln was faced with a difficult choice. Being unsure of who might be elected president, he did not want to leave the fate of the Union and more specifically the question of slavery up to anyone else. He felt that it was in the best interest of the nation and the people for him to solve the slavery problem before the election regardless of the outcome. This is clear in the last sentence of paragraph three. Certainly we have learned in recent years that the president does NOT always have to obtain the support of Congress before he acts, thus eliminating choice D. Additionally, his actions beyond that of Congress are also constitutional within the defined limits of that document, thus eliminating choice A.

360. (D) Reasoning within the Text. Being from Texas and having personal experience with Copperhead snakes, I can assure you the author had additional experiences as did the people who gave this moniker to Mr. Pendleton. These are very stealthy animals that will peacefully exist in private but will strike quickly when provoked. Without that foreknowledge about this snake, you can deduce from the passage that McClellan was "saddled with" Pendleton. Since the democratic party had the solid platform for the ending of the war immediately (and McClellan couldn't even support that as stated in paragraph five), one can understand that Pendleton was the driving force for the presidential ticket more so than McClellan.

361. (B) Reasoning within the Text. For this question, we must start with the foundation of blame laid at the feet of the president and his party for the poor progress in the war. This is the indication that he had no friends either in the government or in the nation. However, when presented with an election, and the possibility of another course of action if another (the adversary) were elected president, now his supporters suddenly become more vocal and positive for his leadership. This may very well have occurred because of the military successes that were happening for the union or it may have occurred regardless. Yet, these are the roots of his sentiment. Even without an opposition candidate, Lincoln could not get a consensus within his own party.

362. (B) Reasoning within the Text. Based on the passage, the details found within as well as the "story-like" feel of the article, the passage was most likely written by and for historians. Others may not have demonstrated the same interest in such a seemingly mundane topic as a presidential memo. Yet this author through her investigation found an interesting written work as well as a more interesting historical context within which it was written.

363. (B) Reasoning beyond the Text. The valedictory (to say farewell) speech may be given by anyone as their farewell to a group. However, in a graduation ceremony it has become traditional for that person (the Valedictorian) to be the student with the highest GPA. Likewise, the Salutatorian, the individual giving the salutation or welcome to the audience traditionally is the student with the second highest GPA.

364. (C) Reasoning beyond the Text. Several concessions and rewards were a part of the Compromise of 1850. The northern concession of the Fugitive Slave Law was met with resistance by many. However, the failure of the North to actually enforce the law led to no changes in the free states whatsoever. Thus, the concession was simply a political tactic to obtain the reward desired and keep the southern states in the dark to the political deception.

365. (A) Reasoning beyond the Text. While compromise is always valued and recognized as the means to civilized resolution of problems, in some instances, there can be no compromise. This was the case in 1850 and in the following 10 years. While the legislation attempted to appease both sides, the lack of commitment on the side of the northern states was clear proof that no compromise was going to be acceptable.

366. (C) Reasoning beyond the Text. At times in history, the gulf between ideologies has been too expansive to find lasting compromise, as in the Civil War. In modern times, the ever increasing gulf between liberal and conservative ideologies seems to be even wider and may likely rip our country apart if compromise and resolution is not found and made to last.

367. (B) Foundation of Comprehension. Of the selections, southerner was the only one not mentioned and discussed in the fourth paragraph of the text.

368. (D) Reasoning beyond the Text. In our society today, there is zero room for compromise and the only tolerance that is demanded is unidirectional: away from Christianity. Thus, each of the selections would likely be emblazoned on Twitter accounts, in blogs across the country, and repeated several times per hour on media news outlets around the nation. Even Henry Clay likely would have been unable to facilitate a compromise in Congress today.

369. (A) Foundation of Comprehension. Although new states were being added to the USA, this was not one of the "major" areas in which Clay was working on a compromise and trying to heal the country and reunite all political members under the same government.

Chapter 18: Linguistics

370. (D) Reasoning beyond the Text. In much the same way as the Egyptians used hieroglyphs (pictorial representations) to convey ideas and messages, today emoji are used to accomplish the same goal via electronic messaging.

371. (A) Foundation of Comprehension. Geography is the only selection that was not listed in paragraph two as a driving rationale for the change in languages.

372. (B) Foundation of Comprehension. Change is a certainty in life and just as animals evolve over time, either rapidly or slowly, language changes. This fluid, evolving, and dynamic process may happen through mistakes, newly introduced words from other cultures, or new words that are created to describe a new idea or technology.

373. (B) Foundation of Comprehension. In paragraph four, the three main aspects of language change are listed: vocabulary, sentence structure, and pronunciation. Thus, context is the negative selection for this question.

374. (B) Reasoning beyond the Text. Without the Internet, the ability to share in an instant your thoughts and ideas with a worldwide audience would be impossible. Society could have used a term like journal; but, the word that became accepted by the online community was blog. This would never have been possible had the technology of the Internet not become available and accessible to everyone.

375. (D) Foundation of Comprehension. In the next-to-last paragraph of the passage the author directly states that "children serve as agents for language change." Such direct and strong statements that relate directly to the main theme of the passage are information that you must map and note to better and more efficiently move through the question and selection portion of CARS.

376. (A) Foundation of Comprehension. Although words may be borrowed from other languages and incorporated into the new language with a new usage, this was not one of the four questions listed at the end of the passage as used by linguists.

377. (A) Reasoning beyond the Text. The etymological fallacy as described in the passage are words whose meanings must stay the same throughout time and cultures. Of the list, the word that has remained fairly unchanged throughout the centuries and into modern day is Genesis which still means beginning.

378. (C) Foundation of Comprehension. This was a statement made by the author in paragraph four of the passage. Swell was used as "slang" in the teens and twenties only to be replaced by cool in the sixties when it went "viral" (became very popular almost overnight). The other terms in the list may in fact have positive meaning or alternative meanings in popular culture but would be more contemporary words when compared to the usage of "swell."

379. (B) Reasoning within the Text. Within the sciences, meta- is often used at a prefix that denotes final or the end of a process. In this case the meta-commentary is the exclamation for a statement that results in a final emphasis on the message being given. This is often heard and seen in popular music not only in contemporary times but also in the tumultuous period surrounding the Vietnam war. While there is often a rebellious nature to these statements that are better understood by a certain social group, the definition being used here is specific to the wording and the message of what it means to be "COOL."

380. (D) Reasoning beyond the Text. This is another instance where the two choices that seem very similar can cause you to spend too much time considering which is the best. An eclipse is in fact a temporary event that will resolve or return in time. This could have lead you to pick selection C. However, in paragraph two, the discussion of Chet Baker clearly illustrates the disdain the author has for Baker being seen in a more positive (i.e., popular) light than Miles Davis. Thus, Miles Davis's popularity didn't wane, much like the light from the sun doesn't decrease when an eclipse happens. It is simply that Chet Baker became more popular and "overshadowed" the popularity of Miles Davis like the moon blocking the light of the sun.

Distractors: Selections A and B can be quickly eliminated since no mention of a retirement was found in the passage anywhere. Being able to quickly eliminate a selection is often more beneficial than rapidly identifying one you like. Elimination will ensure that you have read the selections and for obvious positive or negative reasons cast them aside, your chances of the correct response are drastically increased.

381. (B) Reasoning within the Text. The author clearly believes that Miles Davis specifically and African American musicians generally are the authors and creators of what it means to be cool. His statements about Chet Baker (a white musician) actually being a bad imitation of the "cool" of Miles Davis is a testament to that belief. Additionally, in paragraph five and his mention of the art exhibit called "American Cool," he mentions cool from African American coming from more places than jazz and that this transitioned to mostly white musicians who were NOT cool in his own definition.

Distractors: While I am confident that this particular author would recognize all of the selections as true statements, the one with which he would most adamantly agree, as the passage supports, would be the foundations of cool being with the early black musicians and not the white musicians.

382. (A) Foundation of Comprehension. As much as the passage is about cool, it is more about cool as an example of slang and how words can mean similar things to most yet different things to a wide ranging audience. These words may not be so simply defined in the text of a dictionary but are more sculpted by the feelings and sentiments of the society in which the word has been adopted.

383. (D) Foundation of Comprehension. In the opening sentence of the passage, Schleyer, who is credited for creating Volapük, is said to have been a German priest.

384. (B) Reasoning within the Text. Umlauts are terms that may have escaped your memory from English courses as a student or simply were linguistic instruments that are rarely taught in secondary public schools or universities. While the definition may not have been in your immediate recollection, in the third paragraph, he mentions the gloomy u and o and other vowel sounds in reference to the umlaut. Thus your selection should have been based on that association with the discussion of vowels.

385. (A) Foundation of Comprehension. Even in 1879, English was rapidly becoming a language spoken worldwide and common in most countries. Thus Schleyer reasoned that to build a universal language, he should begin with the one which was becoming widely used and accepted already.

386. (B) Reasoning beyond the Text. In this case selection B is for Bostonians. Even if this question presented you a problem, you could easily eliminate Texas and Southerners from the list. These two regions not only use the r sound but abuse the r sound and thus would find a language lacking the r sound foreign. Bostonians on the other hand have long since rejected the r sound and would find no difficulty in using such a language. For them "car" has always simply been "ca_". Thus, they as a group may very likely slide comfortably into Volapük speaking.

387. (B) Foundation of Comprehension. Of the spin-off languages derived from Volapük that are listed in the final paragraph, the only one of the selections not found in the passage is Grük. This word is used however in the lymric published by a newspaper in jest of Volapük and that familiarity may have caused you to return to the passage.

388. (B) Reasoning beyond the Text. Language brings people and communities together into a cohesive unit of common ground. Thus, so many languages exist in the world for this very reason. Why learn a language to communicate with someone across the world when you may seldom or never have that opportunity. The social language is a bonding glue to hold people together. Thus, to form a stronger or a new group of like-minded individuals, languages change and are created to meet their needs.

389. (B) Reasoning within the Text. Most are probably familiar with gumbo from Louisiana as a dish much like a soup or a stew that contains many different ingredients. Since the author is talking about regional differences in the English language as well as how all of these locales have come together and are using the same language, it reasons that the term gumbo refers to the singular language containing many diverse elements.

390. (A) Foundation of Comprehension. The acronym DARE is used in place of the *Dictionary of American Regional English*. Understand that as you read through these passages, the comprehension questions are as much to challenge your speed as they are to examine your ability to remember the terms. If you are not mapping and recalling, it will force you to return to the passage and that will use up much needed time that could be used on other questions and passages.

391. (D) Reasoning within the Text. Rather than display the state map of the United States, boundaries are drawn around locales based upon where terms are used to distinguish the most commonly used term for an object or an item. Thus for one item, the U.S. may be divided into several regionally distinct areas based on the most common term used in that location.

392. (B) Foundation of Comprehension. In paragraph five only "slatchy" was used to describe this weather condition in Nantucket (New England).

393. (C) Reasoning beyond the Text. Most of these terms are likely familiar to the modern soft drinker today with the exception of polypop. Coke is a general term used in the southern states while soda is that reference for mid-western states, especially Wisconsin. Minnesotans are accustomed to the use of pop as their designation for soft drinks. Polypop has never been used to refer to soft drinks. However it was a term used in the 40s and 50s to refer to a powdered drink beverage much like Kool-Aid today.

394. (B) Foundation of Comprehension. Taken from a region in Georgia, a third-shift mosquito refers to a firefly, as was described in paragraph four of the passage.

395. (D) Foundation of Comprehension. As stated in the first paragraph, the Navajo code talkers served in all six Marine divisions and in other Marine groups during World War II.

396. (B) Reasoning within the Text. This may have been a difficult selection for you to distinguish the best choice between A and B. In fact, in writing this question it was difficult to decide which I would select myself. However, the passage is rich in specific and numerical details as well as anecdotal statements, which makes the passage as much of a story as an informational piece. Those are some of the inherent skills of a historian over that of a journalist.

397. (B) Reasoning within the Text. In the heat of a battle, life and death can be determined in a matter of a few seconds. Thus, when code talkers could, in 20 seconds, do the job of a code machine, which took 30 minutes to translate a code, the troops had reason to love and protect their talkers.

398. (B) Reasoning within the Text. The Navajo code, the only code never to be broken, remained in use by the Marines into a portion of the Vietnam War. Thus, its use as a military code has only recently been rendered obsolete to a point that the information could be released.

399. **(C)** Foundation of Comprehension. Of all the qualities of the Navajo language that made it perfectly suited to be used as a code, selection C is incorrect. In fact, the Navajo language was an unwritten language according to the author in paragraph three.

400. **(A)** Reasoning beyond the Text. The translated Navajo word meant "turtle" and started with a T. That was the first clue to this selection. Additionally, with these special code words, many of the terms looked in some way like the word for which they were code. In that regard and in relationship to the first letter, T, the code was used to mean a tank.

401. **(B)** Foundation of Comprehension. In the first sentence of the passage, the theaters of battle in which the code talkers operated are listed. The Philippines is the only one not listed.

402. **(C)** Foundation of Comprehension. While you may have been tempted to choose A for this answer, C is the best choice. While parents do spend a lot of time with a baby, it isn't the time spent that teaches the baby to say the words. It is however how many times the baby hears the word mommy or daddy during those long periods with their parents that teaches them to associate the word with a certain individual.

403. **(A)** Reasoning beyond the Text. Clearly the ability to vocalize is not simply a cognitive feature of infants but also an anatomical problem. Until the larynx and vocal cords are adequately formed, speaking words isn't physically possible. However, infants do have the potential to use simple sign language gestures to communicate with their parents for such things as drink, food, etc.

404. **(B)** Foundation of Comprehension. In paragraph seven, the author correlates looking patterns to each selection on the list with the exception of letters. While these may be recognized as objects, their association with language would be unlikely.

405. **(C)** Reasoning beyond the Text. Using three or more photos, while it may be a logistical challenge, would greatly eliminate the possibility of random looking for the selections in question and further give statistical reliability to the data obtained. Nonfood items and other adult voices, which are not familiar to the infant, would likely not trigger the recognition the same way as those things familiar and learned by the infant.

406. **(A)** Foundation of Comprehension. Of the list of sound categories in paragraph 13, only selection A, consonants, was not discussed in the passage.

407. **(D)** Foundation of Comprehension. In the closing portion of the passage the author is clear that time spent between the baby and the parent that includes conversation will serve the baby well in learning and understanding. While most parents are already doing so, our modern society, filled with technology and electronic devices, should never rob the child nor the parent these experiences, bonding and learning that will happen between the parent and the baby.

Chapter 19: Political Science

408. (A) Foundations of Comprehension. While Islam does have a defined goal and a sovereign deity, their doctrine and practices range wildly, much like the various religious denominations of Christianity. Thus, ideologically, there isn't a singular set of rules which all Muslims practice completely.

409. (A) Reasoning beyond the Text. Islam and the Muslim world have much more restrictive doctrines and principles than do the citizens of the United States who are protected by the Bill of Rights and the U.S. Constitution. Thus, for any religious group to gain power and survive as leaders, they must uphold our Constitution and thereby protect the rights of all citizens, regardless of race, gender, or religious practice (or lack thereof). For many, this would be the impossible hurdle for this type of relationship.

410. (D) Reasoning within the Text. In this phrase, popular refers to the people choosing a leader, as in an election. The sovereign then is the elected official who presides over the operation of the country as a whole. This is seen in the Muslim world as someone to whom you must subjugate yourself and offer homage. It is completely against the Islamic doctrine to do so to anyone other than the prophet and their God as the author states later in the passage.

411. (B) Foundation of Comprehension. While the author does present information on the possibilities as well as the obstacles for a relationship between Islam and democracy, it is clear, especially in the final portions of the passage, that the author is supportive of such a relationship and feels it would be beneficial. Christianity co-existing with democracy in the United States is an example.

412. (C) Reasoning beyond the Text. Because of the separation of Church and State in the Constitution, anything relating to Christianity is being stripped from our government, our military, or any other affiliated branch of Federal, State, or Local government. Thus, for a religious group to establish themselves as a political party given the stringent doctrines with which they must live and all under the leadership would be expected to follow, it would be impossible for such a group to gain power freely in the United States without a civil war.

413. (B) Reasoning beyond the Text. The longevity of the United States of America can be found in the words of our Constitution. It governs our society and sets forth principles and doctrines of freedoms in our country. With this statement, the author suggests that Islam should take a more primary role in setting doctrine with democracy being a basic framework within which to operate. This completely goes against all things of our country and the Constitution, especially the separation of church and state clause in which our founding fathers stated there should be no government supported religion. That has evolved into the government being unable to remotely display anything related to any religious practice. Thus, any further role of a religious group, such as Islam, that may seek to alter what is stated in the Constitution would be met with fierce resistance.

414. (B) Foundation of Comprehension. As stated in the first paragraph, only Henry Harrison and James Garfield did not give a State of the Union address.

415. (C) Foundation of Comprehension. In the second paragraph, the author is clear that the event that is now the State of the Union address grew out of the mass media of television. With such widespread availability, the president could speak to the people (the voters) and not simply to Congress.

416. (A) Reasoning within the Text. In any form of government and throughout politics, good men are trying to do what they think is right for the country. However, their driving motivation is primarily to gain votes for themselves and their party. Today, nothing seems as transparent and forthright as it was decades ago. Likely this is due to mass media and what all people can now see, slanted by the direction of the reporting news outlet rather than simply judging a politician by the outcomes of their term.

417. (B) Reasoning beyond the Text. In paragraph five, the author describes the role of Everett Dirksen and Gerald Ford in giving the Opposition Response to the president. Of those two, only Gerald Ford was to become president, following the resignation of Richard Nixon in the 70s.

418. (A) Reasoning beyond the Text. The rift between Democrats and Republicans, liberals and conservatives has fractured our country in half. Thus, each portion of the population will despise one set of statements and support the other for their own political agenda.

419. (B) Foundation of Comprehension. In the first paragraph, the author states that the first president to name this speech the State of the Union address was Franklin Roosevelt.

420. (D) Reasoning within the Text. While a glance at the title may not reveal much of the significance of political economy, throughout the passage, the author details its meaning through the life of its creator, Adam Smith. Today, the different political economic systems, such as capitalism, communism, etc., can and do have a major impact on the economy of the country as well as that of the world.

421. (A) Foundation of Comprehension. In paragraph three, the mention of natural liberty is followed by a brief explanation which states that man's self-interest is God's providence. In other words, God's job is to make sure man is provided for by nature and his needs are met.

422. (C) Foundation of Comprehension. Although one may have incorrectly selected politicians (affairs of state), the correct selection would be that of businessmen. This passage is about economics and how politics can affect its performance and health. Thus, other than philosophers, those individuals who had the most to gain or lose are the ones involved in business and would be most interested in his philosophy on the subject.

423. (B) Reasoning within the Text. Smith set out to truly examine all forms of government and how they shaped and influenced the economy of their country and eventually the world. His *Wealth of Nations* was a fully comprehensive work and remains popular today.

424. (D) Reasoning beyond the Text. It is unlikely that much of Smith's philosophy would change even if he spent time in Russia. This was in the mid to late 1700s, so the shift to a capitalist system is still a century away. In light of his other doctrines in his *Wealth of Nations*, it is likely that selection D is and would likely remain his philosophy even in light of a Russian experience.

425. (D) Reasoning beyond the Text. It is doubtful that his philosophy would have changed drastically in light of such catastrophic financial events. However, he would likely remain opposed to government interference, always seen as a hindrance to real fiscal growth and innovation. But, he would have realized the impact that men can also have in a negative manner on the economy and would have slightly altered his natural liberty to include a warning against irreparable business practices.

Chapter 20: Population Health

426. (B) Foundation of Comprehension. This is the only selection not mentioned in the passage.

427. (B) Reasoning beyond the Text. While all selections are plausible explanations for the increase in urbanization, the tone of the authors passage would lead the reader to expect a negative view of urbanization at the expense of the environment and ecology. Thus, urban "sprawl," a negative connotation of the human spreading from the cities into the surrounding areas, would be the most likely clue and the best choice for this question. All distractors may represent individual reasons people may move to or remain in a regional location. However, only selection B has any negative verbiage relating to urbanization.

428. (B) Reasoning beyond the Text. The single perspective in the passage of the negative impact of urbanization on the ecology would lead the reader to infer that the author views urbanization in a negative light and would promote the environment and ecology over human habitations. Thus selection B, which would prevent human/wildlife interactions and preserve the environment would be the most likely choice of this author. Each of the distractors has been employed to varying degrees throughout the world in an attempt to accommodate growing human populations and yet preserve the environment and maintain the ecology. However, each suggested plan would impact the environment and ecology to different degrees. Thus, selection B, restricting human interference with the environment, would be the best selection for this question.

429. (C) Reasoning beyond the Text. While not directly stated, the predicted increase in urbanization that may occur in the next 50 years, given the same rate of growth, suggests that plans have NOT focused on the environment or ecology. Also, the suggestions at the end of the passage for a well thought out strategy for future development supports this assertion. Thus, of the remaining choices, economy (money) has been the primary focus of city planners in the past. Clearly the problem exists because city planners have failed to realize the impact of human growth on the ecology and environment. Efficiency, while always an ideal goal, likely is far less of a priority to cities and their developer when compared to the economy and the increased revenue that will be generated with increased populations.

430. (D) Foundation of Comprehension. The example of bears increasingly entering the suburbs was stated in paragraph six. While all could be pulled from headlines of newspapers in our country, only the interaction of bears and humans was mentioned in this passage.

431. (C) Foundations of Comprehension. From this list, each item is likely true in Liberia and in the ongoing battle against Ebola. However, the author states in paragraphs five and six that the physical contact so often associated with comforting people in grief is impossible since Ebola is transmitted through physical contact. Thus fear is an obstacle in the way of a powerful means with which to lessen the pain of grief and comfort those emotionally hurting people. The other items in the list are more related to the actual transmission of the disease or logistic issues with actually traveling to where the people are located.

432. (C) Foundations of Comprehension. The author talks about all the means through which aid organizations have assisted the people of Liberia through grief counseling, training and education, and community involvement in the prevention of activities that can transmit the disease more readily. However, the one not present in the passage was choice C, the transfer of individuals to the U.S. for treatment. Recall during the crisis in the U.S., several healthcare workers were transported to the hospitals identified by the CDC as the highest level care facilities. However, the vast majority of aid workers in Liberia who became sick, unless they were American and transferred back to the U.S. by the military, remained in Liberia.

433. (B) Reasoning within the Text. All of the actions listed for this question would be worthwhile mechanisms that would help communities and nations deal with terrible crises of any kind. However, so much of the passage was spent discussing the education and the training of the people in Liberia, especially those to help others with grief counseling. Thus, the author would likely feel that the best use of the money available would be to educate and train workers BEFORE the crisis so that the aid and recovery would begin much sooner and help the affected people more rapidly, thus reduce the human suffering.

434. (A) Foundations of Comprehension. In most difficult situations there is a natural pattern for emotionally dealing with the situation and your feelings. The culmination and the conclusion of this process is closure, closing the loop and moving on with the normalcy of life and living. However, for those whose loved ones died from Ebola, that closure was not possible. To prevent the spread of the disease as well as the fear of its spread, the bodies were immediately incinerated. This left the remaining family members with nothing which could assist in the memorial, funeral, ceremony for their dead and lost loved one, nor was there a means with which to obtain the closure for their grief. The author discusses this aspect of the grief process and the difficulty it creates in paragraph seven.

435. (A) Foundations of Comprehension. While the World Health Organization (WHO) does tremendous work worldwide in providing the oversight, organization, funding, etc. to groups and countries in need and in health related crises, the WHO was the only group not recognized in the passage in paragraphs 9 and 10 as organizations with boots on the ground in Liberia providing some kind of aid to the people.

436. (D) Foundation of Comprehension. Through all of the statistics and data, the author is clearly painting a dire picture of the health and quality of life for individuals who do not have the proper care in their country. Furthermore, statements like, "The shocking truth" and in the final sentence, "there is no time to waste," shows how passionate the author is about making people aware of the dire situations in the world and attempting to affect change.

437. (B) Reasoning beyond the Text. Unlike infectious diseases that can be eliminated quickly with medications, NCDs are inherently difficult to treat, long lasting and debilitating. Since these are often caused by an unhealthy lifestyle, education and prevention are the only ways in which the spread of these NCDs will slow and the cost of chronic treatment of the symptoms of these diseases will decrease.

438. (A) Foundation of Comprehension. This was the only NCD not listed anywhere in the passage.

439. (A) Reasoning beyond the Text. The Westernized lifestyle and diet are rich in fats and carbohydrates, each of which lead to substantial health risks when consumed in excess. Thus, as countries "Westernize," these poor eating and lifestyle habits permeate their society and rapidly lead to these health risks and NCDs.

440. (B) Reasoning beyond the Text. Current healthcare systems are designed to treat acute illnesses and eliminate the underlying causes of health problems to return the patient to their normal quality of life. Patients with NCDs, however, are most often unable to recover full function and are thus left with a lower quality of life. Symptoms can be managed but unless their lifestyle changes the conditions will only deteriorate regardless of the medical intervention. Furthermore, the treatment of those chronic NCDs is much more expensive than the treatments for infectious diseases and most countries are simply unable to afford that additional cost and pass it along to their patients.

441. (C) Foundation of Comprehension. Paragraph two ends with the author stating that cancer is the leading cause of death worldwide.

442. (D) Foundation of Comprehension. Cooking over open flames in rural underdeveloped areas of the world is not a preferred way of preparing food: it is the only way. Thus, there are many negative aspects of using an open fire inside of a home. These include all of the above from the list and can be eliminated by the use of cookstoves which will vent the smoke and soot to the outside of the home.

443. (C) Foundation of Comprehension. In the second paragraph, the author describes the challenge in finding someone willing to test the stove and to help work out the logistic details of changing from an open fire system to a cookstove. Once this was working, neighboring households could see the benefits of having the stove in the home and be more willing to try one themselves.

444. (B) Foundation of Comprehension. All of the selections are listed as negatives to using the cook stoves over open fires with the exception of B. In fact, in paragraph five, the author states that cook time is faster using the cook stoves.

445. (C) Reasoning beyond the Text. The time spent with the rural people built trust between them and the PCVs. Without this trust and becoming familiar with the people, it would have taken longer to find those people willing and adventurous enough to try the new stoves. Likely, although the time would have been longer, the stoves would have eventually been seen as a benefit and people would want them in their homes.

446. (D) Reasoning beyond the Text. The stoves are largely provided by USAID so the cost to the individual would not be a major consideration. Floor space and size of the wood is also something that is easily altered and would not be a hindrance to the transition. However, having to purchase all new cookware would be an expense that not many could afford even if those supplies were readily available.

447. (A) Foundation of Comprehension. All of the benefits are listed in the passage with the exception of selection A. In fact, the author makes a point that while the fuel is the same (i.e., wood), the rural people of Peru would have to cut the wood to a smaller size.

448. (A) Foundation of Comprehension. All of the fuels used by individuals for open fires inside their homes were listed in paragraph two and include all of the list with the exception of A.

449. (C) Reasoning with the Text. It is clear from the article that women are largely responsible for obtaining fuel and preparing the food in these rural communities. Thus, time saved for both tasks would benefit women much greater than it would men or the community as a whole directly. Indirectly, better education and more business opportunities for women would have a tremendously positive impact on the growth and development of their society.

450. (B) Reasoning beyond the Text. While we take for granted the fact that when we turn on our cook tops the elements will heat from either natural gas or electricity, not every area in the world has access to these resources which are such a part of our everyday lives. Thus, wood is much more available for these rural people than other types of fuel.

451. (A) Foundation of Comprehension. Countries that already have cookstove programs are listed in paragraph seven and include India, China, and Mexico.

452. (C) Reasoning beyond the Text. In the passage, the author states many benefits to the people, culture, and environment for this switch away from open fires in the home. Thus, any move to further provide a cost effective means to produce cookstoves and get them into the homes would be welcome. If that could happen and also create new job opportunities for the community and stimulate their economy, it would also be viewed most favorably. Thus making the stoves locally would create jobs, reduce shipping costs, and allow them to be made for the needs of their specific culture as described in the passage.

453. (D) Foundation of Comprehension. The problems that could be solved by moving to cookstoves are listed in paragraph seven. Selection D, while likely a beneficial result, it was not discussed in the passage.

Chapter 21: Psychology

454. (A) Reasoning within the Text. Paragraph two, in which decriminalization is discussed, also suggests reduced sensational media coverage as a means to reduce suicide rates. Since modern day media services sensationalize crimes, this would likely tie these two circumstances together and yield a lower media coverage rate (if no longer a crime) and as a result decrease the suicide rate. Since most suicides are spontaneous, there would be little consideration of the taboo or the criminal activity associated with suicide and the victim focuses on the outcome only.

455. (C) Foundations of Comprehension. Pesticide poisoning was stated to be the leading cause of death worldwide and would thus be a target for reduction in suicide rates. Interestingly, this was not expressly mentioned as a method by which to reduce suicide rates.

456. (C) Reasoning beyond the Text. The author discusses the approach of using psychotherapy as a means with which to reduce the suicide rates in paragraph four. This suggests that it is an approach the author supports in this attempt to curb suicide. Thus, while the improvements in healthcare and treatments in the U.S. have not reduced the actual numerical rate, this author would likely agree and argue that this approach has been successful and the rates would have been even higher had they not been in place.

457. (A) Reasoning beyond the Text. Since the author states in paragraph three that most suicides are impulsive, any means by which a victim must expend more time in the search for a way to commit suicide would certainly be time in which they could think through all the ramifications and consequences of their action upon themselves and others. While this may not eliminate suicide it apparently provides enough of a delay that the suicide rate is reduced. Selection B is a rather logic-based argument and not relevant to this question. However, the remainder of the selections may have some truth and value to their isolated statements; but, with respect to the question, they clearly are not as valid as selection A.

458. (B) Foundation of Comprehension. As stated in the passage, 51% of suicides in the U.S. are carried out using firearms. Selections A and C were mentioned as means by which suicides occur and steps in which these can be managed worldwide. However, they are not the most common in the U.S. Selection D is a means by which some individuals may commit suicide, but it was not discussed in this passage.

459. (C) Reasoning beyond the Text. Freedom of the press is not a liberty which allows the news media to say anything and everything it wishes. The right in question gives the news agencies the right to unrestricted reporting of events and the news as it may relate to the country, politics, or political figures. However, in light of the correlation between the suicide rates and sensationalized reporting of suicides, the author would likely agree that there should be regulations and laws that restrict such practices and prevent anything other than the direct reporting of someone's death and not the gory sensationalized details that spur others to suicide.

460. (C) Reasoning within the Text. Throughout the passage, the author is deliberate in his place of blame for the stigma of psychiatry and mental health assistance: it is a self-inflicted injury that hurting people further heap upon themselves. While this has been an issue in human culture since the beginning of psychiatric healthcare, in contemporary times, seeking care has become much more socially acceptable. Yet, there will likely still be pockets that view seeking any healthcare, especially psychiatric care, as a weakness and look negatively upon those individuals. Thus, in light of the passage as a whole, selection C is the best choice since (1) the stigma does remain and (2) it is initiated and it persists internally within the patient.

461. (D) Reasoning within the Text. A person going through a difficult period of their life and having difficulty with their emotions and mental state is not a rare occurrence in our culture. Likewise, people have the fear that seeking help in these times will lead to some if not all of the items listed in response to this question. However, the fear is an internally derived force. It is self-imposed. Likewise, it is seen as a symptom of being unable to control your own emotions like everyone else in the world does (or that the individual erroneously believes they do). In fact, everyone struggles from time to time and that is the normal mode of human existence. However, that fear that somehow you alone are the weak singular individual in the world who cannot do it on your own is the biggest fear and the principle obstacle to overcome for an individual to seek psychiatric help. The author implies these principals in paragraph four of the passage.

462. (D) Foundations of Comprehension. Dealing with psychiatric and emotional problems can be a long and difficult process, as described in the passage. However, with all of the support and guidance that may come from practically each individual or group listed as options for this question, the ultimate person in control of retaining or destroying the stigma associated with mental care is the patient. While this explicit statement may not be found in a specific location in the passage, this theme is woven throughout each and every section of the passage with details about mechanisms being used to assist individuals but them having the final control.

463. (A) Reasoning within the Text. This may have been a more difficult choice for you. Selections C and D are perfectly acceptable methods by which people can help themselves overcome mental difficulties and are discussed in the passage. However, only the first two choices are pertinent to the question at hand. Each seems to be a restatement of the same concept; however, the key to this selection is the word "proud." This word in choice A denotes an internal as well as an external strength within oneself that allows for a new and better way of living in the world. Choice B comes close to that sentiment; yet, understanding and accepting yourself, while important, doesn't quite rise to the level expressed in choice A.

464. (A) Foundations of Comprehension. These selections are based upon the items mentioned in paragraph five of the passage. In this instance, all were mentioned except for bipolar disorder. This should have been a straightforward selection for you. However, bipolar disorder is a common health risk in modern society and you may have equated that with it being mentioned in the list. Hopefully, you mentally noted the list (as you should always) and did not have to return to the passage for this item.

465. (A) Foundation of Comprehension. While the passage does use illustrations from military individuals, its theme is more broadly focused on the stigma society once had for those seeking psychiatric help and how that often prevents people desperately in need from seeking out that help. It also goes on to demonstrate that the stigma is more often in the mind of the individual and not as prevalent in society today.

466. (A) Foundation of Comprehension. When it comes to real estate, they say it's all about location. In this case the location may in fact play a part in the decision to remain in a high risk area. In the next to last paragraph of the passage, place, weather, and beauty of the location are all listed as potential rationales for people remaining. While cost may also and likely does factor into that decision, it was not listed in the passage.

467. (C) Reasoning within the Text. Although there are many specifics of the risks to living in certain locations, the theme of this passage is about "why" people choose to live in certain locations. In fact neighbors may react very differently to the same stimuli and risks as illustrated in the passage. Thus, this work is more about the psychology of the situation rather than the specifics of the destruction, risk, or recovery from natural disasters.

468. (C) Reasoning within the Text. Past experiences either negative or positive will likely influence the decision of each individual in determining where they live and what risk they are able to accept. A devastating loss may likely lead to a move to a safer location, while a near-miss that resulted in no damage may lead an individual to take even greater risks.

469. (B) Foundation of Comprehension. The author lists natural disasters in paragraph two that require people to make risky decisions when choosing that location for a home. Of those listed, tornadoes were not described in the passage.

470. (C) Reasoning within the Text. As stated in paragraph four, the more familiar and known a hazard may be, the less concerned many people will be. With the advancements in severe weather predictions and the precautions people can take ahead of time, the potential for loss of life is far less risky for many and fear does not rise to the level of moving to a different location.

471. (B) Reasoning within the Text. Much can be learned from the past and from history. Thus, scientists may be looking at the occurrence of hazards through time while the people who have lived in a region for generations have the experiences of their ancestors to assist them in picking the best places to live. One example would be in the areas of Texas that flooded. Some people living within closer proximity to the flood waters were out of harm's way although they would be considered by many scientists and insurance agents to be in a flood zone.

472. (D) Foundation of Comprehension. The organs and systems negatively impacted by stress are listed by the author in paragraph two. Of the selections, only urinary system was not found in the passage. While this system is certainly influenced by changes in blood pressure, which may have led you to make an incorrect choice based on your biological knowledge, the question asked for that system NOT listed in the passage.

473. (A) Reasoning beyond the Text. As you prepare for the MCAT examination, even your studies now may foster feelings of anxiety at the mere thought of the actual exam. While many are able to compensate for those debilitating feelings with energy and adrenaline, far too many are simply unable to perform and, with each unanswered question, the stress increases. For this example, the best way to ward off test anxiety is through proper preparation (as you are doing now for the CARS section).

474. (C) Foundation of Comprehension. Of the behaviors controlled by the amygdala and listed in paragraph eight, pleasure is not present in the passage.

475. (A) Foundation of Comprehension. Of the hormonal chain listed in paragraph six of the passage, only the amygdala is not directly involved in the pathway leading to the release of adrenaline.

476. (B) Reasoning beyond the Text. Drill and practice have been used by various militaries for training their soldiers for centuries. This instills a level of confidence in the individuals while at the same time results in instinctual reactions to situations rather than relying on intellectual decisions that are more fluid and influenced by stress.

477. (A) Foundation of Comprehension. According to the author, parents are the greatest source of stress for teens. This may be in the form of expected behaviors, increased performance in school, or even in trying to increase the communication between them and the teen. Regardless, adolescence is a difficult period in the life of every human and it seems from this study that parents only increase the level of stress upon the teen. However, speaking as a parent, the stress is returned in kind!

Chapter 22: Sociology

478. (B) Foundations of Comprehension. This descriptor was used in reference to the reviewing of the data and not about the data itself.

479. (A) Reasoning within the Text. The boss (leader) is typically the highest paid person and final decisions rest with them. While the most educated and highly trained person may have a tremendous impact on decisions in a data-driven business model, in this example they would likely not be as involved. Financial officers may have input and are responsible for cash flow in the business but are not reflected in this phrase. Stockholders, who are the financial backing of a business, may influence the direction of a company by investing or withdrawing their resources. However, in light of this phrase, they are not the group or individual being described.

480. (C) Reasoning within the Text. The passage clearly compares a data-driven business to a scientific investigation. While teachers do use the scientific method either consciously or subconsciously to improve their teaching based on student performance, this career is not mentioned in the passage. Although the passage is about a business model, an accountant may not necessarily use the scientific method that is explicitly compared in this passage. Medical doctors are trained to observe and treat patients, their immediate actions are not dictated by feedback from the patient but from past data and success. Additionally, doctors are not mentioned in this passage.

481. (C) Foundation of Comprehension. Using the scientific method as described in the passage to lead to educated business decisions will reduce risks, improve operations, and likely result in an increase in productivity and success.

482. (D) Reasoning beyond the Text. While an author does pay attention to the genre, niche, and demand of the public, many write because of their skill, joy, and passion for a particular topic and would be least likely to use data to drive their particular style or genre of writing. Each of the aforementioned businesses or individuals will have done considerable research, trial, and error before arriving at financial success in their particular business.

483. (B) Reasoning within the Text. In the final paragraph, the author states that effective decision makers will monitor their data (observe), make changes (experiment), and observe the outcome (evaluate). These are all the steps also described in the scientific method of deductive reasoning. It is simply being applied in the business world in this case for making decisions.

484. (B) Reasoning within the Text. Within the context of the passage, a "cycle" denotes a recurring pattern. While an annual cycle such as seasonally or every year would certainly fit a description of a cycle, in this case the author refers it to child labor. Since the labor occurs throughout the year, the only cycle that could be considered for this reference is the generational cycle that would exist as children grow into adults and have their own children that are then subjected to child labor as their parents had been.

485. (A) Foundations of Comprehension. In paragraph four, the author lists many of the detrimental effects of child labor on the children themselves. Among those listed were developmental deficits, remaining impoverished, lack of educational opportunities, and poor health. Of the options for this question, choice A is the one not listed. While A does mention health, healthcare access is not discussed, so A is the correct choice here.

486. (B) Reasoning beyond the Text. The choices for this question are likely all factors in the existence of child labor worldwide. However, A, C, and D are specific reasons for children still being used in the workforce. The real underlying rational for this to be maintained is the social and cultural acceptance of the practice. Yes, the practical results of children working to the economy, communities, and families are significant; however, the attitude of the practice is much more difficult to change. Until that does change in those countries, any move to eliminate child labor will be met with resistance, and the practical benefits of child labor will be emphasized to outweigh any detrimental consequence for the child. Thus, the greater good will outweigh the individual sacrifice. That will require an entirely new way of thinking to change those cultures.

487. (C) Reasoning within the Text. Often answering these types of questions will involve subtle undertones throughout the passage that either make it difficult to characterize or the writing will simply be neutral and lack any designators that allow for that classification. This is NOT the case with this passage and this author. Throughout the passage, the author uses words and phrases such as "plight of children" in paragraph two and "hazardous to a child" or "trap children."

488. (A) Reasoning beyond the Text. Anyone who has ever had a job can attest to the fact that most employees, especially in the U.S., will always want the best conditions and the best pay for the work they perform. Thus, this is a standard practice among business owners and human resources personal. Typically if individuals do not like the work, they can find another job (within reason of course). However, this is still not the best choice for this negative response question. Children certainly would complain less about work conditions than adult workers. Costs will always be a bottom line factor when it comes to businesses and their operation. Thus, this would be a major motivation to hire children at a lower cost than adults. This leaves the number of children versus adults in the workforce as a possibility. While this statistic may be accurate, it is likely to be the least important one from the list that would motivate these businesses to employ children rather than adults.

489. (C) Foundation of Comprehension. The author is very clear that outside pressure and legal actions have done little to restrict or slow the practice of child labor. However, according to the article, education and societal buy-in has led to some promising reductions in the child labor numbers. Thus, greater education and examples from within those countries will hopefully continue to reduce this debilitating practice.

490. (D) Reasoning beyond the Text. Throughout the centuries, mankind has been unable to always resolve conflicts based on sacred values. These most often lead to war or violence as listed in each selection above. ISIS uses terrorism to try and achieve their goals, the crusades ended largely in a stalemate with Christians leaving the Middle East, and the Native Americans were driven from their land by the colonists who were wanting to expand westward.

491. (C) Foundation of Comprehension. The research team is listed in paragraph three and includes Northwestern, Harvard, New School, and University of Michigan.

492. (C) Reasoning within the Text. In paragraph nine, the author describes the research and how modern social cultures deal with conflict among sacred values. Toward the end of that paragraph, extremist groups are discussed and are said to be motivated toward violence by a different set of traits and circumstances.

493. (A) Reasoning beyond the Text. Soldiers are the weapons through which leaders attempt to resolve conflict by force. The cost of human life can never equate to any outcome achieved through war. Thus, obtaining the motivations and feelings of the soldiers who are facing the possibility of death for their country, society, and beliefs would have important information to share with the research team.

494. (B) Foundation of Comprehension. The organizations listed as using the rational actor theory to guide their business decisions are listed in paragraph four and include World Bank, NGOs, U.S. military, and diplomatic services.

495. (A) Foundation of Comprehension. The results of the research have led governments to move toward a devoted actor theory when dealing with extremists like ISIS. This is discussed in the final two paragraphs of the passage.

496. (D) Reasoning beyond the Text. Politics have been a system used by mankind for as long as man has been on the planet. In our modern system, while politicians are seen as public servants with the desire to facilitate the will of the people, the stereotype of politicians and the mechanisms within which they operate are very different. In fact, their willingness to serve the greater good would eliminate the defector and the reciprocator groups. Additionally, cooperators are clearly the "losers" in this passage as they help anyone regardless of any reward themselves. Thus by elimination we are left with the shunner (which seems ironic because politicians are so public and visible). However, politicians do help the society and they will help others (who are also supporting their causes, programs, and bills).

497. (C) Reasoning within the Text. In the final paragraph of the passage, the author suggests that cooperators will not last long in society, and that defectors will be "invaded" by shunners, and that reciprocators and shunners may transition back and forth. Thus, defectors will be socially excluded from society and be unable to find anyone who is willing to help them in any way.

498. (A) Foundation of Comprehension. The passage describes how members of society will offer and barter their assistance to the group and to individual members of the society. Surprisingly, the author states that the cooperator will "lose" because nice guys finish last when they give their services without any compensatory actions of others. Thus, the "give and take" described in this passage details how this maintains the social order of the group (society).

499. (B) Reasoning beyond the Text. The number of people on welfare and other assistance programs in the U.S. is at an all-time high. These programs have always been intended to be a "hand up" rather than a hand out. However, individuals once on the dole rarely exit the cycle and remain there for most of their lives. In that regard, those individuals are using the tax money contributed by the members of society without giving anything back to anyone. Thus, in light of society, these individuals would be defectors who are draining the financial recourses of the country and still consuming the materials that everyone needs to live.

500. (C) Reasoning beyond the Text. Similar to the previous question, the welfare roles are filled with people who have settled into the role of the defector. These new programs are seeking to force people to move at least into the shunner role if not into the reciprocator role. In this way, people will contribute to society and likely receive the training required to help them escape the welfare role and build a career of their own.

SOURCES

1. "USPS Historic Properties." www.achp.gov/historicpostoffices.pdf
2. Margaret Schroeder, "Building Big." *Humanities,* Volume 21, Number 5, September/October 2000.
3. "The Supreme Court Building." www.supremecourt.gov/about/courtbuilding.aspx
4. Nicholas Jeeves, "The Serious and the Smirk: The Smile in Portraiture." publicdomainreview.org/2013/09/18/the-serious-and-the-smirk-the-smile-in-portraiture/
5. Lynn Waddell, "The Highwaymen, A School of African-American Artists." *Humanities,* Volume 35, Number 5, September/October 2014.
6. Rebecca Gross, "The Importance of Taking Children to Museums." arts.gov/art-works/2014/importance-taking-children-museums
7. "To Make Beautiful the Capitol." www.gpo.gov/fdsys/pkg/GPO-CPUB-113spub10/pdf/GPO-CPUB-113spub10-3.pdf
8. Rebecca Gross, "Cosmic Creativity: An Artist's View of Space." arts.gov/NEARTS/2013no3-kind-of-beauty/cosmic-creativity
9. "Full Exposure: Ballet East Brings Modern Dance to East Austin." arts.gov/NEARTS/2009v2-first-steps/full-exposure
10. Sherry Goodill, "The Healing Power of Dance." arts.gov/art-works/2011/healing-power-dance
11. Janet Mansfield Soares, "Grassroots Modern: New York Dancers Take to the Country." www.neh.gov/humanities/2010/septemberoctober/feature/grassroots-modern
12. Derek Lee, "Yemeni Communities Unite Against Child Marriage." www.usaid.gov/news-information/frontlines/haitiwomen-development/yemeni-communities-unite-against-child-marriage
13. Ira Forman, "All Countries Must Speak Out Against Anti-Semitism." blogs.state.gov/stories/2014/09/03/all-countries-must-speak-out-against-anti-semitism
14. Embassy Nairobi, "The Importance of Press Freedom." blogs.usembassy.gov/nairobi/hello-world/
15. Franklin D. Roosevelt, "Franklin D. Roosevelt: First Inaugural Address." www.bartleby.com/124/pres49.html
16. Rebecca Gross, "Literature's Invisible Art: A Look at Literary Translation." arts.gov/NEARTS/2014v1-opening-world-international-art/invisible-art-translation
17. Rebecca Gross, "Sherman Alexie: Plainspoken Inspiration." arts.gov/NEARTS/2013v4-inspiration-quotient/sherman-alexie

18. Edward Wakeling, "Lewis Carroll and the Hunting of the Snark." publicdomainreview.org/2011/02/22/lewis-carroll-and-the-hunting-of -the-snark/

19. Danny Heitman, "The White Pages." www.neh.gov/humanities/2014/ januaryfebruary/feature/the-white-pages

20. Rebecca Gross, "Reading in Sunshine: Chicago's Printers Row Lit Fest." arts.gov/NEARTS/2011v3-celebration-look-art-festival/reading-sunshine

21. "Setting Themselves Apart: New World Symphony Mentors a New Generation of Leaders." arts.gov/NEARTS/2008v5-music-our-ears/ setting-themselves-apart

22. Carole C. Lee, "The Reach of African Music." *Humanities*, Volume 20, Number 6, November/December 1999.

23. Jack Neely, "The Philosopher at Fontana." www.tva.gov/heritage/ext/ index.htm

24. Robert Pasnau, "The Islamic Scholar Who Gave Us Modern Philosophy." www.neh.gov/humanities/2011/novemberdecember/feature/ the-islamic-scholar-who-gave-us-modern-philosophy

25. Adam Berenbak, "Congressional Play-by-Play on Baseball: Ethics in the National Pastime Become Subject of Hearings." www.archives.gov/ publications/prologue/2011/summer/baseball.html

26. Trisha Creekmore, "Conversational Journalism Is Real." www.innovation-series .com/2011/03/15/conversational-journalism/

27. Bobbie Mixon, "Hunting the Spark of Creativity." nsf.gov/discoveries/ disc_summ.jsp?cntn_id=129320&org=NSF

28. Jennifer Kreizman, "Pure Expression: Lady Pink and the Evolution of Street Art." arts.gov/NEARTS/2013v2-ahead-their-time/pure-expression

29. Sarah Bertness and Natalie V. Hall, "#2TweetorNot2Tweet." arts.gov/ art-works/2013/2tweetornot2tweet-sarah-bertness; arts.gov/art-works/ 2013/2tweetornot2tweet-natalie-v-hall

30. "Defining a Cyberbully." www.nsf.gov/discoveries/disc_summ .jsp?cntn_id=121847&org=NSF

31. Sarah Pulliam Bailey, "American Zenophilia." www.neh.gov/humanities/ 2010/marchapril/feature/american-zenophilia

32. "U.S. Policy and Programs in Support of Religious Freedom." www.state .gov/j/drl/rls/irf/religiousfreedom/index.htm#wrapper

33. "Lord of the Dance." www.neh.gov/humanities/2002/novemberdecember/ feature/lord-the-dance

34. Kristofer Schipper, "Taoism: The Story of the Way." *Humanities*, Volume 21, Number 6, November/December 2000.

35. Alfred Dwight Sheffield, "Confucianism". www.bartleby.com/60/223.html

36. Pepper Smith, "Nothing Glamorous At All: A Talk with a Working Actor." arts.gov/NEARTS/2010v1-art-works-how-art-work/nothing-glamorous-all

37. "Scientists Find Earliest 'New World' Writings in Mexico." www.nsf.gov/ discoveries/disc_summ.jsp?cntn_id=100654&org=NSF

38. "Will Baby Crawl?" www.nsf.gov/discoveries/disc_summ.jsp?cntn_id =103153&org=NSF

39. Rachel Galvin, "The Golden Hoard." *Humanities*, Volume 25, Number 6, November/December 2004.

40. Rachel Galvin, "From the Rainforest." *Humanities*, Volume 25, Number 1, January/February 2004.

41. "Four Bands Community Fund Kick-Starts Small Businesses." http://www .acf.hhs.gov/programs/ana/success-story/four-bands-community-fund-kick -starts-small-businesses

42. Dr. James C. Kaufman, "Can Anyone Be Creative?" arts.gov/art-works/ 2014/can-anyone-be-creative

43. Ronica Roth, "Towards Life in the Fast Lane." *Humanities*, Volume 18, Number 5, September/October 1997.

44. Dan Scheuerman, "Planned Paradise: Making the Florida Dream." *Humanities*, Volume 28, Number 5, September/October 2007.

45. Rachel Galvin, "Of Poets, Prophets, and Politics." *Humanities*, Volume 23, Number 1, January/February 2002.

46. "Value of U.S. Mineral Production Decreased in 2013." www.usgs.gov/ newsroom/article.asp?ID=3837#.U_zmwP3wvVI

47. "Helping the New Orleans Region Diversify, Grow, and Create Jobs." www.eda.gov/news/blogs/2013/09/01/success-story.htm

48. Caron Beesley, "How to Estimate the Cost of Starting a Business from Scratch." www.sba.gov/blogs/how-estimate-cost-starting-business-scratch

49. Linda Cureton, "Sourcing Strategies and Innovation." blogs.nasa.gov/ NASA-CIO-Blog/ (June 3, 2012)

50. "One-Woman Juice Empire." www.adf.gov/documents/Success%20Stories/ SuccessStoryBurundi1842FRUITO.htm

51. U.S. Department of Education Office for Civil Rights, "Historically Black Colleges and Universities and Higher Education Desegregation." www2.ed.gov/about/offices/list/ocr/docs/hq9511.html

52. Kathleen Porter, "The Value of a College Degree." www.ericdigests.org/ 2003-3/value.htm

53. Anne C. Richard, "Refugee and Displaced Children: Back to School—or Not?" blogs.state.gov/stories/2014/09/14/refugee-and-displaced-children -back-school-or-not

54. "The Global View." www.tva.gov/heritage/globalview/index.htm

55. "California's Restless Giant—the Long Valley Caldera." pubs.usgs.gov/fs/ 2014/3056/pdf/fs2014-3056.pdf

56. "Ocean Warming Affecting Florida Reefs." www.usgs.gov/newsroom/ article.asp?ID=3996&from=rss_home#.VBbilBYuLX4

57. "A Most Magnificent Ruin: The Burning of the Capitol During the War of 1812." www.aoc.gov/blog/%E2%80%9C-most-magnificent-ruin %E2%80%9D-burning-capitol-during-war-1812

58. Erin Allen, "Abraham Lincoln's 'Blind Memorandum.'" blogs.loc.gov/ loc/2014/08/abraham-lincolns-blind-memorandum/

59. "Civility in the Senate: Henry Clay, 1842." www.senate.gov/artandhistory/ history/idea_of_the_senate/1842Clay.htm

60. Nicole Mahoney, "Language Change." nsf.gov/news/special_reports/ linguistics/change.jsp

61. David Skinner, "How Did Cool Become Such a Big Deal?" www.neh.gov/ humanities/2014/julyaugust/feature/how-did-cool-become-such-big-deal-0

62. Arika Okrent, "Trüth, Beaüty, and Volapük." publicdomainreview. org/2012/10/17/truth-beauty-and-volapuk/

63. Steve Moyer, "'Toad-stranglers,' 'Whoopensockers' and Other Findings from the *Dictionary of American Regional English.*" *Humanities*, Volume 35, Number 4, July/August 2014.

64. "Navajo Code Talkers: World War II Fact Sheet." http://www.history .navy.mil/browse-by-topic/diversity/native-americans-in-the-navy/ navajo-code-talkers-world-war-ii-fact-sheet.html

65. "Six-month-old Word Learners." www.nsf.gov/discoveries/disc_summ .jsp?cntn_id=123378&org=NSF

66. John L. Esposito and John O. Voll, "Islam and Democracy." *Humanities*, Volume 22, Number 6, November/December 2001.

67. "January 17, 1966: Opposition Response to the State of the Union Address." www.senate.gov/artandhistory/history/minute/Opposition_ Response_to_the_State_of_the_Union_Address.htm

68. "Adam Smith and the Development of Political Economy." http://www .econlib.org/library/Smith/smWN.html

69. "Scientists Predict Massive Urban Growth, Creation of 'Megalopolis' in Southeast in Next 45 Years." www.usgs.gov/newsroom/article .asp?ID=3943#.U_zl0_3wvVI

70. "On the Frontlines of the Ebola Response." blog.usaid.gov/2014/08/ on-the-frontlines-of-the-ebola-response-an-inside-look-at-a-program-to -help-the-grieving/

71. "The Changing Face of Health in the South Pacific." blogs.usembassy.gov/ papuanewguinea/

72. Greg "Goyo" Plimpton, "Improved Cookstoves in Peru: A Peace Corps Volunteer's Story." blog.epa.gov/blog/2014/06/improved-cookstoves-in -peru-a-peace-corps-volunteers-story/

73. Hillary Rodham Clinton and Julia Roberts, "'Clean Stoves' Would Save Lives, Cut Pollution." http://statedept.tumblr.com/post/5252453806/ joint-op-ed-by-secretary-clinton-and-julia

74. Thomas Insel, "Preventing Suicide: A Global Imperative." www.nimh.nih .gov/about/director/2014/suicide-a-global-issue.shtml

75. Cmdr. Russell Carr, MC, "Voices from the Field." https://archive.org/ stream/MEDNEWSSept2013/MEDNEWS%20Sept%202013_djvu.txt

76. Paul Slovic, "Why People Live in Wildfire Zones." www.nsf.gov/ discoveries/disc_summ.jsp?cntn_id=111740&org=NSF

77. Adriana Galván, "Stressed Out: Teens and Adults Respond Differently." www.nsf.gov/discoveries/disc_summ.jsp?cntn_id=117610&org=NSF

78. Rebecca Shakespeare, "Making a Decision? Check the Data." www.innovation-series.com/2014/04/03/making-a-decision-check-the-data/

79. Bama Athreya, "Ending Child Labor." blog.usaid.gov/2014/06/ending-child-labor/

80. "Respect for Sacred Values is Key to Conflict Resolution." www.nsf.gov/discoveries/disc_summ.jsp?cntn_id=112944&org=NSF

81. "Why Contribute to the Good of the Group?" www.nsf.gov/discoveries/disc_summ.jsp?cntn_id=100611&org=NSF